Irish Classical Recordings

Irish Classical Recordings

A Discography of Irish Art Music

Axel Klein

Discographies, Number 91
Michael Gray, Series Editor

GREENWOOD PRESS
Westport, Connecticut • London

Library of Congress Cataloging-in-Publication Data

Klein, Axel.
 Irish classical recordings : a discography of Irish art music / Axel Klein.
   p. cm.—(Discographies, ISSN 0192—334X ; no. 91)
  ISBN 0–313–31742–9 (alk. paper)
  1. Music—Ireland—Discography. I. Title. II. Series.
 ML156.2.K54   2001
 016.78′09415′0266—dc21   2001040445

British Library Cataloguing in Publication Data is available.

Library of Congress Catalog Card Number: 2001040445

ISBN: 0–313–31742–9
ISSN: 0192–334X

First published in 2001

Greenwood Press, 88 Post Road West, Westport, CT 06881
An imprint of Greenwood Publishing Group, Inc.
www.greenwood.com

Printed in the United States of America

The paper used in this book complies with the
Permanent Paper Standard issued by the National
Information Standards Organization (Z39.48–1984).

10 9 8 7 6 5 4 3 2 1

Contents

Part I: Recorded Music by Irish Composers

Contents

Part II: Recorded "Irish" Music by Non-Irish Composers

Acknowledgements

Although this book is, alas, a one-man project, meaning endless days and nights of researching and typing, I would like to express my heartfelt gratitude to a number of individuals who helped in special areas. My thanks are due to Pamela St. Clair, my initial acquisitions editor at Greenwood Press, who took on this project without the slightest hesitation, thereby confirming my own belief in the right choice of topic at the right time. The unerring support of her successor Eric Levy certainly helped me proceed when time for delivery ran out.

Many thanks to Carol Acton, Dublin, and her prolonged arm, Dr. Gareth Cox of Mary Immaculate College, University of Limerick, who were prepared to take the trouble and investigate the endless LP-collection of Charles Acton, long-time (1955-87) music critic of *The Irish Times*. Derek Walsh in Dublin, an ardent opera lover and researcher on Irish opera composers and singers, deliberately provided me with details of long sold-out LPs from his collection. Likewise a number of 1960s LPs would never have come to my attention without the active support of Aileen Wall of the Sound Library at Radio Telefís Éireann (RTÉ).

Otherwise perhaps a word to the sources I used would not be out of place: I consulted several (not all!) volumes of catalogs, such as *Gramophone* (lately called the *R.E.D. Classical Catalogue*), the German *Bielefelder Katalog* and the American *Schwann* catalogs. Apart from my own collection of recorded Irish music I made good use of the excellent website of *Gramophone* reviews at *www.gramofile.co.uk* providing details of recordings since 1983 and I even got news of relevant CDs from websites such as *www.cdnow.com*. Online discographies keep thinking of Irish music as traditional or "folk" music – for too many people Ireland is still the land of leprechauns, shamrocks and fiddles. So much for the topicality of the internet.

There is no further literature on this area, apart from an early article by Charles Acton in the Irish-American quarterly *Éire-Ireland*, vol. 3, fall 1968, pp. 113-154, entitled *A Review of Phonograph Records of Irish Interest*, and this is for most of its space concerned with traditional music. Printed discographies exist as very simple and short appendices in Edgar M. Deale (ed.), *A Catalogue of Contemporary Irish Composers* (2nd edition, Dublin 1973, pp. 105-7) and in Brian Boydell (ed.) *Four Centuries of Music in Ireland* (London 1979, pp. 68-70). In consulting and checking these sources I found I had as much trouble as delight, for many items needed correction, not to speak of additions (and, in fact, one deletion, since one LP listed in Boydell never appeared). In the case of individual composers assistance was provided through discography-appendices to biographical publications, and however small this help was I acknowledge it in the cases of Howard Ferguson (A. Ridout, *The Music of Howard Ferguson*, London 1989) and Seán Ó Riada (B. Harrison & G. Freyer, eds., *Integrating Tradition – The Achievement of Seán Ó Riada*, Ballina & Chester Springs, Penn., 1981). I also wish to thank Michael McGlynn for his personal help with regard to the dates and recording details of his own compositions.

The biographical information on the various composers and the dating of the many compositions in this volume were taken from my own research, from the *New Grove Dictionary of Music and Musicians* (mostly the 1980-edition), from the Contemporary Music Centre, Dublin (deepest thanks to Jonathan Grimes), and partly from authors who cooperate with me in my own work as "Irish" advisor on contributions to the new edition of the encyclopedia MGG (*Die Musik in Geschichte und Gegenwart*, Kassel and Stuttgart 1999-2004). When looking at my completed work I note that my dictionary experience has probably produced one further dictionary, because this volume may well be used not only as a discography but also as a biographical dictionary of Irish composers past and present. With regard to my own enthusiasm for the subject (without which I would never have undertaken a task like this) I would also wish for a third function of this book, that it may become a shopping list for everybody interested in Irish culture.

Introduction

This compilation is an attempt to demonstrate the breadth and depth of a musical tradition which seems all but non-existent. Who thinks of classical music when we talk about "Irish Music"? Yet the classical tradition has been alive in Ireland for centuries, and generations of Irish music lovers went to hear the symphonies, operas and chamber works of their fellow countrymen. Musicological scrutiny can find no reason why this music has for so long been neglected by the general public and by international awareness. Social and historical turmoil, Anglo-Irish conflicts in particular, may be attributed to it, but on purely musical grounds there is a wealth of material to be discovered.

Now is the chance. Ever more recording companies are discovering the Green Isle. Music historians in Europe and America are examining the musical past and present of Ireland. Attitudes towards Irishness and influences of foreign cultures are changing. So it is about time that this area receives more attention and that Irish classical music lovers begin building up a collection of a newly found Irish music. Here is the guide to it.

When I started work on this project I did not quite expect to find so much recorded music as to fill more than 200 pages. Yet the apparent wealth of material is deceiving. For if one is looking at the curriculum vitae of those composers with the most recordings to their credit, it will be found that these are composers with a strong foreign, usually English, connection. Some, indeed, have been living in England for so long that with some justification they may be claimed for England as much as for Ireland. This applies, for instance, to Howard Ferguson (1908-1999) and Charles V. Stanford (1852-1924). The life of John Field (1782-1837) is sufficiently familiar to music lovers to know that he spent the second half of his life in Russia. But the history of Irish music, like that of other arts, is just as much the history of Irish emigration. If we justly claim Swift, Goldsmith or Yeats as Irish, in the field of music we can do so with Roseingrave, Balfe and Stanford. The Anglo-Irish culture is – whether one likes it or not – just as much a part of Irish culture as the Bavarian is to the German. So nobody should ask what's Irish about some of the music assembled here.

Besides its value as a survey of the recorded music of a whole country newly discovered for its classical music, this book provides the first full discographies of well-known Irish emigrants like John Field and Charles V. Stanford, 19th-century opera heroes Michael Balfe and Vincent Wallace, as well as of more or less Anglo-Irish composers such as Howard Ferguson and E. J. Moeran. Although these fared well with the recording industry, the deplorable fact remains that most Irish composers are much underrepresented in an international context. Many have never been recorded, such as well-known names of the past like Philip Cogan (1748-1833). Of the early twentieth century we still miss names prominent in their time like Norman Hay (1889-1943) or Ina Boyle (1889-1967). Of living Irish composers we miss especially the large-scale works, such as cantatas and oratorios, which are still unrecorded. This is not sufficiently substituted by the recording of a single song or piano piece, as valuable as this is nevertheless. Irish composers of the twentieth century are – despite all laudable efforts in recent years – still far from being represented adequately on recording media.

And: the number of recordings under a name doesn't necessarily say much about the importance of their creator. Otherwise the discographies of Aloys Fleischmann (1910-1992), Frederick May (1911-1985) or Brian Boydell (1917-2000) would look very different. On the other hand, the occasional and unexpected recording of a piece by Thomas S. Cooke (1782-1848) or Vincent O'Brien (1870-1948) and the – albeit slow – rediscovery of the church music of John A. Stevenson (1761-1833) or Robert Prescott Stewart (1825-1894) provides for a surprising pleasure. Especially the *Irish Composer Series* by Marco Polo and the *20th Century Irish Series* by Black Box Music will, when completed, add immensely to the worldwide knowledge about Irish composition. At the least they lay the basis for such knowledge. We should not forget, too, that most of the recordings compiled here have *not* been made by Irish record companies, an industry which in its homeland is almost wholly focused on traditional, "contemporary-traditional" and pop music.

Finally, the last forty pages are devoted to pieces by foreign composers who had been tempted to write an "Irish" piece of music, either by a certain fascination for Irish folk music or by Irish literature in the form of legends or the writings by famous Irish poets. It should be said at this point, however, that the sole fact that a piece is a setting of a text by an Irish writer has not been a sufficient reason to include it in this discography. So this book is no discography of settings of texts by Joyce, Synge, Yeats or Beckett. Also, this compilation does not include music influenced by Irish tales or legends, although there are numerous examples. I just had to make a cut somewhere to avoid excess volume of this book. The listed pieces in Part II, some of which are fine examples of the 19th-century type of souvenir piece, derive from purely musical connections.

Another reason, admittedly, is that there is a far greater danger here of a possible omission of works, which would not have been in line with the overall aim of comprehensiveness in this book. Another point I must stress, however, is that, notwithstanding that reservation, this very effort does not strictly apply to Part II. To put it more simply: I know there are more recordings of relevant repertory than are listed. Contrary to Part I, here I am concentrating on CD-recordings to give readers a hint at available material for purchase.

Without a claim to absolute completeness (but with a strong effort in this direction), this discography lists all compact discs (CD), long-playing records (LP) and music cassettes (MC) which have been published since the mono-LP age. I did not include gramophone records of 78 rpm, cylinders or open reel tapes. However, a large number of historical recordings have been represented here when they came out on modern CD-issues.

I would be most grateful to hear from readers in cases where I failed to include certain recordings and will ensure that such omissions will be looked after in a future edition. All efforts have been undertaken to give record numbers, names and other data correctly – but nobody is perfect. If readers would like to exchange ideas or send me any relevant message, please do so using my e-mail address, draxel.klein@epost.de.

Abbreviations

A	Alto voice
acc	Accordion
arr	arranged/arrangement
Art.-Dir.	Artistic Director
B	Bass voice
Bar	Baritone voice
b-cl	Bass clarinet
Bdn	Bodhrán
bn	Bassoon
C-T	Counter-Tenor
CD	Compact disc
ch	Choir
ch-orch	Chamber orchestra
cl	Clarinet
Co.	County
cond	Conductor
db	Double Bass
e-gui	Electric guitar
EP	Extended Playing Record
fl	Flute
gui	Guitar
hp	Harp

hpd	Harpsichord
LP	Long-playing record
mar	Marimbas
MC	Music-cassette
Mez	Mezzo-soprano voice
Nar	Narrator
ob	Oboe
orch	Orchestra
perc	Percussion
pf	Piano
RTÉ	Radio Telefís Éireann (Irish national radio and television service)
S	Soprano voice
satb	Choir of mixed voices (soprano, alto, tenor, bass)
sax	Saxophone
spkr	Speaker
ssaa	female voice choir
str-orch	String orchestra
str-qu	String quartet (2vn, va, vc)
T	Tenor voice
tb	Tuba
trb	Trombone
trp	Trumpet
t-t	Tom-toms
ttbb	male voice choir
t-w	Tin Whistle
U.P.	Uíleann Pipes (Irish bagpipe)
v	Singing voice
va	Viola
vc	Violoncello
vn	Violin

Note: The tonalities of works are abbreviated in capital letters for major scales and small letters for minor scales. *Concerto for Piano and Orchestra in c minor* thus reads *Piano Concerto in c.*

Irish Classical Recordings

PART I

Recorded Music by Irish Composers

Elaine Agnew
(* Larne Co. Antrim 1967)

Elaine Agnew grew up in the Northern Irish countryside and studied at Queen's University, Belfast (BMus 1990), where her composition teachers were Michael Alcorn and Kevin Volans. She continued her studies at Glasgow with James Macmillan and travelled to Iceland and Indonesia on scholarships. Her largest pieces so far are the orchestral works *Tir na nÓg* (1992) and *Strings A-stray* (1994), the latter lending its title to a Black Box CD. Agnew's music is an individual soundworld of contrasts, freely mixing sharply dissonant and quietly consonant material to suit dramatic ideas.

Recorded Work:

Strings A-stray (1994, rev. 1998) str-orch
> Black Box Music BBM 1013, CD (1998): Irish Chamber Orchestra, Fionnuala Hunt (cond):

Michael Alcorn
(* Belfast 1962)

Alcorn studied with David Morris at the University of Ulster at Jordanstown, Co. Antrim (BA 1985), and until 1988 with John Casken at Durham, England, before he returned to Belfast to teach at Queen's University. He particularly engaged in electro-acoustic music, built up relevant facilities at Queen's and is a founder and director of the Irish Electro-Acoustic Music Society. He is also the chairman of the Sonorities Festival of Contemporary Music in Belfast. He was a visiting composer at Stanford University and Simon Fraser University. Most of his music is conceived on a computer or requires a pre-recorded tape.

Recorded Work:

Resonant Air (2000) tape
        Containers / Galway Arts Festival 2000, CD (2000).

Anonymous Medieval and Renaissance

Serious contemporary attempts at performing medieval Irish music from anonymous manuscripts with some degree of authenticity have been very scarce. The sources originate from Irish monasteries and the music is mainly contained in missals, breviaries, antiphonals or similar types of religious manuscript volumes. Only very few LPs and CDs are worth mentioning. The Chant for St. Patrick is the first likely reconstruction of a complete mass for an Irish saint following the Celtic Rite.

Irish Liber Hymnorum (11th cent.)
        Excerpts:
        Brigit bé bithmaith; Ecce fulget; Winter
        Dorian DOR-93177, CD (1999): Altramar.

In Honor of St. Patrick: Chant for His Feast (based on *Dublin Troper* [c. 1360] and antiphonals Trinity College Dublin Mss. 77, 78, 79, 80 [15th cent.])
        Order of St. Benedict Inc., Collegeville, Minnesota, CD (1998): Schola Cantorum of Saint Peter's in the Loop, Chicago, J. Michael Thomson (cond).

        Also from the *Dublin Troper*:
        Angelus ad Virginem
        EMI Ireland IEMC 6005, LP (1975): The Consort of St. Sepulchre, Barra Boydell (cond).

Divine Office Breviary (Trinity College Ms. 80) (early 15th cent.)
        Excerpts:
        Cristo canamus gloriam; Adest dies leticie
        Dorian DOR-93177, CD (1999): Altramar.

Smarmore Tablets (late 15th cent.)
        Dorian DOR-93177, CD (1999): Altramar.

The Lay of the Forge (16th cent.)
        Dorian DOR-93177, CD (1999): Altramar.

Callino Costurame (1580s or 90s) (v) lute
        EMI Ireland IEMC 6008, LP (1977): Lucienne Purcell (v), Andrew Robinson (lute).

        (with additions and variations:)
        Dorian DOR-90235, CD (1997): Baltimore Consort.

Fitzwilliam Virginal Book (c. 1609-1619) hpd
        (arranged excerpts:)
        The Irish Ho-Hoane; The Irishe Dumpe
        Dorian DOR-90235, CD (1997): Baltimore Consort.

Michael William Balfe
(* Dublin 1808, † Rowney Abbey, Herts. 1870)

Balfe was born in Pitt Street, now Balfe Street, Dublin, at a time, when the "golden era" of Anglo-Irish music was just over, but could still be felt. He grew up in Wexford, but was sent to Dublin for tuition after his talents had been discovered. His earliest teacher was the Irish composer William O'Rourke (or Rooke, 1794-1847). After the death of his father in 1823 he moved to England, where he began to sing in operas and play violin in various orchestras. Further tuition and musical engagements led him to Rome (1825), Milan, Paris, and several Italian opera stages until 1833, when he returned to England. He became the most prominent and most successful composer of English-language operas in the 19th century, only to be rivalled by his fellow-countryman, Vincent Wallace (and later in the century by Gilbert & Sullivan). His first British success was *The Siege of Rochelle* (1835), followed by *The Maid of Artois* (1836), *The Bohemian Girl* (1843) and *The Rose of Castile* (1857). Many of his song compositions became successful, too; *By Killarney's Lakes* (1862) still having a folk-song-like popularity in south-west Ireland. He also wrote two cantatas and some chamber music.

Recorded Works:

The Siege of Rochelle (1835) opera
        Excerpts:

'Twas in that Garden Beautiful
Melba 301082, CD (2000): Deborah Riedel (S), Australian Opera and
Ballet Orchestra, Richard Bonynge (cond).

When I Beheld the Anchor Weigh'd
British Music Society BMS 422, CD (1998): Campbell Russell (T),
John Talbot (pf).

The Maid of Artois (1836) opera
Excerpts:
The Rapture Dwelling in my Heart; Yon Moon o'er the Mountain
Melba 301082, CD (2000): Deborah Riedel (S), Australian Opera and
Ballet Orchestra, Richard Bonynge (cond).

Le puits d'amour (1843), opera
Excerpt:
Rêves d'amour, rêves de gloire
Decca 440 679-2DH, CD (1993): Sumi Jo (S), English Chamber
Orchestra, Richard Bonynge (cond).

The Bohemian Girl (1843), opera
Argo 433 324-2, 2CD (1991): Nova Thomas (S), Patrick Power (T),
Jonathan Summers (Bar), Bernadette Cullen (Mez), John del Carlo (B),
Timothy German (T), RTÉ Philharmonic Choir, National Symphony
Orchestra of Ireland, Richard Bonynge (cond).

Excerpts:
Overture
Dutton Laboratories CDSJB 1999, 2CD (2000, recorded 1934):
anonymous orchestra, John Barbirolli (cond).

*Overture, The Heart Bow'd Down, I Dreamt I Dwelt in Marble Halls,
When Other Lips and Other Hearts, Waltz, Love Smiles but to Deceive,
Galop.*
EMI CSD 3651, LP (1968): Veronica Dunne (S), Uel Deane (T), Eric
Hinds (Bar), anonymous orchestra, Havelock Nelson (cond).

Galop
Lyrita SCRS 99, LP (1978): Philharmonia Orchestra, Nicholas
Braithwaite (cond).

I Dreamt I Dwelt in Marble Halls
Decca SET 247-8, LP (1963): Joan Sutherland (S), London Symphony
Orchestra, Richard Bonynge (cond).

Re-issued on Decca 425 048 2DX, CD (199?); Decca 425 850-2DWO, CD / -4DWO, MC (1993).

Griffin GC CD / MC 4009, CD / MC (1994): Patricia Sabin (S), Margaret Lion (pf).

The Heart Bow'd Down
Pearl Gemm CDS 9059/61, 3CD (1994, recorded 1913): Henri Scott (Bar), Original Broadway Cast.

International Record Collectors Club IRCC-CD 810, CD (1994, recorded 1927): Clarence Whitehill (Bar), anonymous orchestra.

Then You'll Remember Me
Symposium 1163, CD (1996, recorded 1914): John McCormack (T), anonymous orchestra.

When Other Lips and Other Hearts
Symposium SYMCD 1163, CD (1994, recorded 1914): John McCormack (T), anonymous orchestra.

Pearl Gemm CD 9319, CD (1989, recorded 1926): Heddle Nash (T), anonymous orchestra.

Kiwi-Pacific Records CDSLD-82. CD, (1994, recorded 1991): Patrick Power (T), National Symphony Orchestra of Ireland, Richard Bonynge (cond) (extract from complete Argo recording).

RCA Victor Red Seal 09026 68030-2, CD (1996): Jerry Hadley (T), English Chamber Orchestra, Richard Bonynge (cond).

ASV CD AJA 5227, CD (1999) *(same recording as Pearl Gemm above).*

Sventurata Ildegonda – Chiuso nell'Armi (1843) (Aria in Angelo Mariani's opera *Ildegonda nel Carcere*)
Decca SXL 6501, LP (1971): Huguette Tourangeau (Mez), L'Orchestre de la Suisse Romande, Richard Bonynge (cond).

The Daughter of St. Mark (1844) opera
Rare Recorded Editions SRRE 141-2, 2LP (1974): Frances Black (S), Geoffrey Shovelton (T), Nigel Beavan (Bar), Malcolm King (B), Gala Opera Group, anonymous orchestra, Ken Jones (cond).

Excelsior (c. 1855) T, Bar, orch
  Pearl Gemm 9455, CD (1991, recorded 1926): Malcolm McEachern
  (T), Harold Williams (Bar), Aeolian Orchestra.

  Pearl Gemm 9989, CD (1992, recorded 1934): Tom Burke (T), Foster
  Richardson (Bar), anonymous orchestra.

Trust Her Not (c. 1855) S, Mez, pf
  Centaur CRC 2075, CD (1990): Ellen Frohnmayer (S), Philip Frohnmayer (Bar), Logan Skelton (pf).

  EMI CDC7 54411-2, CD (1992): Felicity Lott (S), Ann Murray (Mez),
  Graham Johnson (pf).

The Rose of Castile (1857), opera
  Rare Recorded Editions RRE 191/2, 2LP (197?, recorded 1951):
  Maureen Springer (S), Angela O'Connor (Mez), James Cuthbert (B),
  Murray Dickie (T), Wexford Festival Chorus, Radio Éireann Light
  Orchestra, Dermot O'Hara (cond).

  Excerpts:
  The Convent Cell
  Melba 301082, CD (2000): Deborah Riedel (S), Australian Opera and
  Ballet Orchestra, Richard Bonynge (cond).

  'Twas Rank and Fame
  RCA Victor Red Seal 09026 68030-2, CD (1996): Jerry Hadley (T),
  English Chamber Orchestra, Richard Bonynge (cond).

Satanella (1858) opera
  Rare Recorded Editions RRE 173/4, 2LP (197?): Jasmine Tateossian
  (S), Stephanie Debret (S), Susan Devlin (A), David Flint (T), Jack
  Donert (Bar) et al, Addison Orchestra, Brian Galloway (cond).

  Excerpts:
  Oh Could I but His Heart Enslave; There's a Power Whose Sway
  Melba 301082, CD (2000): Deborah Riedel (S), Australian Opera and
  Ballet Orchestra, Richard Bonynge (cond).

Thomas Moore's Irish Melodies (arr. 1859) v, pf
  Excerpt:
  The Harp that Once through Tara's Halls
  EMI EX 290007 3, 2LP (1984, recorded 1930): John McCormack (T),
  Edwin Schneider (pf).

Arrangement for orchestra:
Symposium 1152, CD (1994, recorded 1926): John O'Sullivan
(T), anonymous orchestra, Hamilton Harty (cond).

The Puritan's Daughter (1861) opera
Excerpt:
Bliss for ever Past
Melba 301082, CD (2000): Deborah Riedel (S), Australian Opera and
Ballet Orchestra, Richard Bonynge (cond).

By Killarney's Lakes (1862) v, pf
Pearl Gemm CD 9411, CD (1991, recorded in the 1920s): Tom Burke
(T), anonymous orchestra.

Claremont CDESG 785058, CD (1995, recorded 1934): Richard Crooks
(T), anonymous orchestra.

Nimbus NI 7854, CD (1993, recorded 1910): John McCormack (T),
Victor Orchestra.

Romophone 82006-2, CD (1996) (same recording as above).

Arrangement for choir and piano:
EMI CLP 3532, LP (1966): Feis Éireann Group of Singers, Eileen
O'Grady (pf + cond).

Arrangement for violin and orchestra:
Pearl Past CD 9744, CD (1991): Alfredo Campoli (vn), Raymonde
Orchestra, Walter Goehr (cond).

Arrangement for cornet and piano:
Crystal 450, CD (1996, recorded 1901): Herbert L. Clarke (corn),
anonymous pianist.

Come into the Garden, Maud (18??) v, pf
ASV CD AJA 5119, CD (1993, recorded 1915): John McCormack (T),
anonymous orchestra, Walter B. Rogers (cond).

Pearl Gemm CD 9112, CD (1994, recorded 1926): Walter Widdop (T),
anonymous pianist.

Griffin GCCD 4009, CD/MC (1994): Graham Titus (Bar), Margaret
Lion (pf).

Belart 461316-2, CD (1996): Stuart Burrows (T), John Constable (pf).

Dutton Laboratories CDLX 7031, CD (1999, recorded 193?): Heddle Nash (T), Gerald Moore (pf).

The Sands of Dee (18??) v, pf
Symposium 1074, CD (1989): Peter Allanson (Bar), Stephen Betteridge (pf).

British Music Society BMS 422, CD (1998): Katy Morell (S), John Talbot (pf).

Il Talismano (unfinished, completed by Michael Costa in 1874) opera
Excerpts:
Che Calmo Asil, Placida Notte; Nella Dolce Trepidanza
Melba 301082, CD (2000): Deborah Riedel (S), Australian Opera and Ballet Orchestra, Richard Bonynge (cond).

Gerald Barry
(* Clarecastle Co. Clare 1952)

Gerald Barry is one of the foremost Irish composers of his generation and among them the most well-known internationally. In 1973 he completed his Bachelor of Music course at University College Dublin (MA 1975) and continued his studies in Amsterdam (with Peter Schat, 1973-4), Cologne (with Karlheinz Stockhausen and Mauricio Kagel, 1975-81) and Vienna (with Friedrich Cerha, 1977-8). He taught at University College Cork from 1982 to 1986 and since then lives as freelance composer in Dublin. He is a member of Aosdána. His music has been praised for its bold originality and wit as well as for its careful construction, but, as a CD-booklet-writer notes, it is "not music for the faint-hearted".

Recorded Works:

Things that Gain (1977) pf
Black Box Music BBM 1011, CD (1998): Kevin Volans.

"————" (1979) 2cl/b-cl, va, vc, mar, pf
NMC D022, CD (1994): Nua Nós, Dáirine Ní Mheadhra (cond).

"Ø" (1979) 2pf
Black Box Music BBM 1011, CD (1998): Kevin Volans & Gerald Barry.

Diner (1980) orch
    Marco Polo 8.225006, CD (1997): National Symphony Orchestra of
    Ireland, Robert Houlihan (cond).

Au Milieu (1981) pf
    NMC D022, CD (1994): Noriko Kawai.

Sur les Pointes (1981) pf
    NMC D022, CD (1994): Noriko Kawai.

Sur les Pointes (1981) orch
    Marco Polo 8.225006, CD (1997): National Symphony Orchestra of
    Ireland, Robert Houlihan (cond).

Water Parted (1981-4) C-T, pf
    Black Box Music BBM 1011, CD (1998): Nicholas Clapton (C-T),
    Catherine Edwards (pf).

Five Chorales (1981-4) 2pf
    Black Box Music BBM 1011, CD (1998): Kevin Volans & G. Barry.

String Quartet No. 1 (1985, rev. 1994) str-qu
    Black Box Music BBM 1011, CD (1998.): The Xenia Ensemble.

Of Queen's Gardens (1986) orch
    Marco Polo 8.225006, CD (1997): National Symphony Orchestra of
    Ireland, Robert Houlihan (cond).

Swinging Tripes and Trillibubkins (1986) pf
    NMC D022, CD (1994): Noriko Kawai.

Chevaux-de-frise (1988) orch
    Marco Polo 8.225006, CD (1997): National Symphony Orchestra of
    Ireland, Robert Houlihan (cond).

Bob (1989) cl, cl+b-cl, vn, vc, mar, pf
    NMC D022, CD (1994): Nua Nós, Dáirine Ní Mheadhra (cond).

Triorchic Blues (1990) pf
    NMC D022, CD (1994): Noriko Kawai.

Flamboys (1991) orch
    Marco Polo 8.225006, CD (1997): National Symphony Orchestra of
    Ireland, Robert Houlihan (cond).

Hard D (1992) ch-orch
Marco Polo 8.225006, CD (1997): Members of the National Symphony Orchestra of Ireland, Robert Houlihan (cond).

Challenge CHR 70057, CD (1998): Orkest de Volharding, Jurjen Hempel (cond).

Triorchic Blues (1992) vn
NMC D022, CD (1994): Michael d'Arcy.

Piano Quartet No. 1 (1992) vn, va, vc, pf
NMC D022, CD (1994): Nua Nós, Dáirine Ní Mheadhra (cond).

The Triumph of Beauty and Deceit (1992) opera
Largo 5135, CD (1998): Nicholas Clapton (C-T), Denis Lakey (C-T), Richard Edgar-Wilson (T), Adrian Clarke (Bar), Stephen Richardson (B), The Composers Ensemble, Diego Masson (cond).

Sextet (1993) cl/b-cl, trp, db, 2mar, pf
NMC D022, CD (1994): Nua Nós, Dáirine Ní Mheadhra (cond).

CMC CD01, promotion-CD (1995) (same recording as above).

La Jalousie Taciturne (1996) ch-orch
Black Box Music BBM 1013, CD (1998): Irish Chamber Orchestra, Fionnuala Hunt (cond).

Piano Quartet No. 2 (1996) vn, va, vc, pf
Black Box Music BBM 1011, CD (1998): Eilís Cranitch (vn), Michèle Minne (va), Elizabeth Wilson (vc), Gerald Barry (pf).

Before The Road (1997) 4cl
Black Box Music BBM 1011, CD (1998): Antony Lamb (cl), Victoria Medcalf (cl), Andrew Webster (cl), Robert Ault (cl).

Thomas Bateson
(* England after 1570, † Dublin 1630)

Thomas Bateson belongs to the Elizabethan madrigal school and was for many years its most western representative. Probably born in Cheshire, he was organist at Chester Cathedral from 1599 before he left for Ireland in 1609. Until he died 21 years later he was organist of Christ Church Cathedral, Dublin. He is also among the earliest musical students of Trinity College, where he graduated Bachelor of Music in 1612 and Master of Arts in 1622. The music he left for posterity was all written in Dublin and printed in London. It is contained in two volumes of madrigals dating from 1604 and 1618. Though there have been greater composers in his time, Bateson's music is very elaborated and distinctive.

Recorded works:

The First Set of Madrigals (1604) vv
Excerpts:
Come Follow Me, Fair Nymphs
Argo ZRG 658, LP (1970): Purcell Consort.

Down From Above Falls Jove
HMV HQS 1080, LP (1967): Ambrosian Consort.

Phyllis, Farewell
New Irish Recording Co. DEB 002, LP (1974): Culwick Choral Society, Eric Sweeney (cond).

Telarc CD-80328, CD (1983): Quink Vocal Ensemble.

Sister Awake
Turnabout TV 34202 S, LP (1969): Purcell Consort.

The Nightingale
CRDC 4055, MC (1978): Camerata of London.
Re-issued on CRD 3355, CD (1989).

Koch Discover International DICD 920388, CD (1996): Terpsichore.

Titanic TI 238, CD (1998): Salomone Trio.

Those sweet delightful lillies
Telarc CD-80328, CD (1983): Quink Vocal Ensemble.

With Bitter Sighs
Unicorn UNS 254, LP (1972): The Scholars.

Holy, Lord God Almighty (1612) satb
Priory PRCD 639, CD (1999) Christ Church Cathedral Dublin Choir, Mark Duley (cond).

Christ Church Cathedral Recording / Four Courts Press CCCD1, CD
(1999). Christ Church Cathedral Dublin Choir, Mark Duley (cond)
(different recording from above).

Walter Beckett
(* Dublin 1914, † Dublin 1996)

Beckett was one of the lesser active composers of the mid-twentieth century. He
studied at the Read School, the Royal Irish Academy of Music (RIAM) and at
Trinity College, Dublin, graduating Bachelor of Music in 1936 and Doctor of
Music in 1942. In 1946 he left for Venice and was for several years the foreign
correspondent in musical matters for the Irish Times. From 1963 to 1972 he
lived in Warrickshire and Coventry, England, before returning to Ireland. He
taught harmony and counterpoint at the RIAM from 1972 to 1985, when ill-
health prevented further creative work. Among his main works is a *Suite for
Orchestra* (1945), a *Dublin Symphony* (1989) and a *Quartet for Strings* (1980).

Recorded Works:

Quartet for Strings (1980) str-qu
          Chandos CHAN 9295, CD (1994): Vanbrugh Quartet.

Cornphíopa Dhoire (arr.) orch
          Gael-Linn CEF 004, LP (c. 1960): Radio Éireann Light Orchestra,
          Éimear Ó Broin (cond).

Down by the Sally Gardens (arr.) v, instr. quintet
          Argo ZRG 5434 (stereo), RG 434 (mono), LP (1965): Bernadette
          Greevy (Mez), members of the Radio Éireann Symphony Orchestra.

Seóirse Bodley
(* Dublin 1933)

Bodley is one the most important Irish composers of the older generation and
was probably, in the 1960s and 1970s, the most modern voice sounding from
Ireland. He studied at University College Dublin, 1952-5 (doctorate 1959) and at
the Musikhochschule Stuttgart, Germany (with Johann Nepomuk David, 1957-
59). He taught music at UCD from 1959 to 1998. From three visits to the famous
summer courses of new music at Darmstadt (1963-5) he returned to Ireland with
an awareness of modern continental trends in music which resulted in many

pieces of great complexity. From c. 1972 he combined these modern influences with elements from Irish traditional music, producing a highly original music of contrasts. His works from the early 1980s returns to a more simple language maintaining many qualities of his earlier styles in more subtle reflections. Bodley's case is certainly one of an often misunderstood and today far too little recorded composer.

Recorded Works:

Music for Strings (1952) str-orch
> Decca (USA) DL 9843, LP (1958): Radio Éireann Symphony Orchestra, Milan Horvat (cond).

I Will Walk with My Love (arr. 195x) SATB
> Harmonia Mundi HMS 30691, LP (1965): RTÉ Singers, Waldemar Rosen (cond).

> New Irish Recording Co. DEB 002, LP (1974): Culwick Choral Society, Eric Sweeney (cond).

Prelude, Toccata and Epilogue (1963) pf
> New Irish Recording Co. NIR 001, LP (1971): Charles Lynch.

Chamber Symphony No. 1 (1964) ch-orch
> New Irish Recording Co. NIR 012, LP (1974): New Irish Chamber Orchestra, André Prieur (cond).

String Quartet (1968) str-qu
> New Irish Recording Co. NIR 006, LP (1973): RTÉ String Quartet.

The Narrow Road to the Deep North (1977) pf
> Gael-Linn CEF 085, LP/MC (1980): John O'Conor.

Mass of Peace (1976) spkr, satb, org
> Network Tapes NTO 55C, MC (1977): Clonliffe College Choir, Seóirse Bodley (cond).

Mass of Joy (1978) spkr, satb, fl, 2trp, org, perc
> Network Tapes NTO 102C, MC (1979): (no performers mentioned).

Hymn to St. John of God (1978)
> Network Tapes NTO 102C, MC (1979): (no performers mentioned).

A Girl (1980) Mez, pf
>   Gael-Linn CEF 085, LP/MC (1980): Bernadette Greevy (Mez), John
>   O'Conor (pf).

The Naked Flame (1987) Mez, pf
>   Echo Classic Digital, CD (1996): Aylish Kerrigan (Mez), Seóirse
>   Bodley (pf).

Carta Irlandesa (1988) Mez, pf
>   Echo Classic Digital, CD (1996): Aylish Kerrigan (Mez), Seóirse
>   Bodley (pf).

Symphony No. 4 (1991) orch
>   Marco Polo 8.225157, CD (2001): National Symphony Orchestra of
>   Ireland, Colman Pearce (cond).

Symphony No. 5 "The Limerick Symphony" (1991) orch
>   Marco Polo 8.225157, CD (2001): National Symphony Orchestra of
>   Ireland, Colman Pearce (cond).

String Quartet No. 2 (1992) str-qu
>   Excerpt (3rd movt.):
>   CMC CD02, promotion-CD (1997): Degani String Quartet.

By the Margin of the Great Deep (1995) Mez, pf
>   Echo Classic Digital, CD (1996): Aylish Kerrigan (Mez), Seóirse
>   Bodley (pf).

Undated arrangements:

Laoi Chainte an Tombac (arr) satb
>   Corkfest Records 94, CD (1994): Cór Naomh Múire, Fintan O Murchu
>   (cond).

Táim Gan Im Gan Ór (arr.) orch
>   Gael-Linn CEF 004, LP (c. 1960): Radio Éireann Light Orchestra,
>   Éimear Ó Broin (cond).

Brian Boydell
(* Dublin 1917, † Howth Co. Dublin 2000)

Boydell was a familiar name to many Irish music lovers, concert-goers and radio listeners through his many activities as conductor, teacher and broadcaster. He started his career in natural sciences, obtaining a university degree in Cambridge (1938). He studied music at Heidelberg (1935), London (1938-9) and Dublin (1940-2) and was Professor of Singing at the Royal Irish Academy of Music from 1944 to 1952. From 1962 to 1982 he was Professor of Music at Trinity College, Dublin.

Boydell's music of the 1940s and 1950s was among the most modern achievements of the time in Ireland. Conservative in an international context, his music is part of a parallel, more traditional movement to the serial avantgarde, to which he could find no relationship. Though his main orchestral works have been recorded, much fine music still has to be discovered by the recording media.

Recorded Works:

In memoriam Mahatma Gandhi op. 30 (1943) orch
Marco Polo 8.223887, CD (1997): National Symphony Orchestra of Ireland, Colman Pearce (cond).

String Quartet No. 1 op. 31 (1949) str-qu
Deutsche Grammophon 32291, LP (c. 1956): Benthien Streichquartett.

Goasco GXX 002-4, MC (1985): Academica Quartet.

Violin Concerto op. 36 (1953-54) vn, orch
Marco Polo 8.223887, CD (1997): Maighread McCrann (vn), National Symphony Orchestra of Ireland, Colman Pearce (cond).

Megalithic Ritual Dances op. 39 (1956) orch
Decca (USA) DL 9843, LP (1956): Radio Éireann Symphony Orchestra, Milan Horvat (cond).

Marco Polo 8.223887, CD (1997): National Symphony Orchestra of Ireland, Colman Pearce (cond).

String Quartet No. 2 op. 44 (1957) str-qu
Chandos CHAN 9295, CD (1994): Vanbrugh Quartet.

Dance for an Ancient Ritual op. 39a (1959) pf
New Irish Recording Co. NIR 001, LP (1971): Charles Lynch.

Capriccio op. 48 (1959) pf
New Irish Recording Co. NIR 001, LP (1971): Charles Lynch.

Three Yeats Songs op. 56a (1965) v, pf
Columbia (Japan) JX-32, LP (196?): *(performers?).*

Symphonic Inscapes op. 64 (1968) orch
New Irish Recording Co. NIR 011, LP (1974): RTÉ Symphony
Orchestra, Albert Rosen (cond).

Three Pieces op. 70 (1973) gui
Black Box Music BBM 1002, CD (1998): John Feeley.

Masai Mara op. 87 (1988) orch
Marco Polo 8.223887, CD (1997): National Symphony Orchestra of
Ireland, Colman Pearce (cond).

Adagio and Scherzo op. 89 (1991) str-qu
CMC CD01, Promotion-CD (1995): Vanbrugh Quartet.

Viking Lip-Music op. 91 (1996) brass band
Rondo Grammofon RCD 8358, CD (1997): Royal Danish Brass.

John Buckley
(* Templeglantine Co. Limerick 1951)

The name of John Buckley became established with the Dublin Festival of Twentieth Century Music (1969-84) as a voice of the young, modern generation breaking the bonds with traditionalism in Ireland. Although many pieces by Buckley refer to Irish myths and landscapes, his approach is frankly avantgarde, with musical models in Lutoslawski or Ligeti. The graduate of the Royal Irish Academy of Music (1969-74) and the University of Cardiff (with Alun Hoddinot, 1978-82) lives as a freelance composer in Dublin since 1982. He is a member of Aosdána. Among his main works are orchestral pieces such as *Taller than Roman Spears* (1977), *Symphony No. 1* (1988) and an *Organ Concerto* (1992), but he has written for many solo-instruments, chamber music combinations and an opera called *The Word upon the Window-Pane* (1991).

Recorded Works:

Three Pieces (1973) fl
Black Box Music BBM 1012, CD (1999): William Dowdall.

Wind Quintet (1976) fl, ob+c.a., cl, hn, bn
  Goasco GXX 001-4, MC (1985): Ulysses Wind Quintet.

Oileáin (Islands) (1979) pf
  Marco Polo 8.223784, CD (1999): Anthony Byrne.

Five Epigrams (1980) fl, ob
  Goasco GXX 001-4, MC (1985): Madeleine Berkeley (fl), Helmut
  Seeber (ob).

Sonata for Unaccompanied Violin (1983) vn
  Goasco GXX 001-4, MC (1985): Alan Smale.

  CMC 001S-4, MC (1991): Alan Smale.

Boireann (1983) fl, pf
  Goasco GXX 001-4, MC (1985): William Dowdall (fl), Gillian Smith
  (pf).

Fantasia No. 1 (1984) rec
  Black Box Music BBM 1012, CD (1999): Aidin Halpin.

And Wake the Purple Year (1985) pf
  Marco Polo 8.223784, CD (1999): Anthony Byrne.

Fantasia No. 2 (1987) rec
  Black Box Music BBM 1012, CD (1999): Aidin Halpin.

Symphony No. 1 (1988) orch
  Marco Polo 8.223876, CD (1999): National Symphony Orchestra of
  Ireland, Colman Pearce (cond).

Winter Music (1988) pf
  Marco Polo 8.223784, CD (1999): Anthony Byrne.

Abendlied (1989) S, pf
  Altarus AIR-CD-9010, CD (1996): Penelope Price Jones (S), Philip
  Martin (pf).

Three Lullabies for Deirdre (1989) pf
  Anew Records NEWD 406, CD (1994): Roy Holmes.

  Marco Polo 8.223784, CD (1999): Anthony Byrne.

Arabesque (1990) alto-sax
    Black Box Music BBM 1012, CD (1999): Kenneth Edge.

Concerto for Organ and Orchestra (1992) org, orch
    Marco Polo 8.223876, CD (1999): Peter Sweeney (org), National Symphony Orchestra of Ireland, Colman Pearce (cond).

Sonata for Solo Horn (1993) hn
    CMC CD01, Promotion-CD (1995): Cormac Ó hAodáin.

    Black Box Music BBM 1012, CD (1999): Cormac Ó hAodáin.

The Silver Apples of the Moon, the Golden Apples of the Sun (1993) pf
    Marco Polo 8.223784, CD (1999): Anthony Byrne.

In Lines of Dazzling Light (1995) vn, cl, hn, bn, pf
    Black Box Music BBM 1012, CD (1999): Darragh Morgan (vn), Guy Cowley (cl), Clare Hutchings (hn), Philip Gibbon (bn), Ian Pace (pf), Mikel Toms (cond).

Saxophone Quartet (1996) 4sax
    Black Box Music BBM 1024, CD (1999): Quartz Saxophone Quartet.
    Re-issued on Black Box Music BBM 1012, CD (1999).

Three Preludes (1996) pf
    Marco Polo 8.223784, CD (1999): Anthony Byrne.

Concerto for Alto Saxophone and String Orchestra (1997) alto-sax, ch-orch
    Black Box Music BBM 1013, CD (1998): Kenneth Edge (alto-sax), Irish Chamber Orchestra, Fionnuala Hunt (cond).

Airflow (1998) fl
    Black Box Music BBM 1012, CD (1999): William Dowdall.

Edward Bunting
(* Armagh 1773, † Dublin 1843)

Edward Bunting was organist at St. Anne's Church, Belfast, when in 1792 he was commissioned to attend the Belfast Harpers Festival to note down the tunes of the last itinerant Irish harpers. He became a founding member of Irish Harp Societies and came to live in Dublin in 1819. He collected more than 260 Irish folk tunes and published them in three collections dated 1796, 1809 and 1840.

He published harmonic arrangements for the piano in the style of his time (sometimes as songs with new English texts) and not the original melodies as he heard them. The following short list only includes pieces that were recorded in Bunting's original arrangement.

Recorded Works:

A General Collection of the Ancient Irish Music (arr. 1796) pf
> Excerpts:
> *Love in Secret*
> Hyperion CDA 66774, CD (1995): Timothy Roberts.
>
> *Madam Cole; Thomas O'Burk*
> Ossian OSS CD 65, CD (1992): Rodney Baldwin (hpd).

David Byers
(* Belfast 1947)

Byers studied composition with Raymond Warren at Queen's University, Belfast (1965-7), and with the help of the Manson Scholarship with James Iliff at the Royal Academy of Music, London. He received the Macauley Fellowship in 1972. During the year 1972-3 he studied with Henri Pousseur at the Conservatoire Royale de Musique at Liège, Belgium. He has been working at BBC Northern Ireland for a number of years. Beginning as a composer much interested in sound experiments, Byers later consciously reduced his musical language to more simple means sometimes bordering on the archaic.

Recorded Works:

Dragons (1979) org
> Priory Records PR 178-A, LP (1985): Norman Finlay.

Verses (1982) org
> Priory Records PR 178-A, LP (1985): Norman Finlay.

Rob Canning
(* Dublin 1974)

Canning is among the youngest composers represented in this volume. He studied at the University of Wales at Cardiff (BMus 1997) and completed post-gradual studies at University College Dublin in 2000. In 1998 he gained first prize in the composer class of the "Musician of the Future" competition of Radio Telefís Éireann and also won the 1999 "New Music for Sligo" competition. He is often working in the electro-acoustic medium.

Recorded Work:

Continuum (2000) cl, tape
      Containers / Galway Arts Festival 2000, CD (2000): Paul Roe (cl).

Turlough Carolan
(* near Nobber Co. Meath 1670, † Ballyfarnon Co. Roscommon 1738)

Carolan was one of the last blind harpers in Ireland marking the end of the old Gaelic society and the spreading of Anglo-Irish culture which occurred during his lifetime. Blinded by smallpox when he was 18, he learned to play the Irish harp and travelled the country with the aid of a guide. His worklist consists of more than 200 melodies which he composed for the people he visited and often carried their name as titles. They are preserved in various contemporary collections and often appear with accompaniments which will not have been his own. They show influences of Irish traditional music and of contemporary baroque music which he encountered on his travels to Dublin. He is said to have met Francesco Geminiani and Dean Jonathan Swift.

Today his music appears in innumerable arrangements impossible to list here; therefore this compilation is limited to what can be regarded as authentic. The only CD which can be called authentic follows the harp accompaniments as given in a 1748 fragment of a collection published by Carolan's son, which is in the possession of the National Library of Ireland.

Recorded Works:

Betty O'Brien
Carolan's Concerto (Mrs. Power)
Carolan's Receipt
Dr. John Hart
Elizabeth McDermott Roe
Fanny Power
Farewell to Music
Grace Nugent
James Betagh
Lord Inchiquin
Mabel Kelly

Madam Maxwell
Planxty Hugh O'Donnell
Planxty John O'Connor
Planxty Johnston
Planxty Morgan Magan
Sí Bheag is Sí Mhór
Sir Arthur Shaen
The Fairy Queen
The Parting of Companions
William O'Flinn
 Gael-Linn CEFCD 156, 2CD (1992): Gráinne Yeats (Ir hp).

Charles Thomas Carter
(* Dublin c. 1735, † London 1804)

Carter was at various times between 1751 and 1769 organist and choir-master at
St. Werburgh's and St. Peter's Churches, Dublin. He then pursued a career as an
opera composer in London, his outstanding success being *Just in Time*,
performed in May 1792 at Covent Garden. Carter's biography and works are
often confused with those of another Irish composer named Thomas Carter
(1769-1800) and with Timothy Carter (c. 1715-1772), possibly his father. He
was best known as a composer of songs for the fashionable London Vauxhall
Gardens concerts. His only recorded song on CD is contained in his first London
song-collection for this occasion.

Recorded Work:

Oh Nanny wilt thou gang with me (1773) v, vn, pf
 Vox Classics 7537, CD (1996): Julianne Baird (S), Nancy Wilson (vn),
 Mary Jane Newman (pf).

Rhona Clarke
(* Dublin 1958)

Rhona Clarke was a talented musician from early age on. She studied at University College Dublin (Teachers Diploma 1978, BMus 1980) and taught music

at various schools in Dublin. She has been active in many school projects introducing new music and encouraging musical creativity. Some of her early pieces
won composers' competitions such as *Six Short Piano Pieces* (1982), the choral
work *Suantraí Ghráinne* (1983) and *Sisyphus* (1985) for flute, clarinet and string
trio. Her first orchestral score was *A Great Rooted Tree* (1991). She also wrote
electro-acoustic music such as *Pied Piper* (1994) for flute, tape and live
electronics.

Recorded Works:

Five Songs (1998) S, pf
     Excerpts:
     The Old Men Admiring Themselves in the Water; Autobiography
     Association of Irish Composers AIC 001, Promotion-CD (1999): Judith
     Mok (S), Dearbhla Collins (pf).

Siobháin Cleary
(* Dublin 1970)

Cleary graduated from St. Patrick's College, Maynooth (BA 1991) and from
Queen's University, Belfast (MA 1993). She has successfully taken part in
competitions in Ireland and England and received awards in Italy and France.

Recorded Works:

Threads (1992, rev. 1994) orch
     Vienna Modern Masters VMM 3041, CD (1997): Moravian Philhar-
     monic Orchestra, Jiri Mikula (cond).

Deuce! (1995) 2vn
     Association of Irish Composers AIC 001, Promotion-CD (1999): Brona
     Cahill & Michael d'Arcy.

Thomas Simpson Cooke
(* Dublin 1782, † London 1848)

Cooke was one of the most prolific opera-composers of his time on the British
Isles, a famous tenor and an important theatrical manager in London. He was the

leader of the orchestra at Dublin's Crow Street Theatre and kept a music shop until 1812, when he left for London. He became musical director of the Vauxhall Gardens concerts, and of the opera houses at Covent Garden and Drury Lane.

Cooke wrote music for more than 50 operas, not all of them through-composed and most being of a lighter kind. Lesser known are his works for chamber music instrumentations and vocal ensembles, one of the latter – a glee – being the only recorded piece of music by Cooke so far.

Recorded Work:

Strike the lyre (18??) 4 male vv
> Conifer CDCF 145 (= CD), CFC 145 (= LP), MCFC 145 (= MC)
> (1987): Pro Cantione Antiqua, Mark Brown (cond).

Frank Corcoran
(* Borrisokane Co. Tipperary 1944)

Corcoran was born outside the mainstream of art music in Ireland. From 1961 to 1964 he studied Greek, Latin, philosophy and music theory at St. Patrick's College, Maynooth, then until 1967 theology at the Lateran-University at Rome. Finally he studied composition at Dublin (Royal Irish Academy of Music, with A.J. Potter 1967-9) and at Berlin (Musikhochschule, with Boris Blacher, 1969-71). From 1971 to 1979 he worked as a school music inspector for the Irish Department of Education and in 1976 was a founder member of the Association of Irish Composers. In 1982 he became Professor of Composition at Stuttgart, Germany, and from 1983 at Hamburg, where he continues to teach composition and theory at the Musikhochschule. "Self Help" was his own initiative, when no national or international recording company was interested in contenporary Irish music.

Recorded Works:

The Quare Hawk (1974) fl
> Self Help 101, LP (1980): Madeleine Berkeley.

Gestures of Sound and Silence (1976) str-qu
> Self Help 101, LP (1980): Testore Quartet.

Piano Trio (1978) vn vc pf
> Self Help 101, LP (1980): Hesketh Trio.

Mythologies (1979) perc
   Self Help 101, LP (1980): Roger Doyle.

String Quartet No. 2 (1979) str-qu
   Self Help 101, LP (1980): Testore Quartet.

Symphony No. 2 (1981) orch
   Marco Polo 8.225107, CD (1999): National Symphony Orchestra of
   Ireland, Colman Pearce (cond).

Music for the Book of Kells (1990) perc-ens, pf
   Black Box Music BBM 1026, CD (1999): Percussion Modern, Frank
   Corcoran (pf), Dieter Cichewiecz (cond).

Three Pieces (1990) gui
   Excerpt: (2nd piece)
   Contemporary Music Centre CMC CD02, Promotion-CD (1997):
   Benjamin Dwyer.

Wind Quintet (1992) fl, ob, cl, hn, bn
   Black Box Music BBM 1026, CD (1999): Stuttgart Wind Quintet,
   Willy Freivogel (cond).

Irische Mikrokosmoi [Scenes from My Receding PAST ...] (1994) ch-orch
   Black Box Music BBM 1013, CD (1998): Irish Chamber Orchestra,
   Fionnuala Hunt (cond).

Symphony No. 3 (1994) orch
   Marco Polo 8.225107, CD (1999): National Symphony Orchestra of
   Ireland, Colman Pearce (cond).

Trauerfelder (1995) 4 perc
   Peermusic Classical PM 003, 3CD (2000): Modern Percussion, Joachim
   Winkler (cond).

Symphony No. 4 (1996) orch
   Marco Polo 8.225107, CD (1999): National Symphony Orchestra of
   Ireland, Colman Pearce (cond).

Mad Sweeney (1996) spkr, ch-orch
   Black Box Music BBM 1026, CD (1999): Frank Corcoran (spkr), Das
   Neue Werk NDR Ensemble, Dieter Cichewiecz (cond).

Sweeney's Vision (1997) tape
>> Black Box Music BBM 1026, CD (1999).

Cormac
(fl. 12th century)

Cormac was a monastic scribe about whom nothing is known except that he wrote a psalter in the mid or late twelfth century. It is interesting as it contains a short three-part vocal composition, the words beginning with "Cormacus scripsit" ("Cormac wrote this"), a very early example of polyphonic music from the British Isles.

Recorded Work:

Cormacus scripsit (12th cent.) vv
>> Amon Ra CD-SAR 63 (= CD), CSAR 63 (= MC) (1995): Sine Nomine.

>> Arranged with additions by Michael McGlynn:
>> Danú 001, CD (1993): Anúna, Michael McGlynn (cond).

Tom Cullivan
(* Cavan 1939)

Cullivan is a talented amateur composer living in county Galway. He began playing the piano at an early age and was deeply influenced by traditional Irish music. He worked as musical director in Galway theatres during the 1960s and 70s. In the years 1985 and 1986 he was chairman of the Association of Irish Composers.

Cullivan's music is rooted in the musical aesthetic of the early nineteenth century. Tonal and romantic throughout, additional traces of traditional Irish music have been used deliberately. His largest works include a symphony, two piano concertos, a ballet and music for many chamber music instrumentations. The "Far Western"-label is his own initiative.

Recorded Works:

Sonata No. 1 in A (1992) vn, pf
> Far Western FW 0001, CD (1997): Carmello Andriani (vn), Pádhraig
> Ó Cuinneagáin (pf).

Sonata No. 2 in D (1996) vn, pf
> Far Western FW 0001, CD (1997): Carmello Andriani (vn), Pádhraig
> Ó Cuinneagáin (pf).

Piano Quintet in C (1996) 2vn, va, vc, pf
> Far Western FW 0001, CD (1997): Cork School of Music Quintet.

Shaun Davey
(* Belfast 1948)

Davey was born in Belfast but lives and works in Dublin. He was praised as "one of Ireland's leading composers of music that combines popular appeal with genuine cultural significance". This means in effect that, although "contemporary", stylistically his music could have been written 150 years earlier. Davey combines the romantic language of 19th-century symphonic music with Irish traditional instruments such as the Uíleann Pipes and he chose to commemorate significant events and figures of Irish history as his topics.

Recorded works:

The Brendan Voyage (1980) U.P., Bdn, orch
> Tara CD 3006, CD (1994): Liam O'Flynn (U.P.), Tommy Hayes (Bdn), unnamed orchestra, Noel Kelehan (cond).

The Pilgrim (1983) Nar, pipe bands, satb, orch
> Tara CD 3032, CD (1994): Mick Lally (Nar), Wallacetone Pipe Band, City of Glasgow Pipes and Drums, Cord Gord'rer Garth' Kerensa, An Tryskell, City of Glasgow Chorus, Lorient Festival Orchestra, Noel Kelehan (cond), Glasgow Philharmonic Orchestra, Iain Sutherland (cond).

Granuaile (1985) S, U.P., t-w, sax, hp/Ir hp, hpd, gui, bouzouki, Bdn, perc, orch
> Tara CD 3017, CD (1994): Rita Connolly (S), Liam O'Flynn (U.P.), Shaun Davey (t-w), Carl Geraghty (sax), Helen Davies (hp + Ir hp), Marian Doherty (hpd), Des Moore (gui), Donal Lunny (Bdn, bouzouki), Noel Eccles (perc), unnamed orchestra, Gareth Hudson (cond).

Relief of Derry Symphony (1989) S, s-sax, U.P., org, brass band, orch
Tara CD 3024, CD (1990): Rita Connolly (S), Gerard McChrystal
(s-sax), Liam O'Flynn (U.P.), William West (org), St. Mary's Concert
Band, Ulster Orchestra, Gearoid Grant (cond).

Edgar M. Deale
(* Dublin 1902, † Dublin 1999)

Deale was an amateur composer with intimate connections to the modern music
scene of Dublin during the 1940s to 60s. He worked as director of the Irish
branch of a Swiss insurance company between 1929 and 1963. He had composition lessons from J. Turner Huggard and William J. Watson, but saw himself
largely as an autodidact. His music has nevertheless often attracted the attention
of professional musicians and ensembles. He was a long-time president of the
Culwick Choral Society and was, with Brian Boydell and Frederick May, one of
the founders of the Music Association of Ireland in 1948.

In Deale's work-list vocal music features prominently. His largest compositions include the cantata *A Pageaunt of Human Lyfe* (1945, rev. 1966),
several large-scale settings of Irish poets and choral arrangements of traditional
music and a *Dublin Suite* (1969) for oboe and piano.

Recorded Works:

Pádraic Colum – Four Facets (1967) pic, T, Nar, satb
New Irish Recording Co. DEB 002, LP (1974): Hans Kohlmann (pic),
Patrick Ring (T), Betty Behan (Nar), Culwick Choral Society, Eric
Sweeney (cond).

Down by the Sally Gardens (arr.) satb
New Irish Recording Co. DEB 002, LP (1974): Culwick Choral
Society, Eric Sweeney (cond).

Follow me up to Carlow (arr.) satb
New Irish Recording Co. DEB 002, LP (1974): Culwick Choral
Society, Eric Sweeney (cond).

Kitty, my love, will you marry me? (arr.) satb
Harmonia Mundi HMS 30691, LF (1965): RTÉ Singers, Waldemar
Rosen (cond).

Love at my heart came knocking (arr.) satb)
>Harmonia Mundi HMS 30691, LP (1965): RTÉ Singers, Waldemar Rosen (cond).

Oft in the Stilly Night (arr.) satb
>New Irish Recording Co. DEB 002, LP (1974): Culwick Choral Society, Eric Sweeney (cond).

Raymond Deane
(* Achill Island, Co. Clare 1953)

From a very early age Raymond Deane was attracted to the sound of the modern European avant-garde. In 1969 he was the youngest participant in the *Ferien-kurse für neue Musik* at Darmstadt. He studied music from 1970 to 1974 at University College Dublin and pursued compositional studies abroad. He studied with Gerald Bennett at Basel (1974-5), with Karlheinz Stockhausen at Cologne (1976-7) and with Isang Yun at Berlin (1978-9). He has spent several years working in Germany and France and since 1993 lives in Dublin again.

>Deane's music is well crafted and sincerely modern, demanding the same level of concentration as modern drama, literature or arts. For those who undertake the effort his music makes rewarding listening for its unique sound-world and originality. Deane is a member of Aosdána.

Recorded Works:

Avatars (1982) pf
>Goasco GXX 003-4, MC (1985): Jimmy Vaughan.

Quaternion (1988) pf, orch
>Marco Polo 8.225106, CD (1999): Anthony Byrne (pf), National Symphony Orchestra of Ireland, Colman Pearce (cond).

Krespel's Concerto: Fantasia on E.T.A. Hoffmann (1990) vn, orch
>Marco Polo 8.225106, CD (1999): Alan Smale (vn), National Symphony Orchestra of Ireland, Colman Pearce (cond).

After-Pieces (1990) pf
>Black Box Music BBM 1014. CD (2000): Hugh Tinney.

Excerpt: *After Pieces I*
Contemporary Music Centre CMC CD01, Promotion-CD (1995):
Raymond Deane.

Seachanges (with Danse Macabre) (1994) picc + fl, pf, perc, vn, vc
Black Box Music BBM 1014, CD (2000): Reservoir, Mikel Toms
(cond).

Catacombs (1994) cl, vn, vc, pf
Black Box Music BBM 1014, CD (2000): Reservoir, Mikel Toms
(cond).

Oboe Concerto (1994) ob, orch
Marco Polo 8.225106, CD (1999): Matthew Manning (ob), National
Symphony Orchestra of Ireland, Colman Pearce (cond).

Dekatriad (1995) ch-orch
Black Box Music BBM 1013, CD (1998): Irish Chamber Orchestra,
Fionnuala Hunt (cond).

Marche Oubliée (1996) vn, vc, pf
Black Box Music BBM 1014, CD (2000): Schubert Ensemble of
London.

Brown Studies (1998) str-qu
Association of Irish Composers AIC 001, Promotion-CD (1999):
Hibernia Trio with Michael d'Arcy (vn).

Black Box Music BBM 1014, CD (2000): Vanbrugh Quartet.

Séamas de Barra
(* Cork 1955)

Séamas de Barra lives and works in Cork. He studied with Aloys Fleischmann at University College Cork (BMus 1977, MA 1980) and is active as a private music teacher. Most of his music is written for voices – a large amount of it being liturgical –, some of which has been published. His largest piece so far is the orchestral *Pezzetto Brioso* (1989). His music is mostly diatonic and he believes that most music has a diatonic base even if a composer denies it.

Recorded Work:

Tibi Laus, tibi Gloria (1992) satb, org
        Priory PRCD 639. CD (1999): Christ Church Cathedral Dublin Choir,
        Andrew Johnstone (org), Mark Duley (cond).

Jerome de Bromhead
(* Waterford 1945)

De Bromhead belongs to the more important names of his generation making a
name for themselves during the era of the Dublin Festival of 20th Century Music
(1969-84). He studied harmony and counterpoint with A.J. Potter and
composition at the Royal Irish Academy of Music with James Wilson (1970-74).
He also studied with Seóirse Bodley (1975) and Franco Donatoni (1978). For a
number of years he worked as a producer with RTÉ until a serious traffic
accident in 1996 forced him to retire. De Bromhead was the first and is still the
most prolific Irish composer of music for the guitar. His work-list includes two
guitar concertos, two symphonies, a chamber opera and many more orchestral,
chamber and solo pieces.

Recorded Work:

Gemini (1970) gui
        Black Box Music BBM 1002, CD (1998) John Feeley.

Donnacha Dennehy
(* Dublin 1970)

Donnacha Dennehy studied at the Royal Irish Academy of Music and at Trinity
College, Dublin. A Fulbright Scholarship enabled him to undertake postgraduate
studies in composition at the University of Illinois, where his teachers included
Salvatore Martriano and William Brooks. Following a brief period at the
Institute of Sonology at The Hague he became a lecturer in music and media
technology at Trinity College. Dennehy is the founder and artistic director of the
Dublin-based Crash Ensemble and is equally proficient in writing instrumental
and electro-acoustic music.

Recorded Work:

Work for Organ (1992) org
        TCD CC 002, CD (1998): David Adams.

Begobs (1995) pf
        Norwegian Radio CD, CD (1996): Nils Anders Mortensen.

        Excerpts:
        Begob II; Begob IV
        Media Café, CD (1995): Camille Goudeseune.

Metropolis Mutabilis (1996) tape
        University of Illinois at Urbana-Champaign EMS 9700, CD (1997).

Junk Box Fraud (1997) 2vv, amplified ensemble, tape
        Black Box Music BBM 1036, CD (2001): Natasha Lohan (v), Stepphie
        Buttrich (v), Crash Ensemble.

Swerve (1998) fl, tape
        Black Box Music BBM 1036, CD (2001): Susan Doyle (fl).

Traces of a Revolutionary Song (1998) brass tentet
        Black Box Music BBM 1036, CD (2001): London Brass.

Derailed (2000) amplified ensemble, tape
        Black Box Music BBM 1036, CD (2001): Crash Ensemble.

Mary Dickenson-Auner

(* Dublin 1880, † Vienna 1965)

Mary Dickenson-Auner was a granddaughter of Sir Richard MacDonnell, a provost of Trinity College, Dublin, and co-founder of the Royal Irish Academy of Music. Against the will of her parents she studied violin, organ and composition at the Royal Academy of Music in London until 1902. She lived in the Czech Republic until 1916 and pursued a career as violinist, playing with many orchestras all over Europe. The turmoil of World War I brought her to Amsterdam and in 1920 to Vienna, where she remained until her death. After 1938, when Nazi Austria prohibited her teaching, she concentrated fully on composition. In the following 25 years she wrote four operas, six symphonies, two oratorios and numerous songs and chamber music works. The *Irish Symphony* of 1941 was her first.

Recorded Work:

Irish Symphony op. 16 (1941) orch
>Thorofon CTH 2259, CD (1994): Moravian Philharmonic Orchestra, Manfred Müssauer (cond).

Roger Doyle
(* Dublin 1949)

Roger Doyle is Ireland's most prolific composer for electronic and electro-acoustic music. He studied piano, music theory and harmony at the Royal Irish Academy of Music, later adding post-graduate studies in composition and instrumentation at the Institute of Sonology at Utrecht (today at Den Haag). He was a Visiting Scholar at the University of Washington at Seattle and worked at the Banff Centre in Canada. A member of Aosdána, Doyle likes working on the stage and has provided some incidental music, e.g. for Oscar Wilde's *Salomé*.

Standing in the tradition of the French Musique concrète, Doyle's electro-acoustic music often incorporates pre-recorded natural sounds. His "master-piece before the age of thirty" was *Rapid Eye-Movements* (1980), which was to be followed by a period of popular music (c. 1983-1989). Between 1990 and 1999 he composed *Babel*, music for an imaginary futuristic tower with specific music for each room and floor.

Recorded Works:

Two Movements for Flute and Strings (1968) fl, str-orch
>Thrust Records THR 3, LP (1975): Dublin Baroque Players, Liam Fitzgerald (cond).
>*Re-issued on* DOM BW 03 / Artware 05, CD (1992).

Piano Suite (1969) pf
>Thrust Records THR 3, LP (1975): Roger Doyle.
>*Re-issued on* DOM BW 03 / Artware 05, CD (1992).

Obstinato (1971) tape
>Thrust Records THR 3, LP (1975).
>*Re-issued on* DOM BW 03 / Artware 05, CD (1992).

Theme from Emptigon (1972) gui, pf, perc, tape
Thrust Records THR 3, LP (1975): Roger Doyle (all instr.).
Re-issued on DOM BW 03 / Artware 05, CD (1992).

Bitter-Sweet Suite (1973) special pf
Thrust Records THR 3, LP (1975): Roger Doyle.
Re-issued on DOM BW 03 / Artware 05, CD (1992).

Ceol Sidhe (1973) U.P., Irish hp, tin whistle
Thrust Records THR 3, LP (1975): Peter Brown (U.P.), Gráinne Yeats
(Ir. hp), Jolyon Jackson (t-w).
Re-issued on DOM BW 03 / Artware 05, CD (1992).

Why is Kilkenny so good? (1974) tape
Thrust Records THR 3, LP (1975).
Re-issued on DOM BW 03 / Artware 05, CD (1992).

Baby Grand (1974) pf 4-hands
CBS Records (Ireland) 61813, LP (1978): Roger Doyle.
Re-issued on DOM BW 03 / Artware 05, CD (1992).

Solar Eyes (1975) tape
CBS Records (Ireland) 61813, LP (1978).
Re-issued on DOM BW 03 / Artware 05, CD (1992).

Oizzo No (1975) fl, cl, pf, vn, va, vc, pf, perc
Thrust Records THR 3, LP (1975): Brian Dunning (fl), John Meehan
(cl), Jolyon Jackson (pf), Kieran Egar (vn), Edward Hamilton (va),
Betty Barrett (vc), Roger Doyle (perc).
Re-issued on DOM BW 03 / Artware 05, CD (1992).

Extra Bit (1975) tape
DOM BW 03 / Artware 05, CD (1992).

Thalia (1976) vv, tape
CBS Records (Ireland) 61813, LP (1978): Annelies Konings (v), Karen
Smoor (v).
Re-issued on DOM BW 04 / Artware 06, CD (1992).

Fin-estra (1977) tape
United Dairies UD 011, LP (1981), CD (1995).

Rapid Eye Movements (1980) tape
United Dairies UD 011, LP (1981), CD (1995).

Austrian (1980) v, trb, dr, pf, synth
>CBS Records (Ireland) CBSA 1252, single record (1981): Operating Theatre.
>*Re-issued on* Kabuki Records KAOT 6, EP (1983).

Positive Disintegration (1980) dr, pf, synth
>CBS Records (Ireland) CBSA 1252, single record (1981): Operating Theatre.
>*Re-issued on* Kabuki Records KAOT 6, EP (1983).

Blue Light and Alpha Waves (1981) v, trb, dr, pf, synth
>CBS Records (Ireland) CBSA 2498, single record (1982): Operating Theatre.
>*Re-issued on* Kabuki Records KAOT 6, EP (1983).

Rampwalk (1981) v, synth
>CBS Records (Ireland) CBSA 2498, single record (1982): Olwen Fouéré (v), Roger Doyle (synth).
>*Re-issued on* Kabuki Records KAOT 6, EP (1983).

No Come (1982) tape
>Kabuki Records KAOT 6, EP (1983).

Elation after Hours (1982) tape
>Kabuki Records KAOT 6, EP (1983).

Gloss and Eggshell (1982) tape
>Kabuki Records KAOT 6, EP (1983).

Atlantean (1983) tape
>Mother Records 12 MUM 4, EP (1986).

>Atlantean ATL 001, LP (1990).

Come Down off that Ceiling (1983) S, tape
>Silverdoor SIDO 008-9, 2CD (2000): Lucy Vigne-Walsh (S).

Part of my Make-Up (1983) S, keyboards
>Mother Records 12 MUM 4, EP (1986): Olwen Fouéré (S), Roger Doyle (keyboards).

Satanasa (1983) keyboards
>Mother Records 12 MUM 4, EP (1986): Roger Doyle.

Arminarm (1983, rev. 1985) S, tape
    Silverdoor SIDO 008-9, 2CD (2000): Elena Lopez (S).

Clear the Drains (1983, rev. 1985) S, tape
    Silverdoor SIDO 008-9, 2CD (2000): Lucy Vigne-Walsh (S).

Fire on the Water I and II (1983, rev. 1985) tape
    Silverdoor SIDO 008-9, 2CD (2000).

Four Lucy Pieces (1983, rev. 1985) v, tape
    Operating Theatre Tapes OTT-462, MC (1989): Lucy Vigne-Walsh.

Physical Missing (1983, rev. 1985) S, tape
    Silverdoor SIDO 008-9, 2CD (2000): Lucy Vigne-Walsh (S).

Pilar (1983, rev. 1985) tape
    Operating Theatre Tapes OTT-462, MC (1989).

    Silverdoor SIDO 008-9, 2CD (2000).

Quiet Slipper Year (1983, rev. 1985) tape
    Operating Theatre Tapes OTT-462, MC (1989).

    Silverdoor SIDO 008-9, 2CD (2000).

Say Yes to the Nice Lady (1983, rev. 1985) S, tape
    Silverdoor SIDO 008-9, 2CD (2000): Lucy Vigne-Walsh (S).

Contempo (1984) tape
    Silverdoor SIDO 008-9, 2CD (2000).

Queen of No Heart (1984) S, vv, keyboards, perc
    Mother Records 12 MUM 4, EP (1986): Elena Lopez (S, v), Olwen
    Fouéré (v), Roger Doyle (keyboards), Seán Devitt (perc).

Spring is Coming with a Strawberry in the Mouth (1984)
    Mother Records 12 MUM 4, EP (1986): Elena Lopez (S, v), Olwen
    Fouéré (v), Roger Doyle (keyboards), Seán Devitt (perc).

    Version for tape
    Silverdoor SIDO 008-9, 2CD (2000).

Seresa I, II and III (1985) tape
    Silverdoor SIDO 008-9, 2CD (2000).

Excerpts:
Seresa I, Seresa II
Operating Theatre Tapes OTT-462, MC (1989).

Chinja Miniatures (1986) tape
Operating Theatre Tapes OTT-462, MC (1989).

Silverdoor SIDO 008-9, 2CD (2000).

Dracula Music (1986) tape
Silverdoor SIDO 008-9, 2CD (2000).

Ordained for Grave Dancing (1986) tape
Operating Theatre Tapes OTT-462, MC (1989).

Silverdoor SIDO 008-9, 2CD (2000).

Sidewards and Pinkways (1986) tape
Operating Theatre Tapes OTT-462, MC (1989).

Silverdoor SIDO 008-9, 2CD (2000).

Budawanny (1987) tape
Helmar Music HMR 002, LP (1987).

Atlantean ATL 001, LP (1990).

Oedipus (1987) tape
Silverdoor SIDO 008-9, 2CD (2000).

Why Orange? (1988) tape
Silverdoor SIDO 008-9, 2CD (2000).

The Love of Don Perlimplin and Belisa in the Garden (1988) S, T, tape
Operating Theatre Tapes OTT 461, MC (1989): Elena Lopez (S), Roger
Doyle (T).

Silverdoor SIDO 008-9, 2CD (2000): Elena Lopez (S), Roger Doyle
(T).

Salomé (1988) pf (one movt. with tape)
Gate 001CD, CD (2000): Roger Doyle.

Trapeze in Full Moon Nights (1998) tape
>Operating Theatre Tapes OTT-462, MC (1989).

>Silverdoor SIDO 003-007, 5CD (1999).

Charlotte Corday and the Lament of Louis XVI (1989) vv, tape
>DOM BW 04 / Artware 06, CD (1992): Olwen Fouéré (v), Paavo Evans-Doyle (v).

Babel (1990-1999) various combinations of vv, instr., tape
>Silverdoor SIDO 003-007, 5CD (1999).

>Excerpts (1990-1994)
>Circa 1, CD (1994).

Babel: The Room of Rhetoric (1990-91) tape
>Silverdoor SIDO 003-007, 5CD (1999).

Babel: Temple Music – Cantilena (1991) v, tape
>Silverdoor SIDO 003-007, 5CD (1999): Elena Lopez.

Babel: The Dressing Room (1991-2) v, sax, pf, tape
>Silverdoor SIDO 002 CD, CD (1997): Elena Lopez (v), Jo O'Grady (sax), Roger Doyle (pf).
>*Re-issued on* Silverdoor SIDO 003-007, 5CD (1999).

Babel: Concert Music – Pagoda Charm (1991-2) v, e-gui, sax, keyboards, tape
>Silverdoor SIDO 002 CD, CD (1997): Cindy Cummings (v), Tim Brady (e-gui), Jo O'Grady (sax), Roger Doyle (keyboards).
>*Re-issued on* Silverdoor SIDO 003-007, 5CD (1999).

Babel: Mansard I (1991-2) pf/tape
>Silverdoor SIDO 002 CD, CD (1997): Roger Doyle (pf).
>*Re-issued on* Silverdoor SIDO 003-007, 5CD (1999).
>Nederlands Blazers Ensemble NBECD001, CD (1999): Roger Doyle (pf).

Babel: Mansard II (1992) bn, tape
>Nederlands Blazers Ensemble NBECD001, CD (1999): Dorian Cooke (bn).

Babel: Temple Music – Earth to Earth (1992) bn, fl, vn, tape
>United Dairies UD 011, CD (1995): Rachel Nolan (bn), Claire Wallace (fl), Ger Flanagan (vn).

Re-issued on Silverdoor SIDO 002 CD, CD (1997) *and on* Silverdoor
SIDO 003-007, 5CD (1999).

Version for wind ensemble (1999):
Nederlands Blazers Ensemble NBECD001, CD (1999): Nederlands
Blazers Ensemble, Dick Heuvels (cond).

Babel: Mr. Brady's Room (1992, rev. 1994) e-gui, tape
Silverdoor SIDO 002 CD, CD (1997): Tim Brady (e-gui).
Re-issued on Silverdoor SIDO 003-007, 5CD (1999).

Babel: The Stairwell (1992-94) vv, vn, cl, gui, pf, tape
Silverdoor SIDO 003-007, 5CD (1999): Paul Nash (v, gui), Lee Heuer-
mann (v), Juliette Kang (vn), Cindy Cummings (cl), Roger Doyle (pf).

Babel: The Morning Show (1992-4) vv, keyboards, tape
Silverdoor SIDO 001 CD, CD (1996): Helen Bledsoe (v), Risteard
Cooper (v), Finn Mac Ginty (v), Peter Vollebregt (v), Roger Doyle (v,
keyboards).
Re-issued on Silverdoor SIDO 003-007, 5CD (1999).

Babel: Squat (1992, rev. 1995) vv, cl, sax, keyboards, pf, tape
Silverdoor SIDO 002 CD, CD (1997): Cindy Cummings (v, cl), Roger
Doyle (sax, keyboards), Trevor Knight (pf).
Re-issued on Silverdoor SIDO 003-007, 5CD (1999).

Babel: Entry Level I + II (1992-5) tape
Silverdoor SIDO 002 CD, CD (1997).
Re-issued on Silverdoor SIDO 003-007, 5CD (1999).

Babel: Yunnus (1992-5) fr hn, tape
Silverdoor SIDO 002 CD, CD (1997): Lorraine Fader.
Re-issued on Silverdoor SIDO 003-007, 5CD (1999).

Nederlands Blazers Ensemble NBECD001, CD (1999): Dick Verhoef.

Under the Green Time (1995) U.P., fl, tape
Nederlands Blazers Ensemble NBECD001, CD (1999): Brian Ó
hUiginn (U.P.), Jeannette Landré (fl).

Excerpt:
Part I (U.P., tape)
Private Recording of Doyle's, distributed via the Contemporary Music
Centre, Dublin, CD (1996): Brian Ó hUiginn (U.P.).

Contemporary Music Centre CMC CD02, Promotion-CD (1997): Brian
Ó hUiginn (U.P.).

Babel: The Entertainments & Leisure Pursuits Show (1988-96) vv, keyb., tape
Silverdoor SIDO 001 CD, CD (1996): Myra Davies (v), Olwen Fouéré
(v), Yvon McDevitt (v), Triona Ryan (v), Neil Connolly (v), Mary
Connolly (v), Jackie Magee (v), Tim Brady (v), Bob Gallico (v), Roger
Doyle (v, keyboards).
Re-issued on Silverdoor SIDO 003-007, 5CD (1999).

Babel: Dark Scenery Court Games (1996) tape
Silverdoor SIDO 003-007, 5CD (1999).

Babel: The Iron language Alphabet (1992-97) trp, tape
Silverdoor SIDO 003-007, 5CD (1999): Ian Smith (trp).

Excerpt:
Nederlands Blazers Ensemble NBECD001, CD (1999): André
Heuvelmann (trp).

Babel: The Nightshow (1992-93, rev. 1997) vv, tape
Silverdoor SIDO 003-007, 5CD (1999): David Olds (v), Elena Lopez
(v), Olwen Fouéré (v), Tim Brady (v), Jonathan Philbin Bowman (v),
Cindy Cummings (v), Mary Doyle (v).

Babel: Spirit Levels I-IV (1993-97) tape
Silverdoor SIDO 003-007, 5CD (1999).

Babel: Mercedes Spring (1996-97) cl, vc, perc, tape
(version for tape only:)
Silverdoor SIDO 003-007, 5CD (1999).

Babel: Surface du Monde (1992-98) vv, acc. U.P., vn, sax, tape
Silverdoor SIDO 003-007, 5CD (1999): Severine Angele (v), Elena
Lopez (v), Cecile Mescam (v), Barbara Gogan (v), Jan de Vries (acc),
Brian O hUiginn (U.P.), Leo Barnes (sax).

Babel: Johnny's Body at 002 (1996-98) v, tape
Silverdoor SIDO 003-007, 5CD (1999): Olwen Fouéré.

Babel: Vertical Fissures in Stone (1998) v, tape
Silverdoor SIDO 003-007, 5CD (1999): Olwen Fouéré.

Babel: Mr. Foley's Final Moments (1998) tape
    Silverdoor SIDO 003-007, 5CD (1999).

Babel: Mall Fountain (1998-99) v, tape
    Silverdoor SIDO 003-007, 5CD (1999): Olwen Fouéré.

Tradarr (1999) v, wind ensemble, db, tape
    Nederlands Blazers Ensemble NBECD001, CD (1999): Sarah Greamish
    (v), Nederlands Blazers Ensemble.

Arthur Duff
(* Dublin 1899, † Dublin 1956)

Duff studied at Trinity College, Dublin, and became a member of the Army
School of Music in 1923. In 1932 he changed to Radio Éireann and was
Assistant Music Director there from 1942 until his early death. He made his
doctorate in music at TCD in 1942 and was a vice-president of the Leinster
Society of Organists and Choirmasters.
    Duff is chiefly remembered for his elegant music for string orchestra,
the *Echoes of Georgian Dublin* being an interesting neo-baroque pastiche. He
also wrote music for a ballet, *The Drinking Horn* (1953) and some songs.

Recorded Works:

The Meath Pastoral (1940) str-orch
    New Irish Recording Co. NIRC 012, LP (1974): New Irish Chamber
    Orchestra, André Prieur (cond).

    Black Box Music BBM 1003, CD (1997): Irish Chamber Orchestra,
    Fionnuala Hunt (cond):

Irish Suite for Strings (1940) str-orch
    Decca (US) DL 9844, LP (1956): Radio Éireann Symphony Orchestra,
    Milan Horvat (cond).

    Black Box Music BBM 1003, CD (1997): Irish Chamber Orchestra,
    Fionnuala Hunt (cond).

Echoes from Georgian Dublin (1955) orch
    New Irish Recording Co. NIRC 012, LP (1974): New Irish Chamber
    Orchestra, André Prieur (cond).

Marco Polo 8.223804, CD (1996): RTÉ Sinfonietta, Proinnséas
Ó Duinn (cond).

Excerpt:
In College Green
K-Tel Celtic Collections CCD135, CD (1999): RTÉ Concert Orchestra,
(no conductor named).

An Fallaing Uaithne (arr.) orch
Gael-Linn CEF 004, LP (c. 1960): Radio Éireann Light Orchestra,
Éimear Ó Broin (cond).

Michele Esposito
(* Castellamare di Stabia 1855, † Florence 1929)

Esposito's places of birth and death suggest a life in Italy, but contrary to that
expectation he lived and worked in Dublin almost all his professional life, from
1882 to 1928. He had earlier been studying music at Naples and had moved to
Paris five years before he came to Dublin. He was Professor of Composition at
the Royal Irish Academy of Music, founded the chamber music series at the
Royal Dublin Society in 1886, founded and directed the Dublin Orchestral
Society (1898-1914) and was active as pianist, concert promotor and adjudicator
at musical competitions.

His music is rooted in the late nineteenth-century romantic era, adding
an unmistakable Irish overtone in many compositions using folk-song or dance
material. Among his largest compositions are the opera *The Tinker and the Fairy*
(1910), an *Irish Symphony* (1902) and the cantata *Deirdre* (1897). He also wrote
for many chamber music instrumentations, piano music, songs and folk-song
arrangements.

Recorded Works:

Visione (1879) pf
Chandos CHAN 9675, CD (1998): Micheál O'Rourke.

A la memoria di Bellini (1885) pf
Chandos CHAN 9675, CD (1998): Micheál O'Rourke.

Three Ballades (c. 1900's) pf
Chandos CHAN 9675, CD (1998): Micheál O'Rourke.

Nocturne and Waltz (c. 1900's) pf
    Chandos CHAN 9675, CD (1998): Micheál O'Rourke.

Reverie (c. 1900's) pf
    JG 001, CD (1994): John Gibson.

    Chandos CHAN 9675, CD (1998): Micheál O'Rourke.

Irish Melodies (arr. c. 1903) vn, pf
    Excerpt:
    Coolin
    Continuum CCD 1051, CD (1992): Fionnuala Hunt (vn), Una Hunt (pf).

    Cala Artists CACD 0503, CD (1996): Geraldine O'Grady (vn), Margaret O'Sullivan (pf).

Three Piano Pieces op. 61 (c. 1910's) pf
    Chandos CHAN 9675, CD (1998): Micheál O'Rourke.

A Village Fete (c. 1910's) pf
    Chandos CHAN 9675, CD (1998): Micheál O'Rourke.

Remembrance op. 63 (1912) pf
    JG 001, CD (1994): John Gibson.

    Chandos CHAN 9675, CD (1998): Micheál O'Rourke.

The Lark in the Clear Air, Irish Melody (1915) v, pf
    ASV CD AJA 5283, CD (1999, recorded 1935): Sydney MacEwan (T), Duncan Morrison (pf).

My Irish Sketch Book op. 71 (c. 1920) pf
    Excerpts:
    The Bard and the Fairy; A Lament; The Rose Tree; The Little Stack of Barley; Coulin
    Chandos CHAN 9675, CD (1998): Micheál O'Rourke.

Nine Preludes (c. 1920's) pf
    Excerpts:
    Preludes No. 1, No. 2, No. 4, No. 5, No. 9
    Chandos CHAN 9675, CD (1998): Micheál O'Rourke.

Impromptu (ca. 1920's) pf
    Chandos CHAN 9675, CD (1998): Micheál O'Rourke.

Silent, O Moyle (arr.) vn, pf
> Continuum CCD 1051, CD (1992): Fionnuala Hunt (vn), Una Hunt (pf).

> Cala Artists CACD 0503, CD (1996): Geraldine O'Grady (vn), Margaret O'Sullivan (pf).

The Lark in the Clear Air (arr.) v, pf
> ASV CD AJA 5283, CD (1999, recorded 1935): Sydney MacEwan (T), Duncan Morrison (pf).

Eibhlís Farrell
(* Rostrevor Co. Down 1953)

Farrell studied with Raymond Warren at Bristol (1970-2) and at Queen's University, Belfast (BMus 1976). She taught for some years in Belfast and since 1983 is engaged as vice-director of the DIT Conservatory of Music (ex-College of Music), Dublin. She took further studies in composition with Robert Moevs and Charles Wuorinen at Rutgers University, New Jersey, from 1988 to 1990. Farrell became a member of Aosdána in 1996.

Among her largest compositions is the oratorio *Exultet* (1989), a *Sinfonia* (1990) and the chamber cantata *The Love-Song of Isabella and Elias Cairel* (1992). Farrell finds inspirations in the music of the middle-ages and early baroque and dislikes artificial elements with classically trained singers. Sonority is of more importance to her than a melodic line or harmonic progression.

Recorded Work:

Skyshapes (1994) fl
> Contemporary Music Centre CMC CD02, Promotion-CD (1997): Madeleine Staunton.

Howard Ferguson
(* Belfast 1908, † Cambridge 1999)

Ferguson was living in England since 1922 and studied composition at the Royal College of Music with R. O. Morris (1925-8) and Ralph Vaughan Williams

(1928-9). For a long time he was active as pianist and accompanist and assisted Myra Hess in the organisation of the famous daily war-time concerts at the National Gallery, London. From 1948 to 1963 Ferguson taught composition at the RCM.

Thanks to his early emigration Ferguson was quite well-known in England, despite his small original œuvre and the fact that he stopped composing in 1959. Almost his complete work-list is recorded on CD. His largest pieces include the late cantatas *Amore Langueo* (1956) and *The Dream of the Rood* (1959). He also arranged Irish traditional music for piano and for string orchestra. After 1959 he became a respected editor of nineteenth-century music.

Recorded Works:

Two Ballads op. 1 (1928/32) Bar, orch
> Chandos CHAN 9082, CD (1992): Brian Rayner Cook (Bar), London Symphony Orchestra, Richard Hickox (cond).

Violin Sonata No. 1 op. 2 (1931) vn, pf
> RCA Victor LCS 22909, LP (1966): Jascha Heifetz (vn), Lillian Steuber (pf).
> *Re-issued on* RCA GK 87872 (= LP), GD 87872 (= CD) (1990) and RCA 09026 61774-2, CD (1994).
>
> Chandos CHAN 9316, CD (1995): Lydia Mordkovitch (vn), Clifford Benson (pf).

Three Medieval Carols op. 3 (1933) Mez, pf
> Sutton Sound SSLP 137, LP (1986): Norma Gray Wilson (Mez), Maureen McParland (Mez), Joanna Pullicino (Mez), Elizabeth Bicker (pf).
>
> Chandos CHAN 9316, CD (1995): John Mark Ainsley (T), Clifford Benson (pf).

Octet op. 4 (1933) ob, bn, hn, str-qu, db
> Hyperion A 66192, LP (1986): Nash Ensemble.
> *Re-issued on* Hyperion CDA 66192, CD (1990).
>
> Dutton Laboratories CDAX 8014, CD (1995, recorded 1941): Leon Goossens (ob), C. James (bn), Dennis Brain (hn), Griller Quartet, V. Watson (db).
>
> Thorofon CTH 2249, CD (1995): Ensemble Acht.

Partita op. 5a (1935/36) orch
    Chandos CHAN 9082, CD (1992): London Symphony Orchestra,
    Richard Hickox (cond).

Partita op. 5b (1935/36) 2pf
    Hyperion A 66130, LP (1984): Howard Shelley & Hilary MacNamara.
    Re-issued on Hyperion CDA 66130, CD (1990).

Four Short Pieces op. 6 (1932-36) cl, pf
    Hyperion A 66014, LP (1981): Thea King (cl), Clifford Benson (pf).
    Re-issued on Hyperion KA 66014 (= MC), CDA 66014 (= CD) (1989)
    and Hyperion CDD 22027, 2CD (1997).

    Chandos CHAN 9079, CD (1992): Einar Jóhannesson (cl), Philip
    Jenkins (pf).

    Chandos CHAN 9316, CD (1995): Janet Hilton (cl), Clifford Benson
    (pf).

Piano Sonata in f op. 8 (1938-40) pf
    Concert Artist CA LPA 1075, LP (1954): Clive Lythgoe.

    Hyperion A 66130, LP (1984): Howard Shelley.
    Re-issued on Hyperion CDA 66130, CD (1990).

    Biddulph LHW 025, CD (1996, recorded 1943): Myra Hess.

Five Bagatelles op. 9 (1944) pf
    Hyperion A 66192, LP (1986): Clifford Benson.
    Re-issued on Hyperion CDA 66192, CD (1990).

    Ensemble/Whitetower ENS 162, MC (1991): Philip Dyson.

Violin Sonata No. 2 op. 10 (1946) vn, pf
    Hyperion A 66192, LP (1986): Levon Chilingirian (vn), Clifford
    Benson (pf).
    Re-issued on Hyperion CDA 66192, CD (1990).

    Continuum CCD 1051, CD (1992): Fionnuala Hunt (vn), Una Hunt (pf).

    Chandos CHAN 9316, CD (1995): Lydia Mordkovitch (vn), Clifford
    Benson (pf).

    Guild GMCD 7120, CD (1996): Oliver Lewis (vn), Jeremy Filsell (pf).

Concerto for Piano and Strings op. 12 (1950-51) pf, str-orch
>EMI EL 7496271-1 (= LP), EL 7496271-4 (= MC), CDC7 49627-2 (= CD) (1987): Howard Shelley (pf), City of London Sinfonia, Richard Hickox (cond).
>*Re-issued on* EMI CDM7 64738-2; CD (1993).

Discovery op. 13 (1951) v, pf
>Decca 6BB 197-8, LP (1953): Kathleen Ferrier (Mez), Ernest Lush (pf).
>*Re-issued on* London/Decca 430 061-2, CD (1991) and Decca 433 802-2DM10, 10CD (1992).

>Hyperion A 66103, LP (1984): Anne Dawson (S), Roderick Barrand (pf).

>Chandos CHAN 9316, CD (1995): John Mark Ainsley (T), Clifford Benson (pf).

>Excerpts:
>*Babylon, Jane Allen*
>Sutton Sound SSLP 137, LP (1986): Martin O'Hagan (Bar), Elizabeth Bicker (pf).

Three Sketches op. 14 (1932-52) fl, pf
>Chandos CHAN 9316, CD (1995): David Butt (fl), Clifford Benson (pf).

Five Irish Folksongs (1953) v, pf
>Chandos CHAN 9316, CD (1995): Sarah Burgess (Mez) Clifford Benson (pf).

>Excerpts:
>*I'm from over the Mountain; The Swan; My Grandfather Died*
>Onslo ACAB 61/67, LP (1966): R. I. Foster (v), M. Earl (pf).

>Sutton Sound SSLP 137, LP (1986): *The Apron of Flowers* (Joanna Pullicino, Mez); *I'm from over the Mountain* (Gordon Speers, B); *Calen-o* (Eric Hinds, Bar); *The Swan* (Richard Woods, Bar); all with Elizabeth Bicker (pf).

Overture for an Occasion op. 16 (1953) orch
>Chandos CHAN 9082, CD (1992): London Symphony Orchestra, Richard Hickox (cond).

Amore Langueo op. 18 (1956) T, chorus, orch
EMI EL 7496271-1 (= LP), EL 7496271-4 (= MC), CDC7 49627-2 (= CD) (1987): Martyn Hill (T), London Symphony Chorus, City of London Sinfonia, Richard Hickox (cond).
Re-issued on EMI CDM7 64738-2, CD (1993).

Love and Reason (1958) C-T, pf
Chandos CHAN 9316, CD (1995): Reiner Schneider-Waterberg (C-T), Clifford Benson (pf).

The Dream of the Rood op. 19 (1959) S, satb, orch
Chandos CHAN 9082, CD (1992): Anne Dawson (S), London Symphony Chorus, London Symphony Orchestra, Richard Hickox (cond).

John Field
(* Dublin 1782, † Moscow 1837)

Field's talents had first been discovered by the Italian-Irish composer Tommaso Giordani, who also arranged his first public appearance in Dublin in 1792. Possibly when Field's father got a better job at an English theatre, the family moved to London and Field was apprenticed to Muzio Clementi, then a famous teacher and owner of a pianoforte shop. It was Clementi, too, who brought the young Field in 1802 to Germany, France and finally to Russia. He lived in St. Petersburg until 1821 and from then mainly in Moscow, where he died.

Field was one of the most respected pianists and piano composers of his time. He developed the lyric piano-piece into a new form, the nocturne, which became the model of refined, sensible, romantic piano music influencing many composers until this day. Quite unlike the works of the same title by Chopin, Field's works were nevertheless their model. Besides 20 nocturnes (there are two more than the known 18 numbered ones) his main works are the seven piano concertos.

Recorded Works:

Fal lal la, Air in The Cherokee (c. 1795) pf
Arts 47180-2, CD (1996): Pietro Spada.

The Favourite Hornpipe Danced by Madame del Caro (c. 1795) pf
Arts 47179-2, CD (1995): Pietro Spada.

Go to the Devil and shake yourself (1797) pf
    Chandos CHAN 9315, CD (1994): Micheál O'Rourke.

    Arts 47179-2, CD (1995): Pietro Spada.

The two Favourite Slave Dances in Black Beard (1798) pf
    Arts 47179-2, CD (1995): Pietro Spada.

Speed the Plough (1799 rev. 1814) pf
    Arts 47179-2, CD (1995): Pietro Spada.

Logie of Buchan, Variations in C (1799) pf
    Arts 47180-2, CD (1996): Pietro Spada.

Piano Concerto No. 1 in E flat (1799) pf, orch
    Unicorn UNS 227, LP (1971): Felicja Blumental (pf), Vienna Chamber
    Orchestra, Hellmuth Froschauer (cond).
    Re-issued on RCA VICS 1533, LP (198?).

    Rare Recorded Editions SRRE 122-3, 2LP (1971): Frank Merrick (pf),
    Damon Orchestra, (first name?) Duncan (cond).

    Claddagh Records CSM 55-58, 4LP (1982): John O'Conor (pf), New
    Irish Chamber Orchestra, Janos Fürst (cond).
    Re-issued on Claddagh CSM 55-57, 3CD (1990), Onyx-Qualiton CD
    101/103, 3CD (1990).

    Chandos CHAN 9368, CD (1995): Micheál O'Rourke (pf), London
    Mozart Players, Matthias Bamert (cond).

    Naxos 8.553770, CD (1997): Benjamin Frith (pf), Northern Sinfonia,
    David Haslam (cond).

Since then I'm doom'd, Variations in C (c. 1800) pf
    Arts 47180-2, CD (1996): Pietro Spada.

Three Sonatas op. 1 (1801) pf
    Hunters Moon HMP 0384, LP (1984, CD 1994): Alan Etherden.

    Chandos CHAN 8787, CD (1990): Micheál O'Rourke.

    Telarc CD-80290, CD (1992): John O'Conor.

    Arts 47178-2, CD (1995): Pietro Spada.

Excerpts:
op. 1, no. 1
Naxos 8.550761, CD (1999): Benjamin Frith.

Cascavelle 3010, CD (2000): Trudelies Leonhardt.

op. 1, no. 2
Naxos 8.550761, CD (1999): Benjamin Frith.

op. 1, no. 3
Naxos 8.550762, CD (2000): Benjamin Frith.

Air russe varié (1808) 2pf
Amon Ra CD-SAR 48, CD (1992): Richard Burnett & Lorna Fulford.

Koch International 3-7287-2H1, CD (1994): Bruce Posner & Donald Garvelmann.

Arts 47183-2, CD (1996): Pietro Spada & Giorgio Cozzolino.

Chandos CHAN 9418, CD (1997): Alexander Bakchiyev & Yelena Sorokina.

Kamarinskaya, air russe favori varié (1809) pf
Chandos CHAN 9315, CD (1994): Micheál O'Rourke.

Arts 47180-2, CD (1996): Pietro Spada.

Divertissement No. 1 in E (1810) str-qu, pf
Chandos CHAN 9534, CD (1997): David Juritz (vn), Jennifer Godson (vn), Sarah-Jane Bradley (va), Julia Desbruslais (vc), Micheál O'Rourke (pf).

Divertissement No. 2 in A (1811) str-qu, pf
Chandos CHAN 9534, CD (1997): David Juritz (vn), Jennifer Godson (vn), Sarah-Jane Bradley (va), Julia Desbruslais (vc), Micheál O'Rourke (pf).

Fantaisie sur l'Andante de Martini op. 3 (1811) pf
Chandos CHAN 9315, CD (1994): Micheál O'Rourke.

Walze tirée d'un rondo (1811) pf
Arts 47183-2, CD (1996): Pietro Spada.

Andante in c (1811) 2pf
Amon Ra CD-SAR 48, CD (1992): Richard Burnett & Lorna Fulford.

Koch International 3-7287-2H1, CD (1994): Bruce Posner & Donald Garvelmann.

Arts 47183-2, CD (1996): Pietro Spada & Giorgio Cozzolino.

La Danse des Ours (1811) 2pf
Amon Ra CD-SAR 48, CD (1992): Richard Burnett & Lorna Fulford.

Koch International 3-7287-2H1, CD (1994): Bruce Posner & Donald Garvelmann.

Arts 47183-2, CD (1996): Pietro Spada & Giorgio Cozzolino.

Rondeau in A flat (1812) str-qu, pf
Chandos CHAN 9534, CD (1997): David Juritz (vn), Jennifer Godson (vn), Sarah-Jane Bradley (va), Julia Desbruslais (vc), Micheál O'Rourke (pf).

Nocturne No. 1 in E flat (1812) pf
Vox STGBY 625, LP (1969): Rena Kyriakou.

Turnabout TV 34349 S, LP (1971): Mary Boehm.

Rare Recorded Editions SRRE 124-5, 2LP (1971): Frank Merrick.

Musical Heritage Society MHS 1450/51, 2LP (1972): Hans Kann.
Re-issued on Tuxedo Music TUXCD 1056, CD (1990).

Claddagh Records CSM 50-51, 2LP (1973) Veronica McSwiney.

Chandos CHAN 8719/20, 2CD (1989): Micheál O'Rourke.

Telarc CD-80199, CD (1990): John O'Conor.

Newport NCD 60130, CD (1992): Maria Rose.

Amon Ra CD-SAR 48, CD (1992): Richard Burnett.

Pavane ADW 7110, CD (1993): Roberte Mamou.
Re-issued on Impogram Impressions 95045, CD (1996).

Athene ATHCD1, CD (1994): Joanna Leach.

Arts 47181-2, CD (1996): Pietro Spada.

Cantando 9611, CD (1996): Stéphane Reymond.

Opus 111 OPS 30-178, CD (1997): Olga Tverskaya.

Naxos 8.550761, CD (1999): Benjamin Frith.

Arbiter 116, 2CD (1999): Ignace Tiegerman.

Nocturne No. 2 in c (1812) pf
Vox STGBY 625, LP (1969): Rena Kyriakou

Nonesuch H-71195, LP (1969): Noël Lee.

Turnabout TV 34349 S, LP (1971): Mary Boehm

Rare Recorded Editions SRRE 124-5, 2LP (1971): Frank Merrick.

Musical Heritage Society MHS 1450/51, 2LP (1972): Hans Kann.
Re-issued on Tuxedo Music TUXCD 1056, CD (1990).

Claddagh Records CSM 50-51, 2LP (1973) Veronica McSwiney.

Chandos CHAN 8719/20, 2CD (1989): Micheál O'Rourke.

Telarc CD-80199, CD (1990): John O'Conor.

Newport NCD 60130, CD (1992): Maria Rose.

Amon Ra CD-SAR 48, CD (1992): Richard Burnett.

Pavane ADW 7110, CD (1993): Roberte Mamou.
Re-issued on Impogram Impressions 95045, CD (1996).

Athene ATHCD1, CD (1994): Joanna Leach.

Arts 47181-2, CD (1996): Pietro Spada.

Cantando 9611, CD (1996): Stéphane Reymond.

Naxos 8.550761, CD (1999): Benjamin Frith.

Nocturne No. 3 in A flat (1812) pf
> Vox STGBY 625, LP (1969): Rena Kyriakou

> Nonesuch H-71195, LP (1969): Noël Lee.

> Turnabout TV 34349 S, LP (1971): Mary Boehm

> Rare Recorded Editions SRRE 124-5, 2LP (1971): Frank Merrick.

> Musical Heritage Society MHS 1450/51, 2LP (1972): Hans Kann.
> *Re-issued on* Tuxedo Music TUXCD 1056, CD (1990).

> Claddagh Records CSM 50-51, 2LP (1973) Veronica McSwiney.

> Chandos CHAN 8719/20, 2CD (1989): Micheál O'Rourke.

> Telarc CD-80290, CD (1992): John O'Conor.

> Newport NCD 60130, CD (1992): Maria Rose.

> Amon Ra CD-SAR 48, CD (1992): Richard Burnett.

> Pavane ADW 7110, CD (1993): Roberte Mamou.
> *Re-issued on* Impogram Impressions 95045, CD (1996).

> Athene ATHCD1, CD (1994): Joanna Leach.

> Arts 47181-2, CD (1996): Pietro Spada.

> Cantando 9611, CD (1996): Stéphane Reymond.

> Naxos 8.550761, CD (1999): Benjamin Frith.

Polonaise en rondeau (1813) pf
> Arts 47183-2, CD (1996): Pietro Spada.

Marche triomphale en honneur des victoires du Général Comte de Wittgenstein
(1813) pf
> Chandos CHAN 9315, CD (1994): Micheál O'Rourke.

> Arts 47183-2, CD (1996): Pietro Spada.

Grande Valse (1813) 2pf
Koch International 3-7287-2H1, CD (1994): Bruce Posner & Donald Garvelmann.

Arts 47183-2, CD (1996): Pietro Spada & Giorgio Cozzolino.

Chandos CHAN 9418, CD (1997): Alexander Bakchiyev & Yelena Sorokina.

Sonata No. 4 in B (1813) pf
Hunters Moon HMP 0384, LP (1984, CD 1994): Alan Etherden.

Chandos CHAN 8787, CD (1990): Micheál O'Rourke.

Telarc CD-80290, CD (1992): John O'Conor.

Arts 47178-2, CD (1995): Pietro Spada.

Air du bon bon roi Henri IV, varié in a (1813) pf
Chandos CHAN 9315, CD (1994): Micheál O'Rourke.

Arts 47180-2, CD (1996): Pietro Spada.

Polonaise en rondeau in E flat (1813) pf
Chandos CHAN 9315, CD (1994): Micheál O'Rourke.

Rondo écossais in B (1814) pf
Chandos CHAN 9315, CD (1994): Micheál O'Rourke.

Piano Concerto No. 4 in E flat (1814) pf, orch
Rare Recorded Editions SRRE 136. LP (1974): Frank Merrick (pf), unnamed orchestra and conductor.

Claddagh Records CSM 55-58, 4LP (1982): John O'Conor (pf), New Irish Chamber Orchestra, Janos Fürst (cond).
Re-issued on Claddagh CSM 55-57, 3CD (1990), Onyx-Qualiton CD 101/103, 3CD (1990).

Chandos CHAN 9442, CD (1996): Micheál O'Rourke (pf), London Mozart Players, Matthias Bamert (cond).

Naxos 8.553771, CD (1999): Benjamin Frith (pf), Northern Sinfonia, David Haslam (cond).

Three Romances, no. 1 in A / Nocturne No. 8 (1815) pf
    Turnabout TV 34349 S, LP (1971): Mary Boehm

    Rare Recorded Editions SRRE 124-5, 2LP (1971): Frank Merrick.

    Musical Heritage Society MHS 1450/51, 2LP (1972): Hans Kann.
    Re-issued on Tuxedo Music TUXCD 1056, CD (1990).

    Claddagh Records CSM 50-51, 2LP (1973): Veronica McSwiney.

    Chandos CHAN 8719/20, 2CD (1989): Micheál O'Rourke.

    Telarc CD-80199, CD (1990): John O'Conor.

    Pavane ADW 7110, CD (1993): Roberte Mamou.
    Re-issued on Impogram Impressions 95045, CD (1996).

    Athene ATHCD1, CD (1994): Joanna Leach.

    ASV CDQS 6106, CD (1994): Allan Schiller.

    Arts 47181-2, CD (1996): Pietro Spada.

    Cantando 9611, CD (1996): Stéphane Reymond.

    Naxos 8.550761, CD (1999): Benjamin Frith.

Quintetto in A flat (1815) str-qu, pf
    Chandos CHAN 9534, CD (1997): David Juritz (vn), Jennifer Godson
    (vn), Sarah-Jane Bradley (va), Julia Desbruslais (vc), Micheál O'Rourke
    (pf).

Romance in E flat / Nocturne No. 9 (1816) pf
    Nonesuch H-71195, LP (1969): Noël Lee.

    Turnabout TV 34349 S, LP (1971): Mary Boehm

    Rare Recorded Editions SRRE 124-5, 2LP (1971): Frank Merrick.

    Musical Heritage Society MHS 1450/51, 2LP (1972): Hans Kann.
    Re-issued on Tuxedo Music TUXCD 1056, CD (1990).

    Claddagh Records CSM 50-51, 2LP (1973): Veronica McSwiney.

Chandos CHAN 8719/20, 2CD (1989): Micheál O'Rourke.

Telarc CD-80199, CD (1990): John O'Conor.

Pavane ADW 7110, CD (1993): Roberte Mamou.
Re-issued on Impogram Impressions 95045, CD (1996).

Athene ATHCD1, CD (1994): Joanna Leach.

Arts 47181-2, CD (1996): Pietro Spada.

Naxos 8.550761, CD (1999): Benjamin Frith.

Nouvelle fantaisie sur le motif de la polonaise Ah quel dommage (1816) pf
Chandos CHAN 9315, CD (1994): Micheál O'Rourke.

Arts 47182-2, CD (1996): Pietro Spada.

Exercice modulé dans tous les tons (1816) pf
Arts 47183-2, CD (1996): Pietro Spada.

Piano Concerto No. 2 in A flat (1816) pf, orch
Vox STGBY 625, LP (1969): Rena Kyriakou (pf), Berlin Symphony
Orchestra, Carl-August Bünte (cond).
Re-issued on Vox CDX 5111, CD (1994?).

Claddagh Records CSM 55-58, 4LP (1982): John O'Conor (pf), New
Irish Chamber Orchestra, Janos Fürst (cond).
Re-issued on Claddagh CSM 55-57, 3CD (1990), Onyx-Qualiton CD
101/103, 3CD (1990).

Telarc CD-80370, CD (1994): John O'Conor (pf), Scottish Chamber
Orchestra, Charles Mackerras (cond).

Chandos CHAN 9368, CD (1995): Micheál O'Rourke (pf), London
Mozart Players, Matthias Bamert (cond).

Naxos 8.553771, CD (1999): Benjamin Frith (pf), Northern Sinfonia,
David Haslam (cond).

Teldec 3984-21475-2, CD (1999): Andreas Staier (pf), Concerto Köln,
David Stern (cond).

Poco Adagio in E flat (from Piano Concerto No. 2) (1816) pf
    Arts 47183-2, CD (1996): Pietro Spada.

Piano Concerto No. 3 in E flat (1816) pf, orch
    Rare Recorded Editions SRRE 116, LP (1968): Frank Merrick (pf),
    unnamed orchestra, Lawrence Foster (cond).

    Turnabout TV 34389 S, LP (1972): Felicja Blumental (pf), Vienna
    Chamber Orchestra, Hellmuth Froschauer (cond).

    Claddagh Records CSM 55-58, 4LP (1982): John O'Conor (pf), New
    Irish Chamber Orchestra, Janos Fürst (cond).
    Re-issued on Claddagh CSM 55-57, 3CD (1990), Onyx-Qualiton CD
    101/103, 3CD (1990).

    Telarc CD-80370, CD (1994): John O'Conor (pf), Scottish Chamber
    Orchestra, Charles Mackerras (cond).

    Chandos CHAN 9368, CD (1995): Micheál O'Rourke (pf), London
    Mozart Players, Matthias Bamert (cond).

    Naxos 8.553771, CD (1999): Benjamin Frith (pf), Northern Sinfonia,
    David Haslam (cond).

    Teldec 3984-21475-2, CD (1999): Andreas Staier (pf), Concerto Köln,
    David Stern (cond).

Nocturne No. 4 in A (1817) pf
    Vox STGBY 625, LP (1969): Rena Kyriakou.

    Nonesuch H-71195, LP (1969): Noël Lee.

    Turnabout TV 34349 S, LP (1971): Mary Boehm.

    Rare Recorded Editions SRRE 124-5, 2LP (1971): Frank Merrick.

    Musical Heritage Society MHS 1450/51, 2LP (1972): Hans Kann.
    Re-issued on Tuxedo Music TUXCD 1056, CD (1990).

    Claddagh Records CSM 50-51, 2LP (1973): Veronica McSwiney.

    Chandos CHAN 8719/20, 2CD (1989): Micheál O'Rourke.

    Telarc CD-80199, CD (1990): John O'Conor.

Newport NCD 60130, CD (1992): Maria Rose.

Amon Ra CD-SAR 48, CD (1992): Richard Burnett.

Pavane ADW 7110, CD (1993): Roberte Mamou.
Re-issued on Impogram Impressions 95045, CD (1996).

Athene ATHCD1, CD (1994): Joanna Leach.

Pearl Gemm CD 9114, CD (1994, recorded 1931): Myra Hess.

Arts 47181-2, CD (1996): Pietro Spada.

Opus 111 OPS 30-178, CD (1997): Olga Tverskaya.

Naxos 8.550761, CD (1999): Benjamin Frith.

Nocturne No. 5 in B flat (1817) pf
Nonesuch H-71195, LP (1969): Noël Lee.

Turnabout TV 34349 S, LP (1971): Mary Boehm.

Rare Recorded Editions SRRE 124-5, 2LP (1971): Frank Merrick.

Musical Heritage Society MHS 1450/51, 2LP (1972): Hans Kann.
Re-issued on Tuxedo Music TUXCD 1056, CD (1990).

Claddagh Records CSM 50-51, 2LP (1973): Veronica McSwiney.

Chandos CHAN 8719/20, 2CD (1989): Micheál O'Rourke.

Telarc CD-80199, CD (1990): John O'Conor.

Newport NCD 60130, CD (1992): Maria Rose.

Amon Ra CD-SAR 48, CD (1992): Richard Burnett.

Pavane ADW 7110, CD (1993): Roberte Mamou.
Re-issued on Impogram Impressions 95045, CD (1996).

Athene ATHCD1, CD (1994): Joanna Leach.

Arts 47181-2, CD (1996): Pietro Spada.

Cantando 9611, CD (1996): Stéphane Reymond.

Opus 111 OPS 30-178, CD (1997): Olga Tverskaya.

Naxos 8.550761, CD (1999): Benjamin Frith.

Nocturne No. 6 in F (1817) pf
Nonesuch H-71195, LP (1969): Noël Lee.

Turnabout TV 34349 S, LP (1971): Mary Boehm.

Rare Recorded Editions SRRE 124-5, 2LP (1971): Frank Merrick.

Musical Heritage Society MHS 1450/51, 2LP (1972): Hans Kann.
Re-issued on Tuxedo Music TUXCD 1056, CD (1990).

Claddagh Records CSM 50-51, 2LP (1973): Veronica McSwiney.

Chandos CHAN 8719/20, 2CD (1989): Micheál O'Rourke.

Telarc CD-80199, CD (1990): John O'Conor.

Newport NCD 60130, CD (1992): Maria Rose.

Amon Ra CD-SAR 48, CD (1992): Richard Burnett.

Pavane ADW 7110, CD (1993): Roberte Mamou.
Re-issued on Impogram Impressions 95045, CD (1996).

Athene ATHCD1, CD (1994): Joanna Leach.

Arts 47181-2, CD (1996): Pietro Spada.

Naxos 8.550761, CD (1999): Benjamin Frith.

Rondeau in A (1817) pf
Arts 47179-2, CD (1995): Pietro Spada.

Rondo in E flat (from Piano Concerto No. 3) (1817) pf
Arts 47179-2, CD (1995): Pietro Spada.

Rondo in E flat (from Piano Concerto No. 4) (1817) pf
Arts 47179-2, CD (1995): Pietro Spada.

Piano Concerto No. 5 in E flat, 'L'incendie par l'orage' (1817) pf, orch
Rare Recorded Editions SRRE 122-3, 2LP (1971): Frank Merrick (pf),
Damon Orchestra, (first name?) Duncan (cond).

Claddagh Records CSM 55-58, 4LP (1982): John O'Conor (pf), New
Irish Chamber Orchestra, Janos Fürst (cond).
Re-issued on Claddagh CSM 55-57, 3CD (1990), Onyx-Qualiton CD
101/103, 3CD (1990).

Chandos CHAN 9495, CD (1996): Micheál O'Rourke (pf), London
Mozart Players, Matthias Bamert (cond).

Rondo in A flat (1818) pf
Arts 47179-2, CD (1995): Pietro Spada.

Miloy moy serdechnoy drug, Variations in d / Chanson russe varié (1818) pf
Chandos CHAN 9315, CD (1994): Micheál O'Rourke.

Arts 47180-2, CD (1996): Pietro Spada.

Rondo in A flat (1818) pf
Chandos CHAN 9315, CD (1994): Micheál O'Rourke.

Rondo in E flat (from Piano Concerto No. 1) (1819) pf
Arts 47179-2, CD (1995): Pietro Spada.

Rondo in A flat (from Piano Concerto No. 2) (1819) pf
Arts 47179-2, CD (1995): Pietro Spada.

Rondeau in G (1819) 2pf
Koch International 3-7287-2H1, CD (1994): Bruce Posner & Donald
Garvelmann.

Arts 47183-2, CD (1996): Pietro Spada & Giorgio Cozzolino.

Chandos CHAN 9418, CD (1997): Alexander Bakchiyev & Yelena
Sorokina.

Piano Concerto No. 6 in C (1819, rev. 1820) pf, orch
Claddagh Records CSM 55-58, 4LP (1982): John O'Conor (pf), New
Irish Chamber Orchestra, Janos Fürst (cond).
Re-issued on Claddagh CSM 55-57, 3CD (1990), Onyx-Qualiton CD
101/103, 3CD (1990).

Chandos CHAN 9442, CD (1996): Micheál O'Rourke (pf), London Mozart Players, Matthias Bamert (cond).

Six Dances (1820) pf
Arts 47183-2, CD (1996): Pietro Spada.

Nocturne No. 7 in A (1821) pf
Vox STGBY 625, LP (1969): Rena Kyriakou.

Turnabout TV 34349 S, LP (1971): Mary Boehm.

Rare Recorded Editions SRRE 124-5, 2LP (1971): Frank Merrick.

Musical Heritage Society MHS 1450/51, 2LP (1972): Hans Kann. *Re-issued on* Tuxedo Music TUXCD 1056, CD (1990).

Claddagh Records CSM 50-51, 2LP (1973): Veronica McSwiney.

Chandos CHAN 8719/20, 2CD (1989): Micheál O'Rourke.

Telarc CD-80290, CD (1992): John O'Conor.

Newport NCD 60130, CD (1992): Maria Rose.

Pavane ADW 7110, CD (1993): Roberte Mamou. *Re-issued on* Impogram Impressions 95045, CD (1996).

Athene ATHCD1, CD (1994): Joanna Leach.

Arts 47181-2, CD (1996): Pietro Spada.

Naxos 8.550761, CD (1999): Benjamin Frith.

Exercise No. 1 in C (1822) pf
Arts 47183-2, CD (1996): Pietro Spada.

Exercise No. 2 in A flat (1822) pf
Arts 47183-2, CD (1996): Pietro Spada.

Nocturne No. 10 in e (1822) pf
Vox STGBY 625, LP (1969): Rena Kyriakou

Nonesuch H-71195, LP (1969): Noël Lee.

Turnabout TV 34349 S, LP (1971) Mary Boehm

Rare Recorded Editions SRRE 124-5, 2LP (1971): Frank Merrick.

Musical Heritage Society MHS 1450/51, 2LP (1972): Hans Kann.
Re-issued on Tuxedo Music TUXCD 1056, CD (1990).

Claddagh Records CSM 50-51, 2LP (1973): Veronica McSwiney.

Chandos CHAN 8719/20, 2CD (1989): Micheál O'Rourke.

Telarc CD-80199, CD (1990): John O'Conor.

Newport NCD 60130, CD (1992) Maria Rose.

Pavane ADW 7110, CD (1993): Roberte Mamou.
Re-issued on Impogram Impressions 95045, CD (1996).

Athene ATHCD1, CD (1994): Joanna Leach.

Arts 47181-2, CD (1996): Pietro Spada.

Opus 111 OPS 30-178, CD (1997): Olga Tverskaya.

Cantando 9611, CD (1996): Stéphane Reymond.

Naxos 8.550762, CD (2000): Benjamin Frith.

Nocturne in B flat (1829) pf
Chandos CHAN 9315, CD (1994): Micheál O'Rourke.

Two Albumleafs in C (Preludio, Largo) (c. 1830) pf
Chandos CHAN 9315, CD (1994): Micheál O'Rourke.

Arts 47183-2, CD (1996): Pietro Spada.

Rondoletto in E flat (1831) pf
Arts 47180-2, CD (1996): Pietro Spada.

Rondo in C (from Piano Concerto No. 5) (1832) pf
Arts 47180-2, CD (1996): Pietro Spada.

Rondo in C (from Piano Concerto No. 6) (1832) pf
Arts 47180-2, CD (1996): Pietro Spada.

Piano Concerto No. 7 in c (1822/32) pf, orch
> Rare Recorded Editions SRRE 138, LP (1974): Frank Merrick (pf),
> unnamed orchestra and conductor.

> Claddagh Records CSM 55-58, 4LP (1982): John O'Conor (pf), New
> Irish Chamber Orchestra, Janos Fürst (cond).
> *Re-issued on* Claddagh CSM 55-57, 3CD (1990), Onyx-Qualiton CD
> 101/103, 3CD (1990).

> Chandos CHAN 9534, CD (1997): Micheál O'Rourke (pf), London
> Mozart Players, Matthias Bamert (cond).

Fantasie sur un air favorit de mon ami N.P. "In the Garden" in a (1832) pf
(+ orch)
> Chandos CHAN 9315, CD (1994): Micheál O'Rourke.

> Arts 47182-2, CD (1996): Pietro Spada (pf solo).

Come again, come again, Introduction and Rondo in E (1832) pf
> Arts 47180-2, CD (1996): Pietro Spada.

Grande Pastorale in E / Nocturne No. 17 (1832) pf
> Nonesuch H-71195, LP (1969): Noël Lee.

> Turnabout TV 34350 S, LP (1971): Mary Boehm

> Rare Recorded Editions SRRE 124-5, 2LP (1971): Frank Merrick.
> Musical Heritage Society MHS 1450/51, 2LP (1972): Hans Kann.
> *Re-issued on* Tuxedo Music TUXCD 1056, CD (1990).

> Claddagh Records CSM 50-51, 2LP (1973): Veronica McSwiney.

> Chandos CHAN 8719/20, 2CD (1989): Micheál O'Rourke.

> Telarc CD-80290, CD (1992): John O'Conor.

> Arts 47182-2, CD (1996): Pietro Spada.

> Naxos 8.550762, CD (2000): Benjamin Frith.

Twelve o'clock, the celebrated Rondo, in E / Nocturne No. 18 (1832) pf
> Nonesuch H-71195, LP (1969): Noël Lee.

> Turnabout TV 34350 S, LP (1971): Mary Boehm

Rare Recorded Editions SRRE 124-5, 2LP (1971): Frank Merrick.

Musical Heritage Society MHS 1450/51, 2LP (1972): Hans Kann. *Re-issued on* Tuxedo Music TUXCD 1056, CD (1990).

Claddagh Records CSM 50-51, 2LP (1973): Veronica McSwiney.

Chandos CHAN 8719/20, 2CD (1989): Micheál O'Rourke.

Telarc CD-80199, CD (1990): John O'Conor.

ASV CDQS 6106, CD (1994): Allan Schiller.

Arts 47182-2, CD (1996): Pietro Spada.

Opus 111 OPS 30-178, CD (1997): Olga Tverskaya.

Cascavelle 3010, CD (2000): Trudelies Leonhardt.

Naxos 8.550762, CD (2000): Benjamin Frith.

The Troubadour, notturno (Nr. 19) in C (1832) pf
Turnabout TV 34350 S, LP (1971): Mary Boehm

Musical Heritage Society MHS 1450/51, 2LP (1972): Hans Kann. *Re-issued on* Tuxedo Music TUXCD 1056, CD (1990).

Arts 47182-2, CD (1996): Pietro Spada.

Nocturne No. 11 in E flat (1833) pf
Vox STGBY 625, LP (1969): Rena Kyriakou.

Turnabout TV 34349 S, LP (1971): Mary Boehm.

Rare Recorded Editions SRRE 124-5, 2LP (1971): Frank Merrick.

Musical Heritage Society MHS 1450/51, 2LP (1972): Hans Kann. *Re-issued on* Tuxedo Music TUXCD 1056, CD (1990).

Claddagh Records CSM 50-51, 2LP (1973): Veronica McSwiney.

Chandos CHAN 8719/20, 2CD (1989): Micheál O'Rourke.

Telarc CD-80199, CD (1990): John O'Conor.

Newport NCD 60130, CD (1992): Maria Rose.

Amon Ra CD-SAR 48, CD (1992): Richard Burnett.

Pavane ADW 7110, CD (1993): Roberte Mamou.
Re-issued on Impogram Impressions 95045, CD (1996).

Athene ATHCD1, CD (1994): Joanna Leach.

Arts 47181-2, CD (1996): Pietro Spada.

Naxos 8.550762, CD (2000): Benjamin Frith.

Nouvelle Fantaisie in G (1833) pf
        Chandos CHAN 9315, CD (1994): Micheál O'Rourke.

Arts 47182-2, CD (1996): Pietro Spada.

Nocturne No. 12 in G (1834) pf
        Nonesuch H-71195, LP (1969): Noël Lee.

Turnabout TV 34350 S, LP (1971): Mary Boehm.

Rare Recorded Editions SRRE 124-5, 2LP (1971): Frank Merrick.

Musical Heritage Society MHS 1450/51, 2LP (1972): Hans Kann.
Re-issued on Tuxedo Music TUXCD 1056, CD (1990).

Claddagh Records CSM 50-51, 2LP (1973): Veronica McSwiney.

Chandos CHAN 8719/20, 2CD (1989): Micheál O'Rourke.

Telarc CD-80199, CD (1990): John O'Conor.

Newport NCD 60130, CD (1992): Maria Rose.

Amon Ra CD-SAR 48, CD (1992): Richard Burnett.

Pavane ADW 7110, CD (1993): Roberte Mamou.
Re-issued on Impogram Impressions 95045, CD (1996).

Athene ATHCD1, CD (1994): Joanna Leach.

Arts 47181-2, CD (1996): Pietro Spada.

Opus 111 OPS 30-178, CD (1997): Olga Tverskaya.

Naxos 8.550762, CD (2000): Benjamin Frith.

Nocturne No. 13 in d (1834) pf
Nonesuch H-71195, LP (1969): Noël Lee.

Turnabout TV 34350 S, LP (1971): Mary Boehm.

Rare Recorded Editions SRRE 124-5, 2LP (1971): Frank Merrick.

Musical Heritage Society MHS 1450/51, 2LP (1972): Hans Kann.
Re-issued on Tuxedo Music TUXCD 1056, CD (1990).

Claddagh Records CSM 50-51, 2LP (1973): Veronica McSwiney.

Chandos CHAN 8719/20, 2CD (1989): Micheál O'Rourke.

Telarc CD-80199, CD (1990): John O'Conor.

Pavane ADW 7110, CD (1993): Roberte Mamou.
Re-issued on Impogram Impressions 95045, CD (1996).

Athene ATHCD1, CD (1994): Joanna Leach.

Arts 47181-2, CD (1996): Pietro Spada.

Cascavelle 3010, CD (2000): Trudelies Leonhardt.

Naxos 8.550762, CD (2000): Benjamin Frith.

Terzenübung in C (1834) pf
Arts 47183-2, CD (1996): Pietro Spada.

Variations in B flat, Within a Mile of Edinboro Town (1835) pf
Arts 47180-2, CD (1996): Pietro Spada.

Nocturne No. 14 in C (1836) pf
Turnabout TV 34350 S, LP (1971): Mary Boehm.

Rare Recorded Editions SRRE 124-5, 2LP (1971): Frank Merrick.

Musical Heritage Society MHS 1450/51, 2LP (1972): Hans Kann.
Re-issued on Tuxedo Music TUXCD 1056, CD (1990).

Claddagh Records CSM 50-51, 2LP (1973): Veronica McSwiney.

Chandos CHAN 8719/20, 2CD (1989): Micheál O'Rourke.

Telarc CD-80199, CD (1990): John O'Conor.

Newport NCD 60130, CD (1992): Maria Rose.

Amon Ra CD-SAR 48, CD (1992): Richard Burnett.

Pavane ADW 7110, CD (1993): Roberte Mamou.
Re-issued on Impogram Impressions 95045, CD (1996).

Athene ATHCD1, CD (1994): Joanna Leach.

Arts 47181-2, CD (1996): Pietro Spada.

Opus 111 OPS 30-178, CD (1997): Olga Tverskaya.

Cascavelle 3010, CD (2000): Trudelies Leonhardt.

Naxos 8.550762, CD (2000): Benjamin Frith.

Nocturne No. 15 in C (1836) pf
Nonesuch H-71195, LP (1969): Noël Lee.

Turnabout TV 34350 S, LP (1971): Mary Boehm.

Rare Recorded Editions SRRE 124-5, 2LP (1971): Frank Merrick.

Musical Heritage Society MHS 1450/51, 2LP (1972): Hans Kann.
Re-issued on Tuxedo Music TUXCD 1056, CD (1990).

Claddagh Records CSM 50-51, 2LP (1973): Veronica McSwiney.

Chandos CHAN 8719/20, 2CD (1989): Micheál O'Rourke.

Telarc CD-80199, CD (1990): John O'Conor.

Newport NCD 60130, CD (1992): Maria Rose.

Pavane ADW 7110, CD (1993): Roberte Mamou.
Re-issued on Impogram Impressions 95045, CD (1996).

Athene ATHCD1, CD (1994): Joanna Leach.

Arts 47181-2, CD (1996): Pietro Spada.

Naxos 8.550762, CD (2000): Benjamin Frith.

Nocturne No. 16 in F (1836) pf (+ str-qu ad lib)
Turnabout TV 34350 S, LP (1971): Mary Boehm.

Rare Recorded Editions SRRE 124-5, 2LP (1971): Frank Merrick.

Musical Heritage Society MHS 1450/51, 2LP (1972): Hans Kann.
Re-issued on Tuxedo Music TUXCD 1056, CD (1990).

Claddagh Records CSM 50-51, 2LP (1973): Veronica McSwiney.

Chandos CHAN 8719/20, 2CD (1989): Micheál O'Rourke.

Telarc CD-80199, CD (1990): John O'Conor.

Arts 47182-2, CD (1996): Pietro Spada.

Newport NCD 60130, CD (1992): Maria Rose.
Athene ATHCD1, CD (1994): Joanna Leach.

Chandos CHAN 9534, CD (1997): David Juritz (vn), Jennifer Godson (vn), Sarah-Jane Bradley (va), Julia Desbruslais (vc), Micheál O'Rourke (pf).

Naxos 8.550762, CD (2000): Benjamin Frith.

Andante inédit in E flat (c. 1836) pf
Chandos CHAN 9315, CD (1994): Micheál O'Rourke.

Arts 47183-2, CD (1996): Pietro Spada.

Sehnsuchts-Walzer in E (pubd. 1845) pf
Chandos CHAN 9315, CD (1994): Micheál O'Rourke.

Aloys Fleischmann
(* Munich 1910, † Cork 1992)

Fleischmann was born in Munich, but his parents had been living in Ireland since 1906. He studied at University College Cork (1928-32) and completed his studies at the Staatliche Akademie für Tonkunst at Munich with Joseph Haas (1932-4). On his return to Cork he became Professor of Music at UCC, a position he held until his retirement in 1980. Fleischmann is the founder of the Cork Symphony Orchestra, which he conducted from 1934 to 1992, and of the International Choral Festival at Cork, which he directed between 1954 and 1987 and within which he instituted the important Seminar on Contemporary Choral Music from 1964.

Besides his many contributions to Irish music as a teacher, educator, musicologist and organiser, Fleischmann found the time for a distinctive opus of original composition. Many pieces would deserve more attention and his small discography is in no relation to his real importance as a composer.

Recorded Works:

Suite for Piano (1933) pf
    New Irish Recording Co. NIR 001, LP (1971): Charles Lynch.

Three Songs for High Voice (1937) S/T, pf/orch
    Excerpt:
    Marbhna Eoghain Ruaidh Uí Néill
    Black Box Music BBM 1022, CD (1998): Kathleen Tynan (S),
    Dearbhla Collins (pf).

Piano Quintet (1938) pf, str-qu
    Marco Polo 8.223888, CD (1996): Hugh Tinney (pf), Vanbrugh
    Quartet.

Elizabeth MacDermot Roe (1941) str-orch
    Black Box Music BBM 1003, CD (1997): Irish Chamber Orchestra,
    Fionnuala Hunt (cond).

Redmond Friel
(* Derry 1907, † Belfast? 1979)

Together with T.C. Kelly and Éamonn Ó Gallchobhair, (James) Redmond Friel was one of the most prominent representers of the conservative side of Irish art music after c. 1940, concentrating on arranging traditional music for various forces and composing original music in a similar vein. He studied privately with the Northern Irish composer Norman Hay (1889-1943) and at St. Mary's College of Education, London. He was headmaster of the Waterside Boys' School and member of the music staff at St. Columb's College, Derry. Among his orchestral music is a *Symphonic Movement* (1949) and a ballet and concert suite on *The Children of Lir* (1950).

Recorded Works:

Tiochfaidh an Samradh (arr. 1952) satb
> Harmonia Mundi HMS 30691, LP (1965): RTÉ Singers, Waldemar Rosen (cond).

An Cnocán Fraoich (arr.) orch
> Gael-Linn CEF 004, LP (c. 1960): Radio Éireann Light Orchestra, Éimear Ó Broin (cond).

Stephen Gardner
(* Belfast 1958)

Gardner studied at the University of Ulster at Jordanstown and at the University of Wales at Cardiff from 1984 to 1989. He has received a Vaughan Williams Scholarship and a Draper's Fellowship as well as several commissions from leading Irish and British musicians and ensembles.

In his music Gardner acknowledges influences as diverse as J. S. Bach, James Macmillan, Witold Lutoslawski, Miles Davis and Pink Floyd. Major works have been the orchestral *Wanting, Not Wanting* (1992), premiered by the Ulster Orchesra and several other orchestral and chamber pieces.

Recorded Works:

The Milesian Equation (1993) cl, vn, va, vc
> Contemporary Music Centre CMC CD01, Promotion-CD (1995): Concorde.

Bernard Geary
(* Cork 1934)

Geary studied at University College Cork with Aloys Fleischmann. He is living in Dublin since 1970 and has been active as an organist, pianist, teacher and broadcaster. His moderately modern music is romantic in expression and includes orchestral, choral and chamber music. His CD of piano and choral music is a private initiative.

Recorded Works:

Two Cameos (1979) pf
        SDG CD 610, CD (2000): Anthony Byrne.

Éist le Fuaim na hAbhann (1981) satb, pf
        SDG CD 610, CD (2000): Cantairí Ógra Átha Cliath, Brian Ó Dubhgaill (cond), Anthony Byrne (pf).

The Divine Image (1985) satb, pf
        SDG CD 610, CD (2000): Cantairí Ógra Átha Cliath, Brian Ó Dubhgaill (cond), Anthony Byrne (pf).

Liquid Emotion (1996) satb
        SDG CD 610, CD (2000): Cantairí Ógra Átha Cliath, Brian Ó Dubhgaill (cond).

Sonatina (1996) pf)
        SDG CD 610, CD (2000): Anthony Byrne.

A Dream Garden (1997) satb, pf
        SDG CD 610, CD (2000): Cantairí Ógra Átha Cliath, Brian Ó Dubhgaill (cond), Anthony Byrne (pf).

And Lastly Came Cold February (2000) pf
        SDG CD 610, CD (2000): Anthony Byrne.

Ave Verum (2000) satb
        SDG CD 610, CD (2000): Cantairí Ógra Átha Cliath, Brian Ó Dubhgaill (cond).

Dóchas () satb
        SDG CD 610, CD (2000): Cantairí Ógra Átha Cliath, Brian Ó Dubhgaill (cond).

Scherzo (2000) pf
        SDG CD 610, CD (2000): Anthony Byrne.

John Gibson
(* Dublin 1951)

Gibson is a pianist and composer based in Cork since 1982, where he teaches the piano at the School of Music. He studied at the College of Music, Dublin (1958-60) and at the Royal Irish Academy of Music (1960-71), where his teachers included Rhona Marshall (piano) and A.J. Potter (composition). He also studied music at University College Dublin (1971-3 and 1975-6) and at the Staatliche Hochschule für Tonkunst at Munich (1973-5). As a pianist he visited master classes in Siena, Dartington, Santiago de Compostela and Moscow.

      Gibson's eclectic musical style gives room for daring harmonic progressions and fervour, as in *Nijinsky* (1980), but at the same time his œuvre includes uninspiring, "pretty" folk-music based exercises. The three CDs of his music originate from his own initiative ("JG")

Recorded Works:

(Two of the) *Six Preludes* (1968) pf
        JG 001, CD (1994): John Gibson.

Two Pieces (1968) vn, pf
        JG 002, CD (1997): Ruxandra Colan-Petcu (vn), John Gibson (pf).

Nocturne (1977) pf
        JG 001, CD (1994): John Gibson.

Prayer of Thanksgiving (1978) org
        JG 003, CD (undated [2000]): John O'Brien.

Nijinsky (1980) pf
        Goasco GXX 003-4, MC (1985): Kevin O'Regan.

        JG 001, CD (1994): John Gibson.

Planxty (1980) va, pf
        JG 003, CD (undated [2000]): Niamh Quigley (va), John Gibson (pf).

Slow Dance in 3 & 4 (1992) pf
        JG 001, CD (1994): John Gibson.

Five Irish Airs (1995) vn, pf
        JG 002, CD (1997): Ruxandra Colan-Petcu (vn), John Gibson (pf).

Toccata (1995) pf
        JG 002, CD (1997): John Gibson.

I See his Blood upon the Rose (1996) S, pf / pf
        JG 002, CD (1997): John Gibson (pf).

        JG 003, CD (undated [2000]): Eileen McMahon (S), John Gibson (pf).

Mass of Mercy and Compassion (1996) satb, congregation, cantor, org/pf
        Version for S, A, T, B:
        JG 003, CD (undated [2000]): Zephiro (Rachel Talbot, S, Sarah Lane,
        A, Stuart Kinsella, T, Andrew Redmond, B)

The Music Box (1997?) pf
        JG 002, CD (1997): John Gibson.

Colourvision (1997) pf
        JG 002, CD (1997): John Gibson.

Sliabh Luachra (1997) fl, vn, vc, pf
        JG 002, CD (1997): Johnny McCarthy (fl), Crawford Piano Trio.

Nijinsky 1998 (1998) pf
        JG 003, CD (undated [2000]): John Gibson.

My Soul Longs for Peace (1999) v, pf
        JG 003, CD (undated [2000]): Eileen McMahon (S), John Gibson (pf).

The Light of the World (1999) v, pf
        JG 003, CD (undated [2000]): Eileen McMahon (S), John Gibson (pf).

Tommaso Giordani
(* Naples c. 1733, † Dublin 1806)

Tommaso Giordani first came to England in 1753 with the travelling opera company of his father Giuseppe. In May 1764 they gave their first performance at the Smock Alley Theatre in Dublin and his opera *L'eroe cinese* was the first *opera seria* ever performed in Ireland. After problems with the Irish jurisdiction he left the country in 1768 and returned to Dublin in 1783 to stay for the rest of his life. Giordani became the towering figure of opera in Dublin and composed several stage works using Irish themes, like *The Island of Saints* (1785).

Of Giordani's music little has survived in the recording media. He was an outstanding exponent of the "galant" style, but he is mostly remembered for a single aria, *Caro mio ben*. Apart from his 26 operas he also wrote piano/ harpsichord concertos, several chamber and piano works and many songs (canzonets).

Recorded Works:

Six Quintets op. 1 (1771) hpd, 2vn, va, vc
    Excerpts:
    Quintet No. 3 in A; Quintet No. 5 in C; Quintet No. 6 in G
    Opus 111 OPS 30-233, CD (1999): L'Astrée.

Six Quartets op. 2 (1771) fl, vn, va, vc
    Excerpts:
    Quartet No. 5 in D; Quartet No. 6 in G
    Opus 111 OPS 30-233, CD (1999): L'Astrée.

Six Chamber Concertos op. 3 (c. 1773) fl, 2vn, ch-orch
    Excerpt:
    Concerto in C
    Vanguard Classics 99084, CD (1997): Musica ad Rhenum, Jed Wentz (fl, cond).

Six Concertos op. 14 (1775/6) hpd/pf, str-orch
    Excerpt:
    Concerto No. 1
    Philips 454 476-2, CD (1998): Maria Teresa Garatti (hpd), I Musici.

Sonata in C (c. 1776) hpd/pf/org 4 hands
    Koch Schwann 3-1047-2, CD (1992): Annerös Hulliger (org), Philip Swanton (org).

Six Duettos op. 21 (c. 1780) (4 for vn, vc, 2 for 2vn)
> Excerpt:
> *Duetto II*
> John Marks Records JMR , CD (1998): Arturo Delmoni (vn), Nathaniel
> Rosen (vc).

Queen Mary's Lamentation (1782) v, pf
> Pearl SHE CD 9613, CD (1989): Patricia Wright (S), Jon Gillaspie (pf).

Caro mio ben (1782) v, pf
> Forlane UCD 10902, CD (1986): Montserrat Caballé (S), Miguel
> Zanetti (pf).

> Club 99 CL99-42, CD (1991, recorded 1927): Hermann Jadlowker (T),
> anonymous pianist.

> Decca 436 267-2DH, CD (1992): Cecilia Bartoli (S), György Fischer
> (pf).
> *Re-issued on* Decca 448 300-2DH, CD (-4DH = MC) (1996).

> Preiser 89205, CD (1993, recorded 1930): Heinrich Schlusnus (Bar),
> Franz Rupp (pf).

> RCA 09026 61245-2, CD (1993, recorded 1940): Ezio Pinza (B), Fritz
> Kitzinger (pf).

> Pearl Gemm CDS 9159 (1), CD (1995, recorded 1902): Giuseppe De
> Luca (T), anonymous pianist.

> Decca 455 981-2DH (= CD), -4DH (= MC) (1998): Cecilia Bartoli (S),
> Jean-Yves Thibaudet (pf).

> Erato 3984-23300-2, CD (1998): Sumi Jo (S), Vincenzo Scalera (pf).

> Arrangement with guitar:
> HMV HQS 1436721 (= LP), TC-HQS 1436724 (= MC) (1984): Tito
> Gobbi (Bar), Freddie Philips (gui).

> Arrangements with orchestra:
> HMV CSD 1402, LP (1962): Charles Craig (T), anonymous orchestra,
> Michael Collins (cond).
> *Re-issued on* Testament SBT 1152, CD (1998).

Pan SPAN 6201 (stereo), PAN 6201 (mono), LP (1966): Janet Coster (Mez), Millicent Silver (hpd).

Hungaroton SLPX 1289 (stereo), LPX 1289 (mono), LP (1967): Alexander Sved (Bar), Vienna Musica Antiqua.

Philips 9500 577, LP (1979): Janet Baker (Mez), Academy of St. Martin-in-the-Fields, Neville Marriner (cond).
Re-issued on Philips 465 253-2PH (= CD), -4PH (= MC) (1999).

Decca SXL 7013 (= LP), KSXC 7013 (= MC) (1983): Luciano Pavarotti (T), Philharmonia Orchestra, Piero Gamba (cond).
Re-issued on Decca 417 796-2DM, CD (1990), Decca 430 470-2DH (= CD), -4DH (= MC) (1991).

Philips 412 233-1PH (= LP), -4PH (= MC), -2PH (= CD) (1986): Elly Ameling (S), Gewandhaus Orchestra Leipzig, Kurt Masur (cond).

Eurodisc 672 231, CD (1988): Lucia Popp (S), Munich Radio Orchestra, Kurt Eichenhorn (cond).

Eurodisc GD 69018 (= CD), GK 69018 (= MC) (1990): Fritz Wunderlich (T), Berlin Symphony Orchestra, Gerhard Becker (cond).

Pearl Gemm CD 9450, CD (1991, recorded 1917): Amelita Galli-Curzi (S), anonymous orchestra, Josef Pasternack (cond). *See Romophone-CD (1994) below.*

Philips 434 173-2PM, CD (1992): Janet Baker (Mez), Academy of St. Martin-in-the-Fields, Neville Marriner (cond).

Philips 434 926-2PH, CD (1993): José Carreras (T), English Chamber Orchestra, Vjeksolav Sutej (cond).

Classics for Pleasure CD-CFP 4616, CD (1993): Rudolf Schock (T), Berlin Symphonia, Wilhelm Schüchter (cond).

Romophone 81003-2, CD (1994, recorded 1917): Amelita Galli-Curzi (S), anonymous orchestra, Josef Pasternack (cond). *See Pearl-CD (1991) above.*

EMI CDC5 55271-2, CD (1994): Peter Seiffert (T), Deutsche Oper Berlin Orchestra, Heinz Wallberg (cond).

Naxos 8.553751, CD (1997): Jósef Mukk (T), Budapest Camerata, János Kovács (cond).

Philips 456 543-2PH, CD (1998): Dmitri Hvorostovsky (Bar), Academy of St. Martin-in-the-Fields, Neville Marriner (cond).

Campion RRCD 1345, CD (2000): Inessa Galante (S), London Musici, Mark Stephenson (cond).

Arrangement for violoncello and piano:
Chanterelle HS 2001, CD (1989, recorded 1929): Emmanuel Feuermann (vc), Michael Taube (pf).

Pearl Gemm CD 9077, CD (1994, recorded 1929): Emmanuel Feuermann (vc), Michael Taube (pf).

Arrangement for orchestra:
Memoir Classics CDMOIR 432, CD (1997, recorded 1930): anonymous orchestra.

Deirdre Gribbin
(* Belfast 1967)

Deirdre Gribbin studied composition at Queen's University Belfast and at the Guildhall School of Music and Drama in London. In 1992 she studied for seven months in Copenhagen with Per Norgard and Bent Sorensen. She has received numerous important commissions – among others, for her opera *Hey Persephone!* (1998) which was premiered at the Aldeburgh Festival.

Recorded Works:

Giles (1989) fl
Black Box Music BBM 1015, CD (1999): Madeleine Staunton.

And Now the Shadows are too Long (1993) cl, pf
Black Box Music BBM 1015, CD (1999): Paul Roe (cl), Jane O'Leary (pf).

How to Make the Water Sound (1997) vn, vc, pf
Black Box Music BBM 1015, CD (1999): Alan Smale (vn), David James (vc), Jane O'Leary (pf).

The Sanctity of Trees (1997) gui
>   Black Box Music BBM 1015, CD (1999): Tom Kerstens.

Joseph Groocock

(* Croydon 1913, † Dublin 1997)

Joseph Groocock had been a choral scholar at St. Michael's, Tenbury (England), studied Classics and Music at Christ Church, Oxford, and came to live in Ireland in 1937. He was Director of Music at St. Columba's College, Rathfarnham, and a lecturer at Trinity College, Dublin. He conducted the University of Dublin Choral Society for forty years. His life-long study and enthusiasm was the music of Bach and he excelled in the composition of fugues and canons. He had great qualities as an inspiring teacher.

Recorded Work:

Trio Sonata in C (1986) org
>   TCD CC 002, CD (1998): David Adams.

Ronan Guilfoyle

(* Dublin 1958)

Guilfoyle is one of Ireland's best known jazz musicians. He studied bass and improvisation with Dave Holland at Banff, Canada, and has performed extensively in Europe, Asia and the USA as a bass player. He is Director of the Jazz Department of the Newpark Music Centre in the south of Dublin and has broad teaching experiences. As a composer crossing the borders between jazz and the classical, his works include orchestral and chamber music, among the first being a *Concerto for Jazz Guitar Trio and Orchestra* (1993) – his largest piece so far is his *Concerto for Orchestra* (1995).

Recorded Works:

Sequence of Events (1990) bn, tpt, trb, sax, drums
>   Improvised Music Company IMCD 1005, CD (1997): Ronan Guilfoyle
>   and Ensemble.

Sonata (1994) vn, pf
> Contemporary Music Centre CMC CD02, Promotion-CD (1997):
> Michael d'Arcy (vn), Dearbhla Collins (pf).

Devsirme (1995) s-sax, t-sax, trb, b-gui, drums
> Improvised Music Company IMCD 1008, CD (1997): Brendan Doyle
> (s-sax), Michael Buckley (t-sax), Karl Ronan (trb), Ronan Guilfoyle (b-
> gui), Conor Guilfoyle (drums).

A.K.A. (1996) s-sax, t-sax, trb, b-gui, drums / s-sax, b-gui, drums
> Improvised Music Company IMCD 1008, CD (1997): Brendan Doyle
> (s-sax), Michael Buckley (t-sax), Karl Ronan (trb), Ronan Guilfoyle (b-
> gui), Conor Guilfoyle (drums).

Dice (1996) s-sax, t-sax, trb, b-gui, drums
> Improvised Music Company IMCD 1008, CD (1997): Brendan Doyle
> (s-sax), Michael Buckley (t-sax), Karl Ronan (trb), Ronan Guilfoyle (b-
> gui), Conor Guilfoyle (drums).

Fanfare (1996) s-sax, t-sax, trb, b-gui
> Improvised Music Company IMCD 1008, CD (1997): Brendan Doyle
> (s-sax), Michael Buckley (t-sax), Karl Ronan (trb), Ronan Guilfoyle (b-
> gui).

Obsessive (1996) cl, sax, trb, b-gui, drums
> Improvised Music Company IMCD 1008, CD (1997): Brendan Doyle
> (cl), Michael Buckley (sax), Karl Ronan (trb), Ronan Guilfoyle (b-gui),
> Conor Guilfoyle (drums).

Part One (1996) s-sax, t-sax, trb, b-gui, drums / Jazz trio
> Improvised Music Company IMCD 1006, CD (1995): Guilfoyle-
> Nielsen Trio.
>
> Improvised Music Company IMCD 1008, CD (1997): Brendan Doyle
> (s-sax), Michael Buckley (t-sax), Karl Ronan (trb), Ronan Guilfoyle (b-
> gui), Conor Guilfoyle (drums).

T'Cha (1996) s-sax, t-sax, trb, b-gui, drums
> Improvised Music Company IMCD 1008, CD (1997): Brendan Doyle
> (s-sax), Michael Buckley (t-sax), Karl Ronan (trb), Ronan Guilfoyle (b-
> gui), Conor Guilfoyle (drums).

Transchumance (1996) s-sax, t-sax, trb, b-gui, drums
> Improvised Music Company IMCD 1008, CD (1997): Brendan Doyle (s-sax), Michael Buckley (t-sax), Karl Ronan (trb), Ronan Guilfoyle (b-gui), Conor Guilfoyle (drums).

Sostenuto (1998) tpt, s-, a-, t-, bar-sax, trb, db, pf, drums
> Improvised Music Company IMCD 1014, CD (1998): Improvised Music Ensemble.

Sundials (1998) tpt, s-, a-, t-, bar-sax, trb, db, pf, drums
> Improvised Music Company IMCD 1014, CD (1998): Improvised Music Ensemble.

Philip Hammond
(* Belfast 1951)

Hammond studied at Queen's University, Belfast (BMus 1973), and at the Royal Irish Academy of Music, Dublin. He has been Director of Performing Arts at the Arts Council of Northern Ireland for a number of years besides being active as a pianist, critic and broadcaster. He wrote some educational music for children's choir and claims an educational background for much of his music although he is very well able to write in a serious mode. He wrote many chamber and piano pieces, his largest works being an electro-acoustic composition, *Thanatos* (1977), and a *Fanfare for Orchestra* (1984).

Recorded Work:

Sonata (1983) org
> Priory Records PR 178-A, LP (1985): Norman Finlay.

Carl Gilbert Hardebeck
(* London 1869, † Dublin 1945)

Hardebeck was born of German father and a Welsh mother and came to live in Ireland in 1893. He was organist and teacher in Belfast and won several composition prizes at the Dublin Feis Ceoil. Belfast's "Bloody Sunday" of 1913, World War I and the Irish Civil War contributed to making him an ardent Irish nationalist, who coined the sentence "I believe in God, Beethoven and Patrick

Pearse". In 1922 he was the first Professor of Irish Music at University College Cork, but returned to Belfast in the following year. He lived in Dublin from 1932 arranging Irish traditional music for various instrumental and choral forces (many for educational purposes) for An Gúm, the government publisher of the Republic of Ireland.

Hardebeck was the first classically trained composer to ackowledge the irregular metre of Irish traditional music in his art music arrangements, which consequently abound of frequent bar changes throughout the music. He made very influential arrangements e.g. of *Una Bhán* for voice and piano, many published as early as 1908.

Recorded Works:

Frinseach Tighe Roin (arr.) satb
　　　Harmonia Mundi HMS 30691, LP (1965): RTÉ Singers, Waldemar Rosen (cond).

Is Atuirseach Géar (arr.) satb
　　　Gael-Linn CEF 004, LP (c. 1960): Cór Cois Laoi, Pilib Ó Laoghaire (cond).

Luibin O Luth (arr.) satb
　　　Harmonia Mundi HMS 30691, LP (1965): RTÉ Singers, Waldemar Rosen (cond).

Seo-Tho-lo-Thoil (arr.) satb
　　　Harmonia Mundi HMS 30691, LP (1965): RTÉ Singers, Waldemar Rosen (cond).

Sile ni Gadhra (arr.) satb
　　　Harmonia Mundi HMS 30691, LP (1965): RTÉ Singers, Waldemar Rosen (cond).

Hamilton Harty
(* Hillsborough Co. Down 1879, † Brighton 1941)

Hamilton Harty hailed from the north of Ireland and in 1895 moved to Bray, Co. Dublin, where he was influenced by Michele Esposito. He soon made a name for himself as an accompanist and went to England in 1901 to pursue a career as pianist and conductor. He developed to become one of the best conductors of his time, especially after he took over the Hallé Orchestra in Manchester (1920-33).

Conducting left him little time for composing after 1920. He also conducted in Dublin, London, the United States and Australia.

His music is broadly romantic and often speaks with a clear Irish traditional voice. His *Irish Symphony* (1904) was very popular, but arguably his best works with orchestra are *With the Wild Geese* (1912) and *The Children of Lir* (1938), in both of which he picked up old Irish legends. Harty was knighted in 1925.

Recorded Works:

Sea Wrack (c. 1895) v, pf
EMI CLP 1906, LP (1965): Veronica Dunne (S), Havelock Nelson (pf).

Argo ZRG 5459 (stereo), RG 459 (mono), LP (1966): Bernadette Greevy (Mez), Jeannie Reddin (pf).

Sutton Sound SSLP 137, LP (1986): Carolyn Fullerton (A), Elizabeth Bicker (pf).

Max Sound MSCB 13, MC (1987): Valerie Baulard (Mez), Simon Wright (pf).

Fantasia op. 6 (1902) 2pf
Olympia OCD 680, CD (2000): Bruce Posner & Donald Garvelmann.

Romance and Scherzo op. 8 (1903) vc, pf
Dutton Laboratories CDLX 7102, CD (2000): Andrew Fuller (vc), Michael Dussek (pf).

An Irish Symphony (1904) orch
Chandos ABRD 1027 (= LP), ABTD 1027 (= MC) (1981): Ulster Orchestra, Bryden Thomson (cond).
Re-issued on Chandos DBRD 4002, 4LP (1983); Chandos CHAN 8314, CD (1983); Chandos CHAN 7034, CD (1996); Chandos CHAN 7035, 3CD (1996).

Naxos 8.554732, CD (2000): National Symphony Orchestra of Ireland, Proinnsías Ó Duinn (cond).

Excerpts:
2nd & 3rd movts
Chandos CHAN 6525, CD (1991): (*taken from record above*).

2nd movt.
Lyrita SCRS 99, LP (1978): Philharmonia Orchestra, Nicholas Braithwaite (cond).

BBC Vintage Collection BBC CD-756 (= CD), REH 756 (= LP), ZCR 756 (= MC) (1990, recorded 1929): Hallé Orchestra, Hamilton Harty (cond).

K-Tel Celtic Collections CCD 135, CD (1999): RTÉ Concert Orchestra, (no conductor named).

Irish Fancies (c. 1904) pf
Sutton Sound SSLP 131, LP (1986): Elizabeth Bicker.

Three Traditional Ulster Airs (1905) v, pf
Sutton Sound SSLP 137, LP (1986): Richard Woods (Bar), Eric Hinds (Bar), Elizabeth Bicker (pf)

A Comedy Overture (1906) orch
Chandos ABRD 1027 (= LP), ABTD 1027 (= MC) (1981): Ulster Orchestra, Bryden Thomson (cond).
Re-issued on Chandos DBRD 4002, 4LP (1983); Chandos CHAN 8314, CD (1983); Chandos CHAN 7034, CD (1996); Chandos CHAN 7035, 3CD (1996).

Lane o' the Thrushes (1906) v, pf
EMI CLP 1906, LP (1965): Veronica Dunne (S), Havelock Nelson (pf).

Sutton Sound SSLP 137, LP (1986): Marie O'Connor (S), Elizabeth Bicker (pf).

The Ould Lad (1906) v, pf
Sutton Sound SSLP 137, LP (1986): Gordon Speers (B), Elizabeth Bicker (pf).

Ode to a Nightingale (1907) S, orch
Chandos ABRD 1051 (= LP), ABTD 1051 (= MC) (1982): Heather Harper (S), Ulster Orchestra, Bryden Thomson (cond).
Re-issued on Chandos DBRD 4002, 4LP (1983); Chandos CHAN 8387, CD (1985); Chandos CHAN 7033, CD (1996).

Two Pieces (Waldesstille; Der Schmetterling) (1903) vc, pf
Dutton Laboratories CDLX 7102, CD (2000): Andrew Fuller (vc), Michael Dussek (pf).

Violin Concerto (1908) vn, orch
>Chandos ABRD 1044 (= LP), ABTD 1044 (= MC) (1979): Ralph
>Holmes (vn), Ulster Orchestra, Bryden Thomson (cond).
>*Re-issued on* Chandos DBRD 4002, 4LP (1983); Chandos CHAN 8386,
>CD (1985); Chandos CHAN 7035, 3CD (1996).

Six Songs of Ireland (1908) v, pf
>Excerpt:
>*Lullaby*
>Sutton Sound SSLP 137, LP (1986): Marie O'Connor (S), Elizabeth
>Bicker (pf).

With the Wild Geese (1910) orch
>HMV ASD 2400, LP (1968): Scottish National Symphony Orchestra,
>Alexander Gibson (cond).
>*Re-issued on* HMV Greensleeve ED 290208-1 (= LP) -4 (= MC)
>(1984); Classics for Pleasure CD-CFP 4635, CD (1994).

>Opal 801, LP (1982, recorded 1926): Hallé Orchestra, Hamilton Harty
>(cond).

>Chandos ABRD 1084 (= LP), ABTD 1084 (= MC) (1983): Ulster
>Orchestra, Bryden Thomson (cond).
>*Re-issued on* Chandos DBRD 4002, 4LP (1983); Chandos CHAN 8321,
>CD (1983); Chandos CHAN 7034, CD (1996); Chandos CHAN 7035,
>3CD (1996).

>Naxos 8.554732, CD (2000): National Symphony Orchestra of Ireland,
>Proinnsías Ó Duinn (cond).

Scythe-Song (1910) v, pf
>Sutton Sound SSLP 137, LP (1986): Joanna Pullicino (Mez), Elizabeth
>Bicker (pf).

À la Campagne (1911) ob, pf
>Hyperion A 66206 (= LP) KA 66206 (= MC) (1985): Sarah Francis
>(ob), Peter Dickinson (pf).
>*Re-issued on* Hyperion Helios CDH 55008, CD (1999).

Chansonette (1911) ob, pf
>Hyperion A 66206 (= LP) KA 66206 (= MC) (1985): Sarah Francis
>(ob), Peter Dickinson (pf).
>*Re-issued on* Hyperion Helios CDH 55008, CD (1999).

Orientale (1911) ob, pf
>   Hyperion A 66206 (= LP) KA 66206 (= MC) (1985): Sarah Francis
>   (ob), Peter Dickinson (pf).
>   *Re-issued on* Hyperion Helios CDH 55008, CD (1999).

Variations on a Dublin Air (1912) vn, orch
>   Chandos ABRD 1044 (= LP), ABTD 1044 (= MC) (1979): Ralph
>   Holmes (vn), Ulster Orchestra, Bryden Thomson (cond).
>   *Re-issued on* Chandos DBRD 4002, 4LP (1983); Chandos CHAN 8386,
>   CD (1985); Chandos CHAN 7035, 3CD (1996).

Irish Fantasy (ca. 1912) vn, pf
>   Continuum CCD 1051, CD (1992): Fionnuala Hunt (vn), Una Hunt (pf).

The Stranger's Grave (1913) v, pf
>   Sutton Sound SSLP 137, LP (1986): Norma Gray Wilson (Mez), Eliza-
>   beth Bicker (pf).

In Ireland (1915) fl, pf
>   ASV CD DCA 768, CD (1991): Kenneth Smith (fl), Paul Rhodes (pf).

>   KLT 003, CD (1992): Kirsten Spratt (fl), Elizabeth Mucha (pf).

>   Metier MSVCD 92006, CD (1995): Emily Beynon (fl), Catherine Bey-
>   non (hp).

>   Arrangement for flute and chamber ensemble:
>   Dorian DOR 90250, CD (1997): Chris Norman (fl), Camerata Bari-
>   loche, Fernando Hasaj (cond).

Suite from Handel's Water Music (1920) orch
>   Chandos ABRD 1136 (= LP), ABTD 1136 (= MC) (1979): Ulster
>   Orchestra, Bryden Thomson (cond).
>   *Re-issued on* Chandos CHAN 6583, CD (1993).

Piano Concerto (1922) pf, orch
>   Chandos ABRD 1084 (= LP), ABTD 1084 (= MC) (1983): Malcolm
>   Binns (pf), Ulster Orchestra, Bryden Thomson (cond).
>   *Re-issued on* Chandos DBRD 4002, 4LP (1983); Chandos CHAN 8321,
>   CD (1985); Chandos CHAN 7035, 3CD (1996).

The Londonderry Air (1924) vn, orch
>   Chandos ABRD 1136 (= LP), ABTD 1136 (= MC) (1979): Pan Hon
>   Lee (vn), Ulster Orchestra, Bryden Thomson (cond).

Re-issued on Chandos CHAN 6525, CD (1991); Chandos CHAN 6583, CD (1993).

In Ireland (1935) fl, hp, orch
Chandos ABRD 1084 (= LP), ABTD 1084 (= MC) (1983): Colin Fleming (fl), Denise Kelly (hp), Ulster Orchestra, Bryden Thomson (cond).
Re-issued on Chandos DBRD 4002, 4LP (1983); Chandos CHAN 8321,CD (1983); Chandos CHAN 6583, CD (1993); Chandos CHAN 7034, CD (1996); Chandos CHAN 7035, 3CD (1996).

Naxos 8.554732, CD (2000): National Symphony Orchestra of Ireland, Proinnsías Ó Duinn (cond).

The Children of Lir (1938) S, orch
Chandos ABRD 1051 (= LP), ABTD 1051 (= MC) (1982): Heather Harper (S), Ulster Orchestra, Bryden Thomson (cond).
Re-issued on Chandos DBRD 4002, 4LP (1983); Chandos CHAN 8387, CD (1985); Chandos CHAN 7033; CD (1996).

Five Irish Poems (1938) v, pf
Excerpt:
The Fiddler of Dooney
Sutton Sound SSLP 137, LP (1986) Martin O'Hagan (Bar), Elizabeth Bicker (pf).

A John Field Suite (1939) orch
HMV CSD 3696, LP (1971): English Sinfonia, Neville Dilkes (cond).

Chandos CBR 1005 (= LP), CBT 1005 (= MC) (1979): Ulster Orchestra, Bryden Thomson (cond).
Re-issued on Chandos CHAN 6583, CD (1993).

CBC Records SMCD 5035, CD (1991): Edmonton Symphony Orchestra, Uri Mayer (cond).

Dutton Laboratories CDAX 8012, CD (1995, recorded 1945): Liverpool Philharmonic Orchestra, Malcolm Sargent (cond).

Paul Hayes
(* Dublin 1951)

Paul Hayes studied at the Royal Irish Academy of Music, Dublin, with James Wilson and at University College Dublin with Seóirse Bodley. He composes for a wide variety of instruments and ensembles and has a particular interest in live electronic groupings, music theatre, ballet and modern dance. He is a recipient of the prestigious Varming Prize for composition. Hayes has been living in Japan since the late 1980s.

Recorded Works:

Pre-Prelude for Morton Feldman 1926-1987 (1987) pf
> Association of Irish Composers AIC 001, Promotion-CD (1999): David Adams.

The Love Sonata (1992) ob d'amore, pf
> Contemporary Music Centre CMC CD02, Promotion-CD (1997): Degani Ensemble.

27th January 1995: Lost in Tokyo (1995) pf
> Association of Irish Composers AIC 001, Promotion-CD (1999): David Adams.

Piers Hellawell
(* Derbyshire, England 1956)

After studying with James Wood and Nicholas Maw in England, Piers Hellawell was appointed composer-in-residence at Queen's University Belfast in 1980, where he still lives and teaches. His works have been performed widely, at the ISCM World Music Days and other music festivals. His set of choral pieces, *The Hilliard Songbook Volume One*, was an award-winning CD in 1996. His largest composition so far has been *Drum of the Najd* (1997), a concerto for recorder, percussion and orchestra.

Recorded Works:

Via Dolorosa (198?) org
> Priory Records PR 178-A, LP (1985): Norman Finlay.

Sound Carvings from Rano Raraku (1988) fl, db, pf, perc
Metronome MET CD 1029, CD (1998): Psappha, Tim Williams
(Art.-Dir.).

Truth or Consequences (1991) cl, vc, pf
Metronome MET CD 1029, CD (1998): Psappha, Tim Williams
(Art.-Dir.).

Sound Carvings from the Ice Wall (1994) fl. cl, va, vc, db, pf, perc
Metronome MET CD 1029, CD (1998): Psappha, Paul MacAlindin
(cond), Tim Williams (Art.-Dir.).

High Citadels (1994), cl, pf
Metier MSV CD 92013, CD (1998): Kate Romano (cl), Alan Hicks
(pf).

The Hilliard Songbook Volume One (1995) ttbb
ECM 453 259-2, 2CD (1996): Hilliard Ensemble.

Memorial Cairns (1996) 6vn, 2va, 2vc, db
Metronome MET CD 1029, CD (1998): BT Scottish Ensemble, Piers
Hellawell (cond), Clio Gould (Art.-Dir.).

Sound Carvings from the Water's Edge (1996) 6vn, 2va, 2vc, db
Metronome MET CD 1029, CD (1998): BT Scottish Ensemble, Piers
Hellawell (cond), Clio Gould (Art.-Dir.).

George H. P. Hewson
(* Dublin 1881, † Dublin 1972)

George Hewson began his musical career as a boy chorister at St. Patrick's
Cathedral, Dublin, and has served the choir until his retirement in 1960. During
the early 1920s he became popular in Ireland as one of the only offerers of
classical concerts during the civil war. Hewson was professor of music at Trinity
College, Dublin, from 1935 to 1962 – he also conducted the University of
Dublin Choral Society for more than 20 years.

Recorded Works:

Let us now Praise Famous Men (1937) satb, org
> Priory PRCD 639, CD (1999): Christ Church Cathedral Dublin Choir,
> Andrew Johnstone (org), Mark Duley (cond).

Sunset and Evening Star (19??) satb
> TCDCC001, CD (1997): Trinity College Dublin Chapel Choir, Kerry S.
> Houston (cond).

Magnificat in G (19??) satb, org
> TCDCC001, CD (1997): Trinity College Dublin Chapel Choir, Stephen
> Mailey (org), Kerry S. Houston (cond).

Michael Holohan

(* Dublin 1956)

Michael Holohan lives in Drogheda Co. Louth and much of his work of the past ten years has been inspired by the many prehistoric sites in the area. He studied at University College Dublin and at Queen's University Belfast and attended masterclasses with Olivier Messiaen, Iannis Xenakis, Pierre Boulez and Luciano Berio. He is chairman of the Droichead Arts Centre and was elected to Aosdána, Ireland's academy of creative artists, in 1999.

Recorded Work:

The Lads (2000) cl/b-cl
> Containers / Galway Arts Festival 2000, CD (2000): Paul Roe.

Herbert Hughes

(* Belfast 1882, † Brighton 1937)

Hughes grew up in Belfast and completed his studies with C.V. Stanford at the Royal College of Music, London, in 1901. In 1903, he was a founder member of the Irish Folk Song Society of London and co-editor of its Journal. From 1911 to 1932 he was the music critic of the Daily Telegraph. Hughes was an active folk song collector and collected more than 1,000 melodies, most of them unpublished. Many of these able arrangements deserve high merits for their impressionist qualities. His most important volumes were the *Irish Country Songs* which appeared in 1909, 1915, 1934 and 1936. The following songs all originate from these volumes and are here arranged in alphabetical order for quicker reference.

Recorded Works:

A Ballynure Ballad
> EMI CLP 1906, LP (1965): Veronica Dunne (S), Havelock Nelson (pf).

> Argo ZRG 5459 (stereo), RG 459 (mono), LP (1966): Bernadette Greevy (Mez), Jeannie Reddin (pf).

> Preiser 91081, CD (2000): Robert Brooks (Bar), Ingrid Hedlund (pf).

A Good Roarin' Fire
> Preiser 91081, CD (2000): Robert Brooks (Bar), Ingrid Hedlund (pf).

A Young Maid stood in her Father's Garden
> Hyperion CDA 66627, CD (1993): Ann Murray (Mez), Graham Johnson (pf).

> Preiser 91081, CD (2000): Robert Brooks (Bar), Ingrid Hedlund (pf).

An Irish Elegy
> Preiser 91081, CD (2000): Robert Brooks (Bar), Ingrid Hedlund (pf).

Down by the Sally Gardens
> EMI EX 290007 3, 2LP (1984, recorded 1940): John McCormack (T), Gerald Moore (pf).

> Decca 417 192-2DH, CD (1988, recorded 1949): Kathleen Ferrier (Mez), Phyllis Spurr (pf).
> *Re-issued on* Decca 433 475-2DM, CD (1992); Decca 448 055-2DWO (= CD), -4DWO (= MC) (1996); Decca 458 270-2DH (= CD), -4DH (= MC) (1997).

> Belart 450 020-2, CD (1993) (same recording as Decca above).

> Centaur CRC 2243, CD (1995): Gary Lakes (T), Kevin Murphy (pf).

> Pearl Gemm CDS 9188, 2CD (1995, recorded 1941): John McCormack (T), Gerald Moore (pf).

Testament SBT 1073, CD (1996, recorded 1957): Eileen Farrell (S), George Trovillo (pf).

Symposium 1165, CD (1998) (same recording as Pearl above).

Preiser 91081, CD (2000): Robert Brooks (Bar), Ingrid Hedlund (pf).

How Sweet and how Pleasing the Birds Sing in Tune
Forlane 16784, CD (1998): Ann Murray (Mez), Graham Johnson (pf).

I have a Bonnet trimmed with Blue
Decca 417 192-2DH, CD (1988, recorded 1951): Kathleen Ferrier (Mez), Phyllis Spurr (pf).

Pearl Gemm 9989, CD (1992, recorded 1940): Barbara Mullen (S), Ivor Newton (pf).

Hyperion CDA 66627, CD (1993): Ann Murray (Mez), Graham Johnson (pf).

I know where I'm going
Argo ZRG 5459 (stereo), RG 459 (mono), LP (1966): Bernadette Greevy (Mez), Jeannie Reddin (pf).

Decca 417 192-2DH, CD (1988, recorded 1951): Kathleen Ferrier (Mez), Phyllis Spurr (pf).

Pearl Gemm 9989, CD (1992, recorded 1940): Barbara Mullen (S), Ivor Newton (pf).

ASV CD WHL 2091, CD (1994): Mary Hegarty (S), Ingrid Surgenor (pf).

I will walk with my Love
EMI CLP 1906, LP (1965): Veronica Dunne (S), Havelock Nelson (pf).

Chandos CHAN 8749 (= CD), ABTD 1388 (= MC) (1989): Linda Finnie (Mez), Anthony Legge (pf).

Pearl Gemm 9989, CD (1992, recorded 1940): Barbara Mullen (S), Ivor Newton (pf).

Hyperion CDA 66627, CD (1993): Ann Murray (Mez), Graham Johnson (pf).

Johnny I hardly knew you
>Pearl Gemm 9989, CD (1992, recorded 1941): Barbara Mullen (S), Gerald Moore (pf).

>Forlane 16784, CD (1998): Ann Murray (Mez), Graham Johnson (pf).

Kitty my Love
>Chandos CHAN 8749 (= CD), ABTD 1388 (= MC) (1989): Linda Finnie (Mez), Anthony Legge (pf).

>Centaur CRC 2243, CD (1995): Gary Lakes (T), Kevin Murphy (pf).

Little Boats
>Pearl Gemm CDS 9188, 2CD (1995, recorded 1941): John McCormack (T), Gerald Moore (pf).

Lovely Mollie
>Chandos CHAN 8946, CD (1992): Benjamin Luxon (Bar), David Willison (pf).

Monday, Tuesday
>Hyperion CDA 66627, CD (1993): Ann Murray (Mez), Graham Johnson (pf).

No, not more Welcome
>Pearl Gemm 9989, CD (1992, recorded 1928): William F. Watt (T), anonymous pianist.

>Pearl Gemm CDS 9188, 2CD (1995, recorded 1941): John McCormack (T), Gerald Moore (pf).

Norah O'Neale
>Arrangement for orchestra:
>Nimbus NI 7854, CD (1993, recorded 1929): John McCormack (T), anonymous orchestra, Nathaniel Shilkret (cond).

>Symposium 1166, CD (1998) *(same recording as Nimbus above)*.

O Men from the Fields
>Saga 5345, LP (1973): Sheila Armstrong (S), Martin Isepp (pf).

>ASV CD WHL 2091, CD (1994): Mary Hegarty (S), Ingrid Surgenor (pf).

Oh Breathe not his Name
 Preiser 91081, CD (2000): Robert Brooks (Bar), Ingrid Hedlund (pf).

Roisin Dubh
 EMI CLP 1906, LP (1965): Veronica Dunne (S), Havelock Nelson (pf).

She Moved Through the Fair
 EMI EX 290007 3, 2LP (1984, recorded 1940): John McCormack (T),
 Gerald Moore (pf).

 Chandos CHAN 8946, CD (1992): Benjamin Luxon (Bar), David
 Willison (pf).

 ASV CD AJA 5119, CD (1993, recorded 1941): John McCormack (T),
 Gerald Moore (pf).

 Pearl Gemm CDS 9188, 2CD (1995) (same recording as ASV above).

 HMV Classics 7243 5 73043 2 0, CD (1998, recorded 1978): James
 McCracken (T), John Atkins (pf).

 ASV CD AJA 5283, CD (1999, recorded 1935): Sydney MacEwan (T),
 Duncan Morrison (pf).

 Preiser 91081, CD (2000): Robert Brooks (Bar), Ingrid Hedlund (pf).

The Bard of Armagh
 EMI EX 290007 3, 2LP (1984, recorded 1940): John McCormack (T),
 Gerald Moore (pf).

 Hyperion CDA 66627, CD (1993): Ann Murray (Mez), Graham
 Johnson (pf).

 Centaur CRC 2243, CD (1995): Gary Lakes (T), Kevin Murphy (pf).

 Arrangement for orchestra:
 ASV CD AJA 5119, CD (1993, recorded 1920): John McCormack (T),
 anonymous orchestra, Josef A. Pasternack (cond).

The Cork Leg
 Hyperion CDA 66627, CD (1993): Ann Murray (Mez), Graham
 Johnson (pf).

The Gartan Mother's Lullaby

> Preiser 91081, CD (2000): Robert Brooks (Bar), Ingrid Hedlund (pf).

The Leprehaun

> Hyperion CDA 66627, CD (1993): Ann Murray (Mez), Graham Johnson (pf).

> Preiser 91081, CD (2000): Robert Brooks (Bar), Ingrid Hedlund (pf).

The Little Boats

> Nimbus NI 7854, CD (1993, recorded 1941): John McCormack (T), Gerald Moore (pf).

The Lover's Curse

> Argo ZRG 5459 (stereo), RG 459 (mono), LP (1966): Bernadette Greevy (Mez), Jeannie Reddin (pf).

> Decca 417 192-2DH, CD (1988, recorded 1951): Kathleen Ferrier (Mez), Phyllis Spurr (pf).

> Pearl Gemm 9989, CD (1992, recorded 1928): Margaret Burke-Sheridan (S), Gerald Moore (pf).

> Chandos CHAN 8749 (= CD), ABTD 1388 (= MC) (1989): Linda Finnie (Mez), Anthony Legge (pf).

The Next Market Day

> Pearl Gemm 9989, CD (1992, recorded 1940): Barbara Mullen (S), Ivor Newton (pf).

> Hyperion CDA 66627, CD (1993): Ann Murray (Mez), Graham Johnson (pf).

The Ninepenny Fidil

> Argo ZRG 5459 (stereo), RG 459 (mono), LP (1966): Bernadette Greevy (Mez), Jeannie Reddin (pf).

The Old Turf Fire

> Chandos CHAN 8946, CD (1992): Benjamin Luxon (Bar), David Willison (pf).

> Preiser 91081, CD (2000): Robert Brooks (Bar), Ingrid Hedlund (pf).

The Palatine's Daughter
> Pearl Gemm 9989, CD (1992, recorded 1940): Robert Irwin (Bar),
> Gerald Moore (pf).

The Spanish Lady
> Saga 5345, LP (1973): Sheila Armstrong (S), Martin Isepp (pf).

The Star of the County Down
> EMI EX 290007 3, 2LP (1984, recorded 1939): John McCormack (T),
> Gerald Moore (pf).
> *See also Memoir (1992), ASV (1993), Symposium (1998) below.*

> Chandos CHAN 8946, CD (1992): Benjamin Luxon (Bar), David
> Willison (pf).

> Memoir Classics CDMOIR 418, CD (1992) *(same recording as EMI
> above).*

> ASV CD AJA 5119, CD (1993) *(same recording as EMI above).*

> Centaur CRC 2243, CD (1995): Gary Lakes (T), Kevin Murphy (pf).

> Forlane 16784, CD (1998): Ann Murray (Mez), Graham Johnson (pf).

> Symposium 1166, CD (1998) *(same recording as EMI above).*

> Preiser 91081, CD (2000): Robert Brooks (Bar), Ingrid Hedlund (pf).

> Arrangement for orchestra:
> ASV CD AJA 5085, CD (1991, recorded 1940s or 50s): Cavan
> O'Connor (T), Rae Jenkins and his Orchestra.

The Stuttering Lovers
> Saga 5345, LP (1973): Sheila Armstrong (S), Martin Isepp (pf).

> Chandos CHAN 8749 (= CD), ABTD 1388 (= MC) (1989): Linda
> Finnie (Mez), Anthony Legge (pf).

> Hyperion CDA 66627, CD (1993): Ann Murray (Mez), Graham
> Johnson (pf).

When thro' Life Unblest we Rove
> Forlane 16784, CD (1998): Ann Murray (Mez), Graham Johnson (pf).

Marian Ingoldsby
(* Carrick-on-Suir Co.Tipperary 1965)

Ingoldsby studied with Gerald Barry at University College Cork (BMus 1985, MA 1989). During 1990-1 she studied with Paul Patterson in London. In 1995 she won the prestigious Macauley Fellowship and the Fleischmann Prize from University College Cork. The Elizabeth Maconchy Fellowship in 1996 enabled her to complete a PhD course in composition at University of York, England (2000). She has written some orchestral music and a chamber opera, but her main work consists of chamber and vocal music. She is writing in a freely atonal style with an emphasis on melodic line.

Recorded Work:

Lament (1993) satb
    Corkfest 94, CD (1994): Wilcollane Singers, Anne Dunphy (cond).

Fergus Johnston
(* Dublin 1959)

Fergus Johnston studied at Trinity College Dublin (MusB 1982) and at the Royal Irish Academy of Music where his teachers included Doris Keogh (flute), Tim Hanafin (clarinet) and James Wilson (composition). He also studied for two years with Robert Hanson at Devon (England). A study session with György Ligeti in 1985 led to a creative crisis dropping serial composition as a result. He is attracted by systems of organised chaos and by East Asian philosophy. In 1989 he was awarded the Macauley Fellowship. Johnston became a member of Aosdána, Ireland's academy of the arts, in 1992.

Recorded Works:

Samsara (1991) orch
    Vienna Modern Masters VMM 3035, CD (1996): Ruse Philharmonic Orchestra, Tsanko Delibozov (cond).

Kaleidophone (1992) str-qu, hp, perc
    Contemporary Music Centre CMC CD02, Promotion-CD (1997): Concorde.

"Je goûte le jeu ..." (1997) ch-orch
　　　　Black Box Music BBM 1013, CD (1998): Irish Chamber Orchestra,
　　　　Fionnuala Hunt (cond).

James Joyce
(* Dublin 1882, † Zurich 1941)

Many Joyce readers will know that his poetry and prose contains numerous
allusions to music. In fact, early in his career Joyce even contemplated becoming
a professional singer, possessing a fine tenor voice. That the author of the poetry
collection *Chamber Music* (1907), of the story collection *Dubliners* (1914) and
of *Ulysses* (1922) and *Finnegan's Wake* (1939) was also a composer is not
generally known. In fact, his "work-list" extends to the melody of a song only;
the accompaniment was written by Edmund Pendleton during Joyce's time in
Paris.

Recorded Work:

Bid Adieu (192?) v, pf
　　　　Forlane 16784, CD (1998): Ann Murray (Mez), Graham Johnson (pf).

Thomas C. Kelly
(* Wexford 1917, † Dublin 1985)

T.C. Kelly studied at University College Dublin and was music master at Clon-
gowes Wood College, County Kildare, for many years after 1952. His output
mainly consists of romantic music in traditional Irish style and includes a large
number of arrangements.

Recorded Works:

Three Pieces for Strings (1949) str-orch
　　　　Decca (USA) DL 9844, LP (1956): Radio Éireann Symphony Orches-
　　　　tra, Milan Horvát (cond).

Black Box Music BBM 1003, CD (1997): Irish Chamber Orchestra, Fionnuala Hunt (cond).

Mass for Peace (1976) spkr, satb, org
Network Tapes NTO 55C, MC (1977): Clonliffe College Choir, T.C. Kelly (cond).

O'Carolan Suite for Strings (1978) str-orch
Black Box Music BBM 1003, CD (1997): Irish Chamber Orchestra, Fionnuala Hunt (cond).

Undated arrangements:

Ag Críost an Síol (arr.) vn
Cala Artist 0503, CD (1996): Geraldine O'Grady.

Báidín Fheilimidh (Felemy's Little Boat) (arr.) vn, pf
Cala Artist 0503, CD (1996): Geraldine O'Grady (vn), Margaret O'Sullivan (pf).

Ban-Chnoic Eireann O (arr.) satb
Harmonia Mundi HMS 30691, LP (1965): RTÉ Singers, Waldemar Rosen (cond).

Fanny Power (arr.) vn, vc, pf
Black Box Music BBM 1022, CD (1998): Irish Piano Trio.

Ireland, Mother Ireland (arr.) satb, pf
EMI CLP 3532, LP (1966): Feis Éireann Group of Singers, Eileen O'Grady (pf – cond).

Johnny I hardly knew ye (arr.) satb, pf
EMI CLP 3532, LP (1966): Feis Éireann Group of Singers, Eileen O'Grady (pf + cond).

Lament (arr.) vn, vc, pf
Black Box Music BBM 1022, CD (1998): Irish Piano Trio.

My Mary of the Curling Hair (arr.) vn, pf
Cala Artist 0503, CD (1996): Geraldine O'Grady (vn), Margaret O'Sullivan (pf).

Oft in the Stilly Night (arr.) vn, pf
> Cala Artist 0503, CD (1996): Geraldine O'Grady (vn), Margaret
> O'Sullivan (pf).

The Boys of Wexford (arr.) satb, pf
> EMI CLP 3532, LP (1966): Feis Éireann Group of Singers, Eileen
> O'Grady (pf + cond).

The Breakdown Reel/Bonnie Kate/Miss McLeod's Reel (arr.) 2vn, pf
> Cala Artist 0503, CD (1996): Geraldine O'Grady (vn), Oonagh Keogh
> (vn), Margaret O'Sullivan (pf).

The Derry Air (arr.) vn, pf
> Continuum CCD 1051, CD (1992): Fionnuala Hunt (vn), Una Hunt (pf).

The Gentle Maiden (arr.) vn, pf
> Cala Artist 0503, CD (1996): Geraldine O'Grady (vn), Margaret
> O'Sullivan (pf).

The Lark in the Clear Air (arr.) vn, pf
> Continuum CCD 1051, CD (1992): Fionnuala Hunt (vn), Una Hunt (pf).

> Cala Artist 0503, CD (1996): Geraldine O'Grady (vn), Margaret
> O'Sullivan (pf).

The Mason's Apron/The Piper's Tune (arr) 2vn, pf
> Cala Artist 0503, CD (1996): Geraldine O'Grady (vn), Oonagh Keogh
> (vn), Margaret O'Sullivan (pf).

The Quiet Land of Erin (arr.) vn
> Cala Artist 0503, CD (1996): Geraldine O'Grady.

The Rakes of Mallow (arr.) satb
> New Irish Recording Co. DEB 002, LP (1974): Culwick Choral
> Society, Eric Sweeney (cond).

The Real Old Mountain Dew (arr.) satb, pf
> EMI CLP 3532, LP (1966): Feis Éireann Group of Singers, Eileen
> O'Grady (pf + cond).

The Rose of Tralee (arr.) satb, pf
> EMI CLP 3532, LP (1966): Feis Éireann Group of Singers, Eileen
> O'Grady (pf + cond).

The West's Awake (arr.) satb, pf
>EMI CLP 3532, LP (1966): Feis Éireann Group of Singers, Eileen O'Grady (pf + cond).

Three Lovely Lassies from Bannion (arr.) satb, pf
>EMI CLP 3532, LP (1966): Feis Éireann Group of Singers, Eileen O'Grady (pf + cond).

Úna Bhán (Fair-Haired Una) (arr.) vn
>Cala Artist 0503, CD (1996): Geraldine O'Grady.

>arr. for satb:
>Harmonia Mundi HMS 30691, LP (1965): RTÉ Singers, Waldemar Rosen (cond).

John Kinsella
(* Dublin 1932)

As a composer, John Kinsella was self-taught, but he formally studied violin and viola. He is an avid string quartet member since 1950 and composed four quartets himself. From 1968 he worked as a music producer with RTÉ, becoming Head of Music in 1983. In 1988 he took early retirement to devote his time to composition. Kinsella has written seven symphonies, two violin concertos and much more orchestral music besides songs and chamber music pieces. His musical language changed during the 1980s from a more or less serial aesthetic to neo-romantic sounds.

Recorded Works:

String Quartet No. 2 (1968) str-qu
>NIRC NIR 002, LP (1972): RTÉ String Quartet.

Piano Sonata No. 1 (1971) pf
>Goasco GXX 003-4, MC (1985): Anthony Byrne.

String Quartet No. 3 (1977) str-qu
>Goasco GXX 002-4, MC (1985): Academica Quartet.

>Chandos CHAN 9295, CD (1994): Vanbrugh Quartet.

Last Songs (1983) v, pf
> Altarus AIR-CD-9010, CD (1996): Penelope Price Jones (S), Philip
> Martin (pf).

Nocturne (1990)
> Contemporary Music Centre CMC CD01, Promotion-CD (1995): Irish
> Chamber Orchestra, Fionnuala Hunt (cond).

> Keltia Musique KMCD 63, CD (1996): Irish Chamber Orchestra,
> Fionnuala Hunt (cond) (*same recording as above*).

Symphony No. 3:Joie de vivre (1990) orch
> Marco Polo 8.223766, CD (1997): National Symphony Orchestra of
> Ireland, Proinnsías Ó Duinn (cond).

Symphony No. 4: The Four Provinces (1991) orch
> Marco Polo 8.223766, CD (1997): National Symphony Orchestra of
> Ireland, Proinnsías Ó Duinn (cond).

John F. Larchet
(* Dublin 1884, † Dublin 1967)

John Francis Larchet built the bridge between the 19th and the 20th century in
Irish music. At first he followed in Michele Esposito's footsteps in an unsuccess-
ful attempt to revive the Dublin Orchestral Society. He was music director of the
influential Abbey Theatre from 1907 to 1934. However, Larchet is best remembered for his teaching: he taught harmony and counterpoint at the Royal Irish
Academy of Music (1920-1955) and was professor of music at University
College Dublin (1921-1958). As a composer, he was the last heir to the music of
Stanford and Harty, although it must be said that his music has unique nostalgic
qualities. Some of his songs reach a high artistic level and bridge the gap
between the traditional Irish and the classical approach.

Recorded Works:

The Philosophy of Love (1908) v, pf
> Symposium 1165, CD (1998): John McCormack (T), anonymous pianist
> (possibly Vincent O'Brien).

Pádraic the Fiddiler (1919) (vn,) v, pf (+ vn ad lib)
    Pearl Gemm 9315, CD (1988, recorded 1924): Fritz Kreisler (vn), John McCormack (T), Edwin Schneider (pf).

    Biddulph LAB 068/9, 2CD (1993) (*same recording as above*).

    Marco Polo 8.225098, CD (1998): Bernadette Greevy (Mez), Hugh Tinney (pf).

An Ardglass Boat Song (1920) v, pf
    Marco Polo 8.225098, CD (1998): Bernadette Greevy (Mez), Hugh Tinney (pf).

A Stóirín Bán (1922) v, pf
    Marco Polo 8.225098, CD (1998): Bernadette Greevy (Mez), Hugh Tinney (pf).

The Stranger (1939) v. pf
    ASV CD WHL 2091, CD (1994): Mary Hegarty (S), Ingrid Surgenor (pf).

The Dirge of Ossian & MacAnanty's Reel (1940) orch
    Decca (USA) DL 9844, LP (1956): Radio Éireann Symphony Orchestra, Milan Horvat (cond).

    Black Box Music BBM 1003, CD (1997): Irish Chamber Orchestra, Fionnuala Hunt (cond).

The Wee Boy in Bed (1943) v, pf
    Marco Polo 8.225098, CD (1998): Bernadette Greevy (Mez), Hugh Tinney (pf).

Wee Hughie (1947) v, pf
    Argo ZRG 5459 (stereo), RG 459 (mono), LP (1966): Bernadette Greevy (Mez), Jeannie Reddin (pf).

    Marco Polo 8.225098, CD (1998): Bernadette Greevy (Mez), Hugh Tinney (pf).

Peata an Mhaoir (arr. 1947) satb
    Harmonia Mundi HMS 30691, LP (1965): RTÉ Singers, Waldemar Rosen (cond).

By the Waters of Moyle (1957) orch
> Marco Polo 8.223804, CD (1996): RTÉ Sinfonietta, Proinnséas
> Ó Duinn (cond).

> K-Tel Celtic Collections CCD 135, CD (1999): RTÉ Concert Orchestra,
> (no conductor named).

Mary McAuliffe
(* Cork 1947)

Mary McAuliffe studied at University College Cork and taught music for a number of years before she turned her attention fully to composition. She wrote a large corpus of vocal and choral music, some of it for children, and has had some success with performances at Irish festivals in the USA. Her music is in a direct tonal style with medieval and traditional Irish elements perceivable.

Recorded Works:

By the Lake (1990) ob/C.A., keyb
> International Orphan Aid, CD (1996): Fergus Conaghan (ob, C.A.),
> Mary McAuliffe (keyb).

Morning (1993) keyb
> International Orphan Aid, CD (1996): Mary McAuliffe.

Gloria (1994)
> FMN 1002, CD (1997): Niamh Murray (S), Debbie Clifford (C.A.),
> Colin Block (perc), Dublin County Choir, The Steadfast Band, John
> Dexter (pf, cond).

Song of Adoration (1995)
> FMN 1002, CD (1997): Niamh Murray (S), Debbie Clifford (C.A.),
> Colin Block (perc), Dublin County Choir, Dublin Youth Orchestra,
> John Dexter (pf, cond).

Song of the Orphan Child (1996) children's vv, choir, 2vn, va, vc, trp, keyb, org
> International Orphan Aid, CD (1996): Aisling Dexter (v), Roisin Dexter
> (v), St. Patrick's Cathedral Dublin Choir, Clodagh Vedres (vn), Evelyn
> McGrory (vn), Cheremie Allum (va), Aisling Drury Byrne (vc), Killyan

Bannister (trp), Mary McAuliffe (keyb), Timothy Noone (org), John Dexter (cond).

(dito, short version, same artists) see above

Cormac MacDermott
(* County Roscommon? c. 1580, † London? 1618)

Although the date and place of Cormac MacDermott's birth are unknown, there is a strong possibility that he was born in county Roscommon. In late 1602 or early 1603 he was appointed as harper to the "Royal Musick" at the court of Elizabeth I, probably a "part-time" position, since he continued to be in the services of the 1st Earl of Sailsbury (since c. 1600).

MacDermott must have made a name for himself as a harper before he was called to England. He will have been educated in the old oral harp tradition of Gaelic Ireland, but expanded his technique and musical influences by contact with contemporary English music. Only four of his compositions survived; all are written for consort instrumentations, but it may be reasonably assumed that they were conceived on an Irish harp. This is what the 20th century recordings with harp try to recapture.

Recorded Works:

Cormacke
> Deutsche Harmonia Mundi 05472 77504-2, CD (1999): Andrew Lawrence-King (Irish hp).

Allmane (Sir John Paiton's Pavan)
> Deutsche Harmonia Mundi 05472 77504-2, CD (1999): Andrew Lawrence-King (Irish hp).

Mr Cormake Allman
> Deutsche Harmonia Mundi 05472 77504-2, CD (1999): Andrew Lawrence-King (Irish hp).

Schoc.a.torum Cormacke
> Deutsche Harmonia Mundi 05472 77504-2, CD (1999): Andrew Lawrence-King (Irish hp).

Michael McGlynn
(* Dublin 1964)

Michael McGlynn studied at University College Dublin (BMus 1986). He sang in the RTÉ Chamber Choir and in 1989 founded his own choir called An Uaíthne (since 1993 spelt as Anúna). While at first this choir presented new music by a number of Irish composers including McGlynn, the success of the choir's participation in the original version of the popular dance show *Riverdance* changed the choir's direction. It now fully concentrates on McGlynn's music, a tasteful blend of medieval, impressionist and Irish traditional music. Naturally, choral music features prominently in his work, but he also composed instrumental music and larger scale pieces such as *Sir Gawain and the Green Knight* (1990) and the *O'Malley Mass* (1991). This list only features his original compositions, not the arrangements.*

Recorded Works:

Angels are Singing (1989) T, satb
> Danú 010 / Celtic Heartbeat/Universal UD 53095, CD (1998): Anúna, Michael McGlynn (T + cond).

Codhlaím go Suan (1989) 2S, vn, Ir hp, satb
> Danú 005, CD (1995): Monica Donlon (S), Sara Clancy (S), Aingeala de Burca (vn), Mairéad Ní Fhaoláin (Ir hp), Anúna, Michael McGlynn (cond).
> *Re-issued on* Danú 010 / Celtic Heartbeat/Universal UD 53095, CD (1998).

Incantations (originally titled *Alleluia*) (1989) satb
> Danú 012, CD (2000): Anúna, Michael McGlynn (cond).

Tenebrae I (1989) S, Mez, satb
> Danú 005, CD (1995): Monica Donlon (S), Miriam Blennerhassett (Mez), Anúna, Michael McGlynn (cond).

> Danú 008 / Celtic Heartbeat/Universal UD 53098, CD (1996): Monica Donlon (S), Miriam Blennerhassett (Mez), Anúna, Michael McGlynn (cond).

---

* In the following list, Danú is the label distributed in Ireland; Celtic Heartbeat/ Universal and Gimell/Universal respectively refer to the international distributor.

Agnus Dei (1990) S, Mez, vn, org, satb
Danú 005, CD (1995): Monica Donlon (S), Miriam Blennerhassett (Mez), Aingeala de Burca (vn), Andrew Synott (org), Anúna, Michael McGlynn (cond).

Danú 008 / Celtic Heartbeat/Universal UD 53098, CD (1996): Monica Donlon (S), Miriam Blennerhassett (Mez), Caron Hannigan (vn), Timothy Noone (org), Anúna, Michael McGlynn (cond).
Re-issued on Danú 010 / Celtic Heartbeat/Universal UD 53095, CD (1998).

Codail a Linbh (1990) 2S, Ir hp, satb
Danú 006 / Celtic Heartbeat/Universal UD 53098, CD (1995): Méav Ní Mhaolchatha (S), Monica Donlon (S), Mairéad Ní Fhaoláin (Ir hp), Anúna, Michael McGlynn (cond).

Danú 008 / Celtic Heartbeat/Universal UD 53098, CD (1996): Méav Ní Mhaolchatha (S), Monica Donlon (S), Anne Marie O'Farrell (Ir hp), Anúna, Michael McGlynn (cond).
Re-issued on Danú 010 / Celtic Heartbeat/Universal UD 53095, CD (1998).

Eirí na Gréine / The Rising of the Sun (1990) S, satb, U.P./t-w, vn, perc
Danú CD 002 / Celtic Heartbeat/Universal UD 53089, CD (1994): Katie McMahon (S), Anúna, Declan Masterson (U.P. + t-w), Aingeala de Burca (vn), Noel Eccles (perc), Michael McGlynn (cond).

Raise Up Your Hunting Spear (1990) S, T, 2vn, perc, satb
Danú 005, CD (1995): Katie McMahon (S), John McGlynn (T), Aingeala de Burca (vn), Caron Hannigan (vn), Noel Eccles (perc), Anúna, Michael McGlynn (cond).

Sanctus (1990) satb, Ir hp
Danú CD 001 / Celtic Heartbeat/Universal UD 53085, CD (1993): Anúna, Mairéad Ní Fhaoláin (Ir hp), Michael McGlynn (cond).
Re-issued on Danú 010 / Celtic Heartbeat/Universal UD 53095, CD (1998).

Pater Noster (1991) satb
Danú CD 001 / Celtic Heartbeat/Universal UD53085, CD (1993): Anúna, Michael McGlynn (cond).

Invocation (1992) satb
> Danú CD 001 / Celtic Heartbeat/Universal UD 53085, CD (1993):
> Anúna, Michael McGlynn (cond).

Aisling (1993, rev. 1997) vn, satb, orch
> Danú 009, CD (1997): Anúna, Lesley Hatfield (vn), Ulster Orchestra,
> Michael McGlynn (cond).

Heia Viri (1993) S, satb
> Danú CD 002 / Celtic Heartbeat/Universal UD 53089, CD (1994):
> Monica Donlon (S), Anúna, Michael McGlynn (cond).

The Raid (1993) satb, vn, gui, perc
> Danú CD 001 / Celtic Heartbeat/Universal UD 53085, CD (1993):
> Anúna, Caron Hannigan (vn), John McGlynn (gui), Lloyd Byrne (perc),
> Michael McGlynn (cond).

Goltraí (1994) S, 2gui, t-w, satb
> Danú CD 002 / Celtic Heartbeat/Universal UD 53089, CD (1994):
> Caron Hannigan (S), Benjamin Dwyer (gui), John McGlynn (gui),
> Anúna, Michael McGlynn (t-w + cond).

Hin Barra (1994) T, satb
> Danú CD 002 / Celtic Heartbeat/Universal UD 53089, CD (1994):
> Garrath Patterson (T), Anúna, Michael McGlynn (cond).

Innisfree (1994) S, satb
> Danú CD 002 / Celtic Heartbeat/Universal UD 53089, CD (1994):
> Katie MacMahon (S), Anúna, Michael McGlynn (cond).

Peperit Virgo (1994) Mez, 3va da gamba
> Danú CD 002 / Celtic Heartbeat/Universal UD 53089, CD (1994):
> Máire Lang (Mez), Mark Wilkes (va da gamba), Ann Robinson (va da
> gamba), Lucy Robinson (va da gamba), Michael McGlynn (cond).

Quis est Deus (1994) Mez, S, T, satb
> Danú CD 002 / Celtic Heartbeat/Universal UD 53089, CD (1994):
> Miriam Blennerhassett (Mez), Monica Donlon (S), Anúna, Michael
> McGlynn (T + cond).

Sleepsong (1994) 3S, T, satb, hp
> Danú CD 002 / Celtic Heartbeat/Universal UD 53089, CD (1994):
> Katie MacMahon (S), Sara Clancy (S), Máire Lang (Mez), Michael

McGlynn (T), Anúna, Anne-Marie O'Farrell (cond), Michael McGlynn (cond).

JVC Victor Japan VICP-60517, CD (2000): Boys Air Choir.

Song of Oisín (1994) S, 2gui, t-w, satb
Danú CD 002 / Celtic Heartbeat/Universal UD 53089, CD (1994): Katie MacMahon (S), Padraig Carrol (gui), John McGlynn (gui), Anúna, Michael McGlynn (cond).

Under the Greenwood (1994) T, B, rec, Ir hp, satb
Danú CD 002 / Celtic Heartbeat/Universal UD 53089, CD (1994): Shane Lillis (T), David Clarke (B), Hilda Milner (rec), Mairéad Ní Fhaoláin (Ir hp), Anúna, Michael McGlynn (cond).

Wind on Sea (1994) 2T, vn, t-w, satb
Danú CD 002 / Celtic Heartbeat/Universal UD 53089, CD (1994): John McGlynn (T), Aingeala de Burca (vn), Anúna, Michael McGlynn (T, t-w + cond)

Dúlamán (1995) T, ttbb
Danú 005, CD (1995): Anúna, Michael McGlynn (T + cond).

Danú 008 / Celtic Heartbeat/Universal UD 53098, CD (1996), Anúna, Garrath Patterson (T) Michael McGlynn (cond).

Teldec 16676, CD (1997): Chanticleer, Frank Albinder (cond).

From Nowhere to Nowhere (1995) alto sax
Silva Classics SILKD 6010, CD (1996): Gerard McChrystal.

Danú 009, CD (1997): Kenneth Edge.
Re-issued on Contemporary Music Centre CMC CD03, Promotion-CD (2001).

Geantraí (1995) S, satb
Danú 005, CD (1995): Méav Ní Mhaolchatha (S), Anúna, Michael McGlynn (cond).

Danú 008 / Celtic Heartbeat/Universal UD 53098, CD (1996): Méav Ní Mhaolchatha (S), Anúna, Michael McGlynn (cond).
Re-issued on Keltia Musique KMCD 63, CD (1997).

Maria Matrem Virginem (1995) S, satb
  Danú 005, CD (1995): Monica Donlon (S), Anúna, Michael McGlynn
  (cond).

  Danú 008 / Celtic Heartbeat/Universal UD 53098, CD (1996): Monica
  Donlon (S), Anúna, Michael McGlynn (cond).
  Re-issued on Danú 010 / Celtic Heartbeat/Universal UD 53095, CD
  (1998).

O Viridissima (1995) S, vn, Ir hp, satb
  Danú 005, CD (1995): Katie McMahon (S), Aingeala de Burca (vn),
  Mairéad Ní Fhaoláin (Ir hp), Anúna, Michael McGlynn (cond).

  Danú 008 / Celtic Heartbeat/Universal UD 53098, CD (1996), Eimear
  Quinn (S), Caron Hannigan (vn), Mairéad Ní Fhaoláin (Ir hp), Anúna,
  Michael McGlynn (cond).

Tenebrae II (1995) S, satb
  Danú 005, CD (1995): Máire Lang (S), Anúna, Michael McGlynn
  (cond).

Blackthorn (1996) S, Ir hp, satb
  Danú 007 / Gimell/Universal 462822, CD (1996): Méav Ní
  Mhaolchatha (S), Anne Marie O'Farrell (Ir hp), Anúna, Michael
  McGlynn (cond).
  Re-issued on Hearts of Space CD 11108, CD (1998).

Island (1996) S, Ir hp, satb
  Danú 007 / Gimell/Universal 462822, CD (1996): Eimear Quinn (S),
  Anne Marie O'Farrell (Ir hp), Anúna, Michael McGlynn (cond).

Kyrie (1996) S, satb
  Danú 007 / Gimell/Universal 462822, CD (1996): Monica Donlon (S),
  Anúna, Michael McGlynn (cond).

Salve Rex Gloriae (1996) S, T, 2vn, perc, satb
  Danú 008 / Celtic Heartbeat/Universal UD 53098, CD (1996): Eimear
  Quinn (S), John McGlynn (T), Aingeala de Burca (vn), Caron Hannigan
  (vn), Noel Eccles (perc), Anúna, Michael McGlynn (cond).

The Green Laurel (1996) S, satb
  Danú 007 / Gimell/Universal 462822, CD (1996): Eimear Quinn (S),
  Anúna, Michael McGlynn (cond).
  Re-issued on Green Linnet CD 3125, CD (1999).

The Sea (1996) S, fl, satb
>Danú 007 / Gimell/Universal 462822, CD (1996): Eimear Quinn (S), Bill Dowdall (fl), Anúna, Michael McGlynn (cond).

1901 (1997) S, satb
>Danú 009, CD (1997): Deirdre Gilsenan (S), Anúna, Ulster Orchestra, Michael McGlynn (cond).

Annaghdown (1997) 2S, satb, orch
>Danú 009, CD (1997): Roisín Dempsey (S), Méav Ní Mhaolchatha (S), Anúna, Ulster Orchestra, Michael McGlynn (cond).

August (1997) T, satb
>Danú 009, CD (1997): Anúna, Michael McGlynn (T + cond).

Ave Maria (1997) Mez, orch
>Danú 009, CD (1997): Miriam Blennerhassett (Mez), Ulster Orchestra, Michael McGlynn (cond).

Behind the Closed Eye (1997) sax, satb
>Danú 009, CD (1997): Kenneth Edge (sax), Anúna, Michael McGlynn (cond).

Ceann Dubh Dílis (1997) perc, ttbb
>Danú 009, CD (1997): Lloyd Byrne (perc), Anúna, Michael McGlynn (cond).

Gathering Mushrooms (1997) T, satb, orch
>Danú 009, CD (1997): Anúna, Ulster Orchestra, Michael McGlynn (T + cond).

Midnight (1997) S, satb, orch
>Danú 009, CD (1997): Méav Ní Mhaolchatha (S), Anúna, Ulster Orchestra, Michael McGlynn (cond).

The Coming of Winter (1997) satb, orch
>Danú 009, CD (1997): Anúna, Ulster Orchestra, Michael McGlynn (cond).

The Great Wood (1997) S, satb, orch
>Danú 009, CD (1997): Monica Donlon (S), Anúna, Ulster Orchestra, Michael McGlynn (cond).

Where All Roses Go (1997) T, satb, orch
  Danú 009, CD (1997): Anúna, Ulster Orchestra, Michael McGlynn (T + cond).

Cynara (1998) T, satb
  Danú 012, CD (2000): Anúna, Michael McGlynn (T + cond).

Pie Jesu (1998) satb
  Danú 012, CD (2000): Anúna, Michael McGlynn (cond).

An Oíche (1999) satb
  Danú 012, CD (2000): Anúna, Michael McGlynn (cond).

Armarque cum Scuto (1999) S, perc, satb
  Danú 012, CD (2000): Lucy Champion (S), Paul Maher (perc), Anúna, Michael McGlynn (cond).

Fuígfidh Mise'n Baile Seo (1999) satb
  Danú 012, CD (2000): Anúna, Michael McGlynn (cond).

Ocean (1999) 2S, vn, hp, satb
  Danú 012, CD (2000): Monica Donlon (S), Kira Deegan (S), Michael d'Arcy (vn), Denise Kelly (hp), Anúna, Michael McGlynn (T + cond).

When the War is Over (1999) S, satb
  Danú 012, CD (2000): Monica Donlon (S), Anúna, Michael McGlynn (cond).

Victimae (2000) T, satb
  Danú 012, CD (2000): Anúna, Michael McGlynn (T + cond).

John McLachlan
(* Dublin 1964)

John McLachlan studied music at Trinity College Dublin (MusB 1988) and at various times composition with Kevin Volans, Robert Hanson, Hormoz Farhat and William York. Many of his works have been broadcast in Ireland and internationally. He is the director of the Association of Irish Composers.

Recorded Work:

Two Lyric Sketches (1987) str-qu
>>Association of Irish Composers AIC 001, Promotion-CD (1999):
Hibernia Trio with Kenneth Rice (vn).

Dermot Macmurrough
(* Dublin 1872, † Dublin 1943)

Dermot Macmurrough was one of the pseudonyms of Harold R. White. He began his career as a choir boy in Christ Church Cathedral from 1881 to 1887 and won several composition prizes at early Feis Ceoil competitions. In 1905 he founded the Clef Club, an exclusive choral association which is still extant. From the 1920s until his death he was the music critic of the *Irish Independent* and published concert reviews in many papers of his day. His largest works were the opera *Seán the Post* (1924) and the choral *Hymn to St. Patrick at Tara* (1930). He also wrote many songs, none of which surpassed the popularity of *Macushla* (1910) which is said to have made a rich man of Macmurrough/White.

Recorded Works:

Macushla (1910) v, pf
>>HMV CSD 1446, LP (1962): Charles Craig (T), anonymous orchestra, Michael Collins (cond).
Re-issued on Testament SBT 1152, CD (1998).

>>Pearl Gemm CD 9175, CD (1995, recorded 1931): Heddle Nash (T), Gerald Moore (pf).

>>Dutton Laboratories CDLX 7031, CD (1999, same recording as Pearl Gemm above).

>>Version for orch:
ASV CD AJA 5119, CD (1993, recorded 1911): John McCormack (T), Victor Orchestra.

>>Memoir Classics CDMOIR 418, CD (1993) *(same recording as ASV above)*.

>>Nimbus NI 7854, CD (1993) *(same recording as ASV above)*.

>>Romophone 82006-2, CD (1996) *(same recording as ASV above)*.

Claremont CDGSE 78-50-50, CD (1993, recorded 1933): Richard Crooks (T), anonymous orchestra.

Pearl Gemm CD 9093, CD (1995) (*same recording as Claremont above*).

Virgin Classics VC 7 90705-2, CD (1988): Robert White (T), Monte Carlo Philharmonic Orchestra, Robin Stapleton (cond).

HMV Classics 7243 5 73043 2 0, CD (1998, recorded 1948): Josef Locke (T), Eric Robinson and his Orchestra.

ASV AJA 5359, CD (2000) (*same recording as HMV above*).

Naxos Nostalgia 8.120504, CD (2000) (*same recording as ASV above*).

Arrangement for cornet and orchestra:
Crystal CD 450, CD (1996, recorded 1917): Herbert L. Clarke (cornet), anonymous orchestra.

Elizabeth Maconchy
(* Broxbourne, Herts. 1907, † Norwich 1994)

Although Maconchy was born in England and lived there almost all of her life she regarded herself as an Irish composer. She was from an old Irish family, grew up and went to school in Ireland. She then studied composition with Charles Wood and Ralph Vaughan Williams at the Royal College of Music, London (1923-9) and later with K.B. Jirák in Prague, where she became friendly with Zoltan Kodály. Some of her works were written in Ireland such as the ballet *Puck Fair* (1940) or her *String Quartet No. 5* (1948). Besides 13 string quartets she also wrote three one-act operas, a *Sinfonietta* (1976), two clarinet concertini (1945, 1984) and many other orchestral and chamber pieces. She wrote in an advanced central European style. She was for many years the chairwoman of the Society for the Promotion of New Music, London, and in 1989 she was made a Dame.

Recorded Works:

Have you seen but a bright Lily grow (1930) v, pf
        Hyperion CDA 66709, CD (1994): Anthony Rolfe-Johnson (T), Graham Johnson (pf).

Meditation for his Mistress (1930) v, pf
> Hyperion CDA 66709, CD (1994): Anthony Rolfe-Johnson (T),
> Graham Johnson (pf).

String Quartet No. 1 (1933) str-qu
> Unicorn-Kanchana DKP 9080, CD (1989): Hanson Quartet.

String Quartet No. 2 (1936) str-qu
> Unicorn-Kanchana DKP 9080, CD (1989): Hanson Quartet.

String Quartet No. 3 (1938) str-qu
> Unicorn-Kanchana DKP 9080, CD (1989): Hanson Quartet.

String Quartet No. 4 (1943) str-qu
> Unicorn-Kanchana DKP 9080, CD (1989): Hanson Quartet.

Clarinet Concertino No. 1 (1945)
> Hyperion CDA 66634, CD (1993): Thea King (cl), English Chamber
> Orchestra, Barry Wordsworth (cond).

String Quartet No. 5 (1948) str-qu
> Argo ZRG 5329 (stereo), RG 329 (mono), LP (1964): Allegri Quartet.

> Unicorn-Kanchana DKP 9081, CD (1990): Bingham Quartet.

String Quartet No. 6 (1950) str-qu
> Unicorn-Kanchana DKP 9081, CD (1990): Bingham Quartet.

Nocturne (1951) orch
> ATMA ACD 22199, CD (1999): Foundation Philharmonic Orchestra,
> David Snell (cond).

Overture 'Proud Thames' (1952) orch
> Lyrita SRCS 57, LP (1972): London Philharmonic Orchestra, Vernon
> Handley (cond).

Symphony for Double String Orchestra (1953) 2str-orch
> Lyrita SRCS 116, LP (1982): London Symphony Orchestra, Vernon
> Handley (cond).

String Quartet No. 7 (1955) str-qu
> Unicorn-Kanchana DKP 9081, CD (1990): Bingham Quartet.

Variations on a Theme from Vaughan Williams' 'Job' (1957) vc
    Harmonie 3003, CD (2000): Anthony Cooke.

Serenata Concertante (1962) vn, orch
    Lyrita SRCS 116, LP (1982): Manoug Parikian (vn), London Symphony
    Orchestra, Vernon Handley (cond).

Clarinet Quintet (1963)
    Hyperion CDA 66428, CD (1992): Thea King (cl), Britten Quartet.

String Quartet No. 8 (1967) str-qu
    Unicorn-Kanchana DKP 9081, CD (1990): Bingham Quartet.

String Quartet No. 9 (1968) str-qu
    Argo ZRG 5672, LP (1971): Allegri Quartet.

    Unicorn-Kanchana DKP 9082, CD (1990): Mistry Quartet.

Ariadne (1970) S, orch
    L'Oiseau Lyre SOL 331, LP (1972): Heather Harper (S), English
    Chamber Orchestra, Raymond Leppard (cond).

Three Bagatelles (1972) ob, hpd
    HMV HQS 1298, LP (1973): Evelyn Barbirolli (ob), Valda Aveling
    (hpd).

String Quartet No. 10 (1972) str-qu
    Unicorn-Kanchana DKP 9082, CD (1990): Mistry Quartet.

Siren's Song (1974) satb
    Continuum CCD 1055, CD (1993): Ionian Singers, Timothy Salter
    (cond).
    Re-issued on Usk USK 1216 CD, CD (1995).

String Quartet No. 11 (1976) str-qu
    Unicorn-Kanchana DKP 9082, CD (1990): Mistry Quartet.

Sun, Moon and Stars (1977) S, pf
    British Music Society BMS 420/1, 2CD (1998): Tracey Chadwell (S),
    Pamela Lidiard (pf).

    Metier MSV CD 92025, CD (2000): Alison Smart (S), Katherine
    Durran (pf).

String Quartet No. 12 (1979) str-qu
>Unicorn-Kanchana DKP 9082, CD (1990): Mistry Quartet.

Colloquy (1979) fl, pf
>Lorelt LNT 107, CD (1995): Ingrid Culliford (fl), Dominic Saunders (pf).

Fantasia (1980) cl, pf
>Metier MSV CD 92013, CD (1998): Kate Romano (cl), Alan Hicks (pf).

My Dark Heart (1981) S, fl, ob/C.A., hn, vn, va, vc
>Lorelt LNT 101, CD (1992): Jane Manning (S), Lontano, Odaline de la Martinez (cond).

String Quartet No. 13 (1984) str-qu
>Unicorn-Kanchana DKP 9082, CD (1990): Mistry Quartet.

Clarinet Concertino No. 2 (1984)
>Hyperion CDA 66634, CD (1993): Thea King (cl), English Chamber Orchestra, Barry Wordsworth (cond).

Five Sketches (198?) va
>Gamut GAMCD 537, CD (1994): Philip Dykes.

Three Songs (198?) S, pf
>British Music Society BMS 420/1, 2CD (1998): Tracey Chadwell (S), Pamela Lidiard (pf).

Philip Martin
(* Dublin 1947)

Philip Martin is equally known as pianist and composer. He studied composition from 1965 to 1968 at the Hendon College of Technology, London, with the Hindemith-pupil Franz Reizenstein and also the piano with Louis Kentner. For short periods he also studied with Lennox Berkeley, Elizabeth Maconchy, and Richard Rodney Bennett. He lives in Wiltshire, England since c. 1970. As a composer, Martin concentrates on the piano and wrote more than a hundred songs for his wife, the soprano Penelope Price Jones, but he has also written orchestral and chamber music. His music maintains a strong harmonic and melodic sense with an occasional Irish influence.

Recorded Works:

Rest Sweet Nymphs (1969) v, pf
> Altarus AIR-CD-9009, CD (1994): Penelope Price-Jones (S), Philip
> Martin (pf).

Winter (1969) v, pf
> Altarus AIR-CD-9009, CD (1994): Penelope Price-Jones (S), Philip
> Martin (pf).

The Wayfarer (1971) v, pf
> Altarus AIR-CD-9009, CD (1994): Penelope Price-Jones (S), Philip
> Martin (pf).

This is just to say ... (1972) v, pf
> Altarus AIR-CD-9009, CD (1994): Penelope Price-Jones (S), Philip
> Martin (pf).

The Bereaved Swan (1973) v, pf
> Altarus AIR-CD-9009, CD (1994): Penelope Price-Jones (S), Philip
> Martin (pf).

The Fiddler of Dooney (1973) v, pf
> Altarus AIR-CD-9009, CD (1994): Penelope Price-Jones (S), Philip
> Martin (pf).

> Gregory Wiest GW 95-2.2, CD (1995): Gregory Wiest (T), Oresta
> Cybriwsky (pf).

The Warden (1973) v, pf
> Altarus AIR-CD-9009, CD (1994): Penelope Price-Jones (S), Philip
> Martin (pf).

The Lake Isle if Innisfree (1974) v, pf
> Altarus AIR-CD-9009, CD (1994): Penelope Price-Jones (S), Philip
> Martin (pf).

> Gregory Wiest GW 95-2.2, CD (1995): Gregory Wiest (T), Oresta
> Cybriwsky (pf).

The Stolen Child (1975) v, pf
> Altarus AIR-CD-9009, CD (1994): Penelope Price-Jones (S), Philip
> Martin (pf).

Gregory Wiest GW 95-2.2, CD (1995): Gregory Wiest (T), Oresta Cybriwsky (pf).

Be Still as you are Beautiful (1977) v, pf
Altarus AIR-CD-9009, CD (1994): Penelope Price-Jones (S), Philip Martin (pf).

Birthright (1978) v, pf
Altarus AIR-CD-9009, CD (1994): Penelope Price-Jones (S), Philip Martin (pf).

Four Convictions (1980) v, pf
Altarus AIR-CD-9009, CD (1994): Penelope Price-Jones (S), Philip Martin (pf).

On Wings of Ebony (1980) v, pf
Altarus AIR-CD-9009, CD (1994): Penelope Price-Jones (S), Philip Martin (pf).

Songs for the Four Parts of the Night (1981) S, vn
Altarus AIR-CD-9011, CD (1995): Penelope Price-Jones (S), Ruxandra Colan (vn).

Under the Harvest Moon (1982) v, pf
Altarus AIR-CD-9009, CD (1994): Penelope Price-Jones (S), Philip Martin (pf).

Love Song (1988) v, pf
Altarus AIR-CD-9009, CD (1994): Penelope Price-Jones (S), Philip Martin (pf).

The Rainbow Comes and Goes (1988) pf
Altarus AIR-CD-9011, CD (1995): Philip Martin.

A Thomas Moore Medley (1989) v, pf
Altarus AIR-CD-9009, CD (1994): Penelope Price-Jones (S), Philip Martin (pf).

He wishes for the Cloths of Heaven (1989) v, pf
Altarus AIR-CD-9009, CD (1994): Penelope Price-Jones (S), Philip Martin (pf).

Gregory Wiest GW 95-2.2, CD (1995): Gregory Wiest (T), Oresta Cybriwsky (pf).

I am of Ireland (1989) v, pf
>Altarus AIR-CD-9009, CD (1994): Penelope Price-Jones (S), Philip Martin (pf).

>Gregory Wiest GW 95-2.2, CD (1995): Gregory Wiest (T), Oresta Cybriwsky (pf).

Beato Angelico (1990) orch
>Marco Polo 8.223834, CD (1998): National Symphony Orchestra of Ireland, Kasper de Roo (cond).

Piano Concerto No. 2: A Day in the City (1991) pf, orch
>Marco Polo 8.223834, CD (1998): Philip Martin (pf), National Symphony Orchestra of Ireland, Kasper de Roo (cond).

Echoes under the Stones (1991) v, pf
>Altarus AIR-CD-9009, CD (1994): Penelope Price-Jones (S), Philip Martin (pf).

Harp Concerto (1993) hp, orch
>Marco Polo 8.223834, CD (1998): Andreja Malir (hp), National Symphony Orchestra of Ireland, Kasper de Roo (cond).

Light Music (1993)
>Altarus AIR-CD-9011, CD (1995): Penelope Price-Jones (S), Philip Martin (pf).

Serendipity (1993) vn, vc, pf
>Altarus AIR-CD-9011, CD (1995): Crawford Piano Trio.

>Excerpt (from the above recording):
>Contemporary Music Centre CMC CD01, Promotion-CD (1995).

Two Elegies (1994) vn, pf
>Altarus AIR-CD-9011, CD (1995): Ruxandra Colan (vn), Philip Martin (pf).

Frederick May
(* Dublin 1911, † Dublin 1985)

Frederick May was one of the most promising Irish composers of the first half of the twentieth century, a reputation he established with the *String Quartet in c minor* (1936) and the *Songs from Prison* (1941) for tenor and orchestra. Increasing tinnitus and deafness restricted his output severely and he stopped composing after 1955. Yet, together with Aloys Fleischmann and Brian Boydell he deservedly enjoys a standing as one of Ireland's grandfathers of contemporary music, which is not quite reflected in the quantity of his discography.

Recorded Works:

String Quartet in c (1936) str-qu
        Claddagh CSM 2, LP/MC (1974): Aeolian Quartet.

        Marco Polo 8.223888, CD (1996): Vanbrugh Quartet.

Suite of Irish Airs (1942) str-orch
        Decca (USA) DL 9843, LP (1958): Radio Éireann Symphony Orchestra, Milan Horvat (cond).

E.J. Moeran
(* Heston, Middlesex 1894, † Kenmare Co. Kerry 1950)

Ernest John Moeran's father was Irish and he spent as much time in Ireland as in England after he made Kenmare his second home around 1934. In 1913 he began to study with C.V. Stanford, but World War I interrupted. From about 1919 to 1923 he had occasional lessons on a friendly basis with John Ireland. Moeran wrote many pieces with a strong Irish flavor beginning with the orchestral *In the Mountain Country* (1921), culminating in his *Symphony in g minor* (1937) and the concertos for violin (1942) and cello (1945). His English side is reflected in many works catching Elizabethan renaissance aesthetics, such as his *Whythorne's Shadow* (1931) and the *Serenade in G* (1948).

Recorded Works:

Three Pieces for Piano (1919) pf
        Lyrita RCS 3, LP (1960): Iris Loveridge.

        J. Martin Stafford JMSCD2, CD (1994): Eric Parkin.

Black Box Music BBM 1010, CD (2001): Una Hunt.

Theme and Variations (1920) pf
Lyrita RCS 3, LP (1960): Iris Loveridge.

J. Martin Stafford JMSCD2, CD (1994): Eric Parkin.

Black Box Music BBM 1010, CD (2001): Una Hunt.

Piano Trio in D (1920) vn, vc, pf
British Music Society BMS 418 CD, CD (1997): Cantamen.

ASV DCA 1045, CD (1998): Joachim Trio.

Spring Goeth All in White (1920) v, pf
HMV CSD 3587 (stereo), CLP 3587 (mono), LP (1966): Frederick
Harvey (Bar), Gerald Moore (pf).

Ludlow Town (1920) v, pf
Excerpts:
*When Smoke Stood Up from Ludlow; Farewell to Barn and Stack and
Tree; Say, Lad, Have You Things to Do?*
Saga 5260, LP (1966): John Shirley-Quirk (Bar), Martin Isepp (pf).

In the Mountain Country (1921) orch
Chandos CHAN 8639, CD (1989): Ulster Orchestra, Vernon Handley
(cond).
Re-issued on Chandos CHAN 6525, CD (1991).

String Quartet in A (1921) str-qu
Chandos CHAN 8465 (= CD), ABRD 1168 (= LP), ABTD 1168
(= MC) (1986): Melbourne Quartet.

Naxos 8.554079, CD (1997): Maggini Quartet.

ASV DCA 1045, CD (1998): Vanbrugh Quartet.

On a May Morning (1921) pf
Lyrita RCS 3, LP (1960): Iris Loveridge.

J. Martin Stafford JMSCD2, CD (1994): Eric Parkin.

Black Box Music BBM 1010, CD (2001): Una Hunt.

Toccata (1921) pf
Lyrita SRCS 42, LP (1970): Eric Parkin.

J. Martin Stafford JMSCD2, CD (1994): Eric Parkin.

Black Box Music BBM 1010, CD (2001): Una Hunt.

Stalham River (1921) pf
Lyrita SRCS 42, LP (1970): Eric Parkin.

J. Martin Stafford JMSCD2, CD (1994): Eric Parkin.

Black Box Music BBM 1010, CD (2001): Una Hunt.

Violin Sonata in E (1922) vn, pf
Chandos CHAN 8465 (= CD), ABRD 1168 (= LP), ABTD 1168 (= MC) (1986): Donald Scotts (vn), John Talbot (pf).

Symposium SYMCD 1075, CD (1990, recorded 1937): May Harrison (vn), Charles Lynch (pf).

Rhapsody No. 1 (1922) orch
Chandos CHAN 8639 (= CD), ABRD 1327 (= LP), ABTD 1327 (= MC) (1989): Ulster Orchestra, Vernon Handley (cond).

Three Fancies (1922) pf
Lyrita RCS 3, LP (1960): Iris Loveridge.

Chandos DBRD 2006 (= 2LP), DBTD (= MC) (1983): Eric Parkin.

J. Martin Stafford JMSCD2, CD (1994): Eric Parkin.

Black Box Music BBM 1010, CD (2001): Una Hunt.

Gather ye Rosebuds (1922) satb
British Music Society BMS 417 CD, CD (1996): City Chamber Choir of London, Stephen Jones (cond).

Weep you no more, sad fountains (1922) satb
British Music Society BMS 417 CD, CD (1996): City Chamber Choir of London, Stephen Jones (cond).

Two Legends (A Folk Story, Rune) (1923) pf
Lyrita SRCS 42, LP (1970): Eric Parkin.

J. Martin Stafford JMSCD2, CD (1994): Eric Parkin.

Black Box Music BBM 1010, CD (2001): Una Hunt.

Six Folksongs from Norfolk (1923), v, pf
Excerpts:
The Pressgang; The Shooting of his Dear
Chandos CHAN 8946, CD (1992): Benjamin Luxon (Bar), David Willison (pf).

Robin Hood borne on his Bier (1923) satb
British Music Society BMS 417 CD, CD (1996): City Chamber Choir of London, Stephen Jones (cond).

Two Songs (The Bean Flower, Impromptu in March) (1923) v, pf
Hyperion A 66103, LP (1984): Anne Dawson (S), Roderick Barrand (pf).

Rhapsody No. 2 (1924) orch
Lyrita SRCS 43, LP (1970): London Philharmonic Orchestra, Adrian Boult (cond).
Re-issued on Musical Heritage Society MHS 1411, LP (c. 1972).

Chandos CHAN 8639 (= CD), ABRD 1327 (= LP), ABTD 1327 (= MC) (1989): Ulster Orchestra, Vernon Handley (cond).

Summer Valley (1925) pf
Lyrita RCS 3, LP (1960): Iris Loveridge.

Kingdom/Conifer KCLCD 2017 (= CD), CKCL 2017 (= MC) (1990): Christopher Headington.

J. Martin Stafford JMSCD2, CD (1994): Eric Parkin.

Black Box Music BBM 1010, CD (2001): Una Hunt.

Bank Holiday (1925) pf
Lyrita SRCS 42, LP (1970): Eric Parkin.

EMI SDD 444, LP (1974): John McCabe.

J. Martin Stafford JMSCD2, CD (1994): Eric Parkin.

Black Box Music BBM 1010, CD (2001): Una Hunt.

Far in a Western Brookland (1925) v, pf
> Hyperion CDA 66471-2, 2CD (1995): Anthony Rolfe Johnson (T), G. Johnson (pf).

In Youth is Pleasure (1925) v, pf
> Eclipse ECS 545, LP (1970, recorded 1956): Peter Pears (T), Benjamin Britten (pf).

The Merry Month of May (1925) v, pf
> Argo ZRG 5439 (stereo) RG 439 (mono), LP (1965): Peter Pears (T), Benjamin Britten (pf).

> Belart 461 550-2, CD (1997, recorded 1964): Peter Pears (T), Viola Tunnard (pf).

Irish Love Song (1926) pf
> Lyrita RCS 3, LP (1960): Iris Loveridge.

> J. Martin Stafford JMSCD2, CD (1994): Eric Parkin.

The White Mountain (1927) pf
> Lyrita SRCS 42, LP (1970): Eric Parkin.

> J. Martin Stafford JMSCD2, CD (1994): Eric Parkin.

> Black Box Music BBM 1010, CD (2001): Una Hunt.

Seven Poems of James Joyce (1929) v, pf
> Excerpt:
> *Bright Cap*
> Forlane 16784, CD (1998): Ann Murray (Mez), Graham Johnson (pf).

Songs of Springtime (1930) satb
> RCB 7, LP (1971): Proteus Chorus.

> Koch Schwann 3-1266-2, CD (1992): East London Chorus, Michael Kibblewhite (cond).

> Chandos CHAN 9182, CD (1993): Finzi Singers, Paul Spicer (cond).

> Vocalis VOC 05952, CD (1994): Bristol Bach Choir, Glyn Jenkins (cond).

British Music Society BMS 417 CD, CD (1996): City Chamber Choir of London, Stephen Jones (cond).

Excerpts:
Spring the Sweet Spring, To Daffodils
EMI CDC 7 49765 2, CD (1988): King's Singers.

Magnificat and Nunc Dimittis in D (1930) satb, org
Priory PRCD 554 (= CD), PRC 554 (= MC) (1996): St. Edmundsbury Cathedral Choir, Scott Farrell (org), Mervyn Cousins (cond).

Te Deum and Jubilate in E (1930) satb, org
Priory PRCD 470 (= CD), PRC 470 (= MC) (1994): Norwich Cathedral Choir, Neil Taylor (org), Michael Nicholas (cond).

Two Pieces (Lonely Waters, Whythorne's Shadow) (1931) ch-orch
HMV CSD 3705, LP (1972): English Sinfonia, Neville Dilkes (cond).
Re-issued on HMV ESD 7101 (= LP), TC-ESD 7101 (= MC), HMV Greensleeve ED 290187-1 (= LP), -4 (= MC) (1984).

EMI CDC7 47945-2 (= CD), EL 270592-1 (= LP), -4 (= MC) (1987): English Chamber Orchestra, Jeffrey Tate (cond).
Re-issued on EMI CDZ7 64200-2, CD (1995).

Chandos CHAN 8807, CD (1990): Ulster Orchestra, Vernon Handley (cond).
Re-issued on Chandos Enchant 7078, CD (1998).

String Trio (1931) vn, va, vc
Pearl SHE 563, LP (198?): Members of the Hanson String Quartet.

Dutton Laboratories CDAX 8014, CD (1995, recorded in 1941): Jean Pougnet (vn), Frederick Riddle (va), Anthony Pini (vc).

Naxos 8.554079, CD (1997): Maggini Quartet.

Six Suffolk Folk Songs (1931) v, pf
Excerpt:
The Isle of Cloy
Chandos CHAN 8946, CD (1992): Benjamin Luxon (Bar), David Willison (pf).

The Sweet O' the Year (1931) v, pf
> ASV Living Era CD AJA 5227, CD (1999, rec. 1945): Heddle Nash
> (T), Gerald Moore (pf).

> Dutton Laboratories CDLX 7031, CD (1999, same recording as above).

Two Pieces (Prelude, Berceuse) (1933) pf
> Lyrita SRCS 42, LP (1970): Eric Parkin.

> J. Martin Stafford JMSCD2, CD (1994): Eric Parkin.

> Black Box Music BBM 1010, CD (2001): Una Hunt.

Nocturne (1934) Bar, satb, orch
> Chandos CHAN 8808, CD (1990): Hugh Mackey (Bar), The
> Renaissance Singers, Ulster Orchestra, Vernon Handley (cond).

Four English Lyrics (1934) v, pf
> Hyperion A 66103, LP (1984): Anne Dawson (S), Roderick Barrand
> (pf).

Symphony in g (1937) orch
> HMV ASD 2913, LP (1973): English Sinfonia, Neville Dilkes (cond).
> *Re-issued on* HMV Greensleeve ED 290187-1 (= LP), -4 (= MC)
> (1984).

> Lyrita SRCS 70, LP (1975): New Philharmonia Orchestra, Adrian Boult
> (cond).

> HMV EM 290462-3 (= 2LP), -5 (= MC) (1985, recorded 1942): Hallé
> Orchestra, Leslie Heward (cond).

> Chandos CHAN 8577 (= CD), ABRD 1272 (= LP), ABTD 1272 (=
> MC) (1988): Ulster Orchestra, Vernon Handley (cond).
> *Re-issued on* Chandos Enchant 7106, CD (1998).

> Dutton Laboratories CDAX 8001, CD (1993) *(same recording as HMV
> above)*.

Diaphenia (1937) v, pf
> ASV Living Era CD AJA 5227, CD (1999, rec. 1937): Heddle Nash
> (T), Gerald Moore (pf).

> Dutton Laboratories CDLX 7031, CD (1999, same recording as above).

Phyllida and Corydon (1939) satb
  Chandos CHAN 9182, CD (1993): Finzi Singers, Paul Spicer (cond).

Violin Concerto (1942) vn, orch
  Lyrita SRCS 105, LP (1979): John Georgiadis (vn), London Symphony
  Orchestra, Vernon Handley (cond).

  Chandos CHAN 8807 (= CD), ABTD 1435 (= MC) (1990): Lydia
  Mordkovitch (vn), Ulster Orchestra, Vernon Handley (cond).
  Re-issued on Chandos Enchant 7078, CD (1998).

  Symposium 1201, CD (1999, recorded 1946): Albert Sammons (vn),
  BBC Symphony Orchestra, Sir Adrian Boult (cond).

Rhapsody in F sharp (1943) pf, orch
  Lyrita SRCS 91, LP (1979): John McCabe (pf), New Philharmonia
  Orchestra, Nicholas Braithwaite (cond).

  Chandos CHAN 8639 (= CD), ABRD 1327 (= LP), ABTD 1327 (=
  MC) (1989): Margaret Fingerhut (pf), Ulster Orchestra, Vernon
  Handley (cond).
  Re-issued on Chandos Enchant 7106, CD (1998).

Prelude (1943), vc, pf
  Lyrita SRCS 42, LP (1970): Peers Coetmore (vc), Eric Parkin (pf).

Overture for a Masque (1944) orch
  Lyrita SRCS 43, LP (1970): London Philharmonic Orchestra, Adrian
  Boult (cond).
  Re-issued on Musical Heritage Society MHS 1411, LP (c. 1972).

  Chandos CHAN 8577 (= CD), ABRD 1272 (= LP), ABTD 1272 (=
  MC) (1988): Ulster Orchestra, Vernon Handley (cond).

Sinfonietta (1944) orch
  Lyrita SRCS 37, LP (1968): London Philharmonic Orchestra, Adrian
  Boult (cond).

  Chandos CHAN 8456 (= CD), ABRD 1167 (= LP), ABTD 1167 (=
  MC) (1986): Raphael Wallfisch (vc), Bournemouth Sinfonietta, Norman
  del Mar (cond).
  Re-issued on Chandos CHAN 7078, CD (1998).

EMI CDC7 49912-2 (= CD), EL 749912-4 (= MC) (1989): Northern Sinfonia, Richard Hickox (cond).
Re-issued on EMI CDM7 64721-2. CD (1994).

BBC Radio Classics 15656 9163-2, CD (1995, recorded 1963): Philharmonia Orchestra, Adrian Boult (cond).

The Jolly Carter (1944) satb
British Music Society BMS 417 CD, CD (1996): City Chamber Choir of London, Stephen Jones (cond).

Cello Concerto (1945) vc, orch
Lyrita SRCS 43, LP (1970): Peers Coetmore (vc), London Philharmonic Orchestra, Adrian Boult (cond).
Re-issued on Musical Heritage Society MHS 1411, LP (c. 1972).

Chandos CHAN 8456 (= CD), ABRD 1167 (= LP), ABTD 1167 (= MC) (1986): Raphael Wallfisch (vc), Bournemouth Sinfonietta, Norman del Mar (cond).
Re-issued on Chandos Enchant 7078, CD (1998).

Fantasy Quartet (1946) ob, vn, va, vc
Altarus AIR-2-9005, LP (1984): John Anderson (ob), Thamyse String Trio.

Chandos ABRD 1114 (= CD), ABTD 1114 (= MC) (1985): Sarah Francis (ob), English String Quartet.
Re-issued on Chandos CHAN 8392, CD (1987).

ASV DCA 1045, CD (1998): Nicholas Daniel (ob), Vanbrugh Quartet.

Symposium 1201, CD (1999, recorded 1947): Leon Goossens (ob), Carter String Trio.

Cello Sonata (1947) vc, pf
Lyrita SRCS 42, LP (1970): Peers Coetmore (vc), Eric Parkin (pf).

Marco Polo 8.223718, CD (1994): Raphael Wallfisch (vc), John York (pf).

Serenade in G (1948) orch
Concert Artist SLPA 2002 (= stereo), LPA 2002 (= mono), LP (1966): Guildford Philharmonic Orchestra, Vernon Handley (cond).
Re-issued on RCF 003, LP (1970).

EMI CDC7 49912-2 (= CD), EL 749912-4 (= MC) (1989): Northern
Sinfonia, Richard Hickox (cond).
Re-issued on CDM7 64721-2, CD (1994).

Chandos CHAN 8808 (= CD), ABTD 1436 (= MC) (1990): Ulster
Orchestra, Vernon Handley (cond).

Symposium 1201, CD (1999, recorded 1948): London Symphony
Orchestra, Basil Cameron (cond).

The Sailor and Young Nancy (1948-9) satb
Collegium COLCD 104 (= CD), COLC 104 (= LP) (1987): Cambridge
Singers, John Rutter (cond).

Somm Recordings SOMMCD 207, CD (1997): Cheltenham Bach Coir,
Brian Kay (cond).

O fair enough are Sky and Plain (late 1940s) v, pf
Hyperion CDA 66471-2, 2CD (1995): Anthony Rolfe Johnson (T),
Graham Johnson (pf).

String Quartet No. 2 in E flat (1946-9?) str-qu
Naxos 8.554079, CD (1997): Maggini Quartet.

ASV DCA 1045, CD (1998): Vanbrugh Quartet.

Songs from County Kerry (1950) v, pf
Excerpts:
*My Love Passed Me By; The Roving Dingle Boy; The Tinker's
Daughter; Kitty I am in Love with You*
Forlane 16784, CD (1998): Ann Murray (Mez), Graham Johnson (pf).

Irish Elegy (arr. 1955 by Desmond Ratcliffe from 2nd movt. of *Serenade*, 1948)
satb
British Music Society BMS 417 CD, CD (1996): City Chamber Choir
of London, Stephen Jones (cond).

Garret Wesley, 1st Earl of Mornington
(* Dublin 1735, † Kensington 1781)

Lord Mornington, as he was commonly known, was a keen violinist, keyboard
player and composer. He succeeded his father as Baron Mornington in 1758 and

in 1760 was created Viscount Wellesley and Earl of Mornington. In 1758 he founded the first Musical Academy in Ireland. From 1764 to 1774 he was the first professor of music at Trinity College, Dublin. Mornington was famous as a composer of part-songs, especially glees and catches, gaining several Irish and English composition prizes. In 1846 Sir Henry Bishop edited a complete collection of his vocal music – his religious music was then believed to be lost. Today his only recorded music consists of two psalm settings.

Recorded Works:

Bow Down Thine Ear and Hear Me (17??) satb, org
  Priory PRCD 409 (= CD), PRC 409 (= MC) (1992): Norwich Cathedral Choir, Neil Taylor (org), Michael Nicholas (cond).

Princes have Persecuted Me Without a Cause (17??) satb, org
  Hyperion CDP 11011, CD (2000): St. Paul's Cathedral Choir, Huw Williams (org), John Scott (cond).

Gráinne Mulvey
(* Dun Laoghaire Co. Dublin 1966)

Gráinne Mulvey studied music with Eric Sweeney at the Waterford Institute of Technology, with Hormoz Farhat at Trinity College Dublin and with Agustín Fernández at Queen's University Belfast. She won the first Elizabeth Maconchy Fellowship for postgraduate composition studies at York University where she completed her DPhil in 1999. In 1998 she was awarded the Macauley Fellowship. Her largest works are a *Symphony No. 1* (1989) and the orchestral *Angst* (1993). Her highly original music has been played and broadcast internationally.

Recorded Works:

Rational Option Insanity (1993) vn, ob, cl, hn, pf
  Black Box Music BBM 1015, CD (1999): Alan Smale (vn), Ruby Ashley (ob), Paul Roe (cl), Lesley Bishop (hn), Jane O'Leary (pf), Proinnsías Ó Duinn (cond).

Sextet Uno (1997) vn, fl, cl, vc, perc, pf
  Black Box Music BBM 1015, CD (1999): Alan Smale (vn), Madeleine Staunton (fl), Paul Roe (cl), David James (vc), Richard O'Donnell (perc), Jane O'Leary (pf), Proinnsías Ó Duinn (cond).

Gerard Murphy
(* Limerick 1947)

Gerard Murphy studied at University College Dublin and is a school teacher in Dublin since 1973. Initially he composed mainly for school purposes; among those works are five school operas. The interest of Austrian/American recording company Vienna Modern Masters in his work recently brought him surprising fame and since 1997 it has been followed by more recordings of his recent orchestral music.

Recorded Works:

Dialects (1994) U.P., orch
> Vienna Modern Masters VMM 3040, CD (1997): Moravian
> Philharmonic Orchestra, Jiri Mikula (cond).

Good Friday: Belfast 10-4-98 (1998) orch
> Vienna Modern Masters VMM 3049, CD (1999): Moravian
> Philharmonic Orchestra, Jiri Mikula (cond).

Piano Concerto No. 1 (2000) pf, orch
> Vienna Modern Masters VMM 3051, CD (2001): Finghin Collins (pf),
> Moravian Philharmonic Orchestra, Jiri Mikula (cond).

Alicia A. Needham
(* Ireland 1870s?, † London 1945)

Not much is known about Alicia Adelaide Needham but that she studied at both the Royal Academy of Music and the Royal College of Music and was one of many female song and ballad composers around the turn of the 19th to the 20th century. The British Library in London holds more than 200 publications of hers, some containing up to twelve pieces, mainly published between 1894 and 1917. Many of her songs had an Irish traditional flavor without being arrangements of traditional repertoire.

Recorded Work:

Husheen (1897), v, pf
> Pearl GEM 0086, CD (2000, recorded 1930): Clara Butt (Mez),
> anonymous pianist.

Havelock Nelson
(* Cork 1917, † Belfast 1996)

Nelson was more known as an organiser and music activist, but also composed a large amount of light and entertaining music. He studied with John F. Larchet at the Royal Irish Academy of Music (1937-43) and took part in summer courses for piano accompaniment with Gerald Moore in 1938 and 1939. In 1943 he took his MusB at Trinity College, Dublin. From 1947 to 1977 Nelson was the official accompanist with BBC Northern Ireland in Belfast and conducted the Studio Opera Group and the Studio Symphony Orchestra. As an adjudicator to international music competitions he travelled as far as Canada, Hong Kong and Jamaica. In 1977 he founded the Trinidad and Tobago Opera Company.

Recorded Works:

The Lark in the Clear Air (arr. 1954) v, pf
> EMI CLP 1906, LP (1965): Veronica Dunne (S), Havelock Nelson (pf).

The Little Pets of Mochua (1961) v or unison chorus, pf
> Marco Polo 8.225098, CD (1998): Bernadette Greevy (Mez), Hugh Tinney (pf).

The Last Rose of Summer (arr. 1964?) vn, pf
> Continuum CCD 1051, CD (1992): Fionnuala Hunt (vn), Una Hunt (pf).

Dirty Work (1985) v, pf
> CRD 3473 (= CD), CRDC 4173 (= MC) (1992): Sarah Walker (Mez), Roger Vignoles (pf).
>
> Marco Polo 8.225098, CD (1998): Bernadette Greevy (Mez), Hugh Tinney (pf).

Vincent O'Brien
(* Dublin 1870, † Dublin 1948)

Vincent O'Brien remains best known as the first singing teacher of Irish celebrities John McCormack and Margaret Burke Sheridan; in fact, James Joyce was his pupil, too. In Irish musical history, however, he is better represented as the long-time organist of the catholic St. Mary's Pro-Cathedral in Dublin (1902-1946) and conductor of the cathedral choir, one of the outstanding choirs in

Ireland at the time. As McCormack's first accompanist, he also travelled with the singer on his first world tour and appeared on McCormack's early gramophone recordings from 1914. O'Brien was also the first music director of Radio Éireann (1926-1941) and conducted the first public concerts of the station's orchestra in the 1930s. He was less important as composer; he wrote the opera *Hester* (1893), some organ and choral music and a number of songs.

Recorded Works:

The Fairy Tree (1930) v, pf
> Argo ZRG 5459 (stereo), RG 459 (mono), LP (1966): Bernadette Greevy (Mez), Jeannie Reddin (pf).

> Hyperion CDA 66818, CD (1995): Robert White (T), Stephen Hough (pf).

> ASV CD AJA 5224, CD (1997, recorded 1930): John McCormack (T), Edwin Schneider (pf).

> Marco Polo 8.225098, CD (1998): Bernadette Greevy (Mez), Hugh Tinney (pf).

Baby Aroon (193?) T, pf
> Symposium 1166, CD (1998, recorded 1935): John McCormack (T), Edwin Schneider (pf).

Éamonn Ó Gallchobháir
(* Dundalk Co. Louth 1906, † Alicante, Spain 1982)

Ó Gallchobháir (anglicised O'Gallagher) studied at the Royal Irish Academy of Music (1927-1935) and was a prolific composer of easy listening songs, piano and chamber music with a very strong Irish traditional influence. He was the most outspoken opponent of modernism in Irish music, publishing articles in the 1930s arguing for an insular atavistic approach to Irish music. He also wrote a number of Gaelic operettas between 1944 and 1962 as well as some ballets on folklore themes, the largest being the 2.5 hour production *Catháir Linn* (1942). He held short-time positions as conductor of the Radio Éireann Light Orchestra (1948) and as music director of the Abbey Theatre (1962).

Recorded Works:

An Sean Duine (1930)
    Gael-Linn GL 18, LP/MC (197?): *(performers?)*.

Rosc Catha na Mumhan (arr. 1936) satb
    Gael-Linn CEF 004, LP (c. 1960): Cór Cois Laoi, Pilib Ó Laoghaire
    (cond).

Óró mo Churaichín (1952)
    Gael-Linn GL 18, LP/MC (197?): *(performers?)*.

Undated arrangements (in alphabetical order):

Ard-Tighe Cuain (arr.) satb)
    Harmonia Mundi HMS 30691, LP (1965): RTÉ Singers, Waldemar
    Rosen (cond).

Báidín Fhéilimidh (arr.)
    Decca 46031, LP (195?): *(performers?)*.

Cor na Siog (arr.) satb
    Harmonia Mundi HMS 30691, LP (1965): RTÉ Singers, Waldemar
    Rosen (cond).

Crúibíní Muice (19??)
    Harmonia Mundi HMS 30691, LP (1965): RTÉ Singers, Waldemar
    Rosen (cond).

Meioreiseac (19??) Ir hp
    Arion ARN 60357, LP (1977), CD (1996): Régis Chenut.

The King of the Fairies (arr) vn, pf
    Cala Artists CACD 0503, CD (1996): Geraldine O'Grady (vn),
    Margaret O'Sullivan (pf).

Jane O'Leary
(* Hartford, Connecticut 1946)

Jane O'Leary (née Strong) is living in Ireland since 1972. She studied at Vassar
College (BA 1968) and at Princeton (MA 1971), where her composition teacher

was Milton Babbitt. She received a doctorate in 1978. She taught at Dublin's College of Music (1974-7) and at University College Galway (1978-83). In 1976 she founded the still active chamber ensemble Concorde, which gave numerous (first) performances of new Irish music. She also filled many positions in Irish musical life as head or member of several organisations. She received the Marten Toonder Award in 1994. Until 1983 O'Leary's music was fairly strictly serial. Since then she allowed more intuitive elements and successfully developed an individual style based on comprehensible harmonies and flowing melodic lines.

Recorded Works:

Cartoline dalla Sicilia (Postcards from Sicily) (1987) pf
> Nardiello CN 115, CD (2000): Catherine Nardiello.

Silenzio della Terra (1993) fl, mar, t-t
> Contemporary Music Centre CMC CD01, promotion-CD (1995): Concorde.

> Capstone Records CPS-8640, CD (1997): Concorde.

Duo for Violin and Cello (1994)
> Capstone Records CPS-8640, CD (1997): Alan Smale (vn), David James (vc).

Four Pieces (1994) gui
> Black Box Music BBM 1002, CD (1998): John Feeley.

Within/Without (2000) cl
> Containers / Galway Arts Festival 2000, CD (2000): Paul Roe.

Seán Ó Riada
(* Cork 1931, † London 1971)

Ó Riada remains the most enigmatic composer in twentieth-century Irish music. Born John Reidy, he studied at University College Cork with Aloys Fleischmann (BMus 1952), was Assistant Music Director at Radio Éireann (1952-4) and came in touch with serialism while spending some time in Paris in 1954. 1955-62 he was music director of the Abbey Theatre, succeeding Frederick May and pre-ceeding Éamonn Ó Gallchobháir. He then became lecturer in Irish music at University College Cork (1963-71).

Ó Riada became a legendary figure through his orchestral scores for Irish documentary movies (like *Mise Éire*, 1959) and his founding of the first band playing Irish traditional music in a group, the Ceóltoirí Chualann (from 1961). Although he continued writing avant-garde compositions (the most notable being *Hercules Dux Ferrariae*, 1957, and the *Theban Cycle*, 1963) for a while, his popularity largely rests on the success of the band. He died early, not fulfilling the hopes of many in Ireland for fusing art music and traditional music.

Recorded Works:

Three Poems by Thomas Kinsella (1954) Mez, pf
> Claddagh Records CSM 1 (= LP), 4 CSM 1 (= MC) (1969): Bernadette Greevy (Mez), Veronica McSwiney (pf).

Four Hölderlin Songs (1956) Mez, pf
> Claddagh Records CSM 1 (= LP), 4 CSM 1 (= MC) (1969): Bernadette Greevy (Mez), Veronica McSwiney (pf).

The Banks of Sullane (1956) orch
> Marco Polo 8.223804, CD (1996): RTÉ Sinfonietta, Proinnséas Ó Duinn (cond).

Nomos No. 1 – Hercules Dux Ferrariae (1957) str-orch
> Claddagh Records CSM 1 (= LP), 4 CSM 1 (= MC) (1969): London Symphony Orchestra, Carlo Franci (cond).

Mise Éire (1959) orch
> Gael-Linn CEF 002, EP (1960): Radio Éireann Symphony Orchestra, Seán Ó Riada (cond).
> *Re-issued on* Gael-Linn CEF 080 (= LP), CEFC 080 (= MC) (1979).

> Gael-Linn CEFCD 134 (= CD), CEF 134 (= LP), CEFCTV 134 (= MC) (1987): RTÉ Concert Orchestra, Elmer Bernstein (cond).

Saoirse? (1959) orch
> Gael-Linn GL 1, EP (1960): Radio Éireann Symphony Orchestra, Seán Ó Riada (cond).
> *Re-issued on* Gael-Linn CEF 080 (= LP), CEFC 080 (= MC) (1979).

> Gael-Linn CEFCD 134 (= CD), CEF 134 (= LP), CEFCTV 134 (= MC) (1987): RTÉ Concert Orchestra, Elmer Bernstein (cond).

The Playboy of the Western World (1962) fl, U.P., t-w, 2acc, 2vn, perc
    Claddagh Records CEF 012, LP (1962): Ceoltóirí Chualann, Seán
    Ó Riada (cond).

Hill Field (1965) Mez, pf
    Claddagh Records CSM 1 (= LP), 4 CSM 1 (= MC) (1969): Bernadette
    Greevy (Mez), Veronica McSwiney (pf).

An Tine Bheo (1966) orch
    Gael-Linn GL 12, EP (1966): Radio Telefís Éireann Symphony
    Orchestra, Seán Ó Riada (cond).
    Re-issued on Gael-Linn CEF 080 (= LP), CEFC 080 (= MC) (1979).

    Gael-Linn CEFCD 134 (= CD), CEF 134 (= LP), CEFCTV 134
    (= MC) (1987): RTÉ Concert Orchestra, Elmer Bernstein (cond).

Ceol na Laoi (c. 1966) orch
    Gael-Linn GL 14, EP (1966): Radio Telefís Éireann Symphony
    Orchestra, Seán Ó Riada (cond).

Sekundenzeiger (1966) Mez, pf
    Claddagh Records CSM 1 (= LP), 4 CSM 1 (= MC) (1969): Bernadette
    Greevy (Mez), Veronica McSwiney (pf).

Lovers on Aran (1968) Mez, pf
    Claddagh Records CSM 1 (= LP), 4 CSM 1 (= MC) (1969): Bernadette
    Greevy (Mez), Veronica McSwiney (pf).

Ceol an Aifrinn (Ó Riada Mass) (1968) vv, satb, org
    Gael-Linn CB 3 (= LP), CBC 3 (= MC) (1971): Cór Cúil Aodha, Seán
    Ó Riada (cond).

Aifreann 2 (Aifreann nua) (1970) vv, satb, org
    Gael-Linn CEF 081 (= LP), CEFC 081 (= MC) (1979): Cór Cúil Aodha,
    Peadar Ó Riada (cond).

Undated arrangements:

Am Aonar Seal (arr.) satb
    Harmonia Mundi HMS 30691, LP (1965): RTÉ Singers, Waldemar
    Rosen (cond).

An Ciarraigheach Malluighthe (arr.) satb
> Harmonia Mundi HMS 30691, LP (1965): RTÉ Singers, Waldemar Rosen (cond).

An Draighnean Donn (arr.) satb
> Harmonia Mundi HMS 30691, LP (1965): RTÉ Singers, Waldemar Rosen (cond).

Cath Chéim an Fhiadh (arr.) satb
> Harmonia Mundi HMS 30691, LP (1965): RTÉ Singers, Waldemar Rosen (cond).

Feirmeoir an Ghallbhaile (arr.) orch
> Gael-Linn CEF 004, LP (c. 1960): Radio Éireann Light Orchestra, Éimear Ó Broin (cond).
>
> Gael-Linn CEF 019, LP (c. 1968): Radio Éireann Light Orchestra, Éimear Ó Broin (cond).

Maidin Luain Cingcise (arr.) satb
> Harmonia Mundi HMS 30691, LP (1965): RTÉ Singers, Waldemar Rosen (cond).

Slán le Máigh (arr.) orch
> Gael-Linn CEF 019, LP (c. 1968): Radio Éireann Light Orchestra, Éimear Ó Broin (cond).

George Alexander Osborne
(* Limerick 1806, † London 1893)

Osborne was one of the virtuoso pianists famed and famous in continental Europe during the nineteenth century, an Irish Thalberg perhaps. In 1825 he emigrated to Brussels, Belgium, and soon joined musical circles. One year later he was in Paris, studying with Pixis, Fétis and Kalkbrenner and became friendly with Chopin and Berlioz. From 1843 the fashionable pianist lived in London. He wrote music for or with piano, among them many popular arrangements of opera excerpts by Rossini, Donizetti or Verdi as well as of his Irish compatriots Michael W. Balfe and Vincent Wallace. There were also some orchestral pieces and two operas, the scores of which seem to be lost. His *La pluie des perles* for piano enjoyed extreme popularity for many years. His pieces are very demanding in technical respects, not all of them living up to the same expectation musically.

Recorded Work:

Duo brillant à quatre mains op. 69 (c. 1850) 2pf
    Koch International 3-7287-2H1, CD (1994): Bruce Posner & Donald
    Garvelmann.

Geoffrey Molyneux Palmer
(* Staines, Middlesex 1882, † Dublin 1957)

Palmer was born in England of Irish parents and came to live in Ireland around
1910. In 1901 he was the youngest Bachelor of Music in Oxford college history
and studied with C.V. Stanford in London (1904-7). He made a name for himself
by writing popular pieces in a folk idiom for song or choral settings. He also
wrote several stage works of which the most successful was the opera *Sruth na
Maoile* (1923). There are some orchestral pieces and the choral cantata *Duain
Chroí Íosa (Hymn to the Sacred Heart)*, published in 1953. He surprised the
musical public in the early 1980s when it was found that he was the first
composer to set Joyce poems (from 1907) – he set 32 of the 36 poems of the
Chamber Music collection. They differ very much from his other work, making
him the most advanced song composer in early twentieth-century Ireland.

Recorded Works:

Chamber Music (32 Joyce-poems) (1907-1939) T, pf
    Indiana University Press, MC (1993): Robert White (T), Samuel
    Sanders (pf).

A.J. Potter
(* Belfast 1918, † Greystones Co. Wicklow 1980)

A(rchibald) J(oseph) Potter studied with Ralph Vaughan Williams at the Royal
College of Music in London (1936-8). He took part in World War II with the
Indian Army at Burma and worked some years in West Africa before returning to
Ireland in the late 1940s. He taught harmomy and counterpoint at the Royal Irish
Academy of Music. Very well aware of modern compositional trends, Potter
wrote the first Irish composition using a twelve-note row (*Variations on a Popular Tune,* 1955), but, curiously enough, he also wrote some of the most entertaining Irish music of his time in a tonal idiom, often applying modern techniques to produce satirical effects. Large serious compositions showed the other

side of Potter, the most well-known being the *Sinfonia de Profundis* (1969). He also composed the TV-opera *Patrick* (1962).

Recorded Works:

Nocturne (1936) pf
> Anew Records NEWD 406, CD (1994): Roy Holmes.

Overture to a Kitchen Comedy (1950) orch
> Marco Polo 8.225158, CD (2001): National Symphony Orchestra of Ireland, Robert Houlihan (cond).

Rhapsody under a High Sky (1952) orch
> Marco Polo 8.223804, CD (1996): RTÉ Sinfonietta, Proinnséas Ó Duinn (cond).

Fantasia Gaelach No. 1 (1952) orch
> Marco Polo 8.225158, CD (2001): National Symphony Orchestra of Ireland, Robert Houlihan (cond).

Variations on a Popular Tune (1955) orch
> Decca (USA) DL 9844, LP (1956): Radio Éireann Symphony Orchestra, Milan Horvat (cond).

> Marco Polo 8.225158, CD (2001): National Symphony Orchestra of Ireland, Robert Houlihan (cond).

Finnegan's Wake (1957) orch
> EMI Ireland STAL (I) 1003, LP (1971): Irish Concert Orchestra, Éimear Ó Broin (cond).

> Marco Polo 8.225158, CD (2001): National Symphony Orchestra of Ireland, Robert Houlihan (cond).

Fantasia Éireannach (1966)
> Gael-Linn CEF 004, LP (c. 1960): Radio Éireann Light Orchestra, Éimear Ó Broin (cond).

> Gael-Linn CEF 019, LP (c. 1968): Radio Éireann Light Orchestra, Éimear Ó Broin (cond).

Ten Epigrams of Hilaire Belloc (1967)
> Excerpt:

Epigram on a Sleeping Friend
> NIRC DEB 002, LP (1974): Culwick Choral Society, Eric Sweeney (cond).

Sinfonia de Profundis (1969) orch
> Marco Polo 8.225158, CD (2001): National Symphony Orchestra of Ireland, Robert Houlihan (cond).

Song of Sweden (c. 1970) orch
> EMI Ireland STAL (I) 1003, LP (1971): Irish Concert Orchestra, Éimear Ó Broin (cond).

Finnegan's Wake (1970) brass band
> EMI TW 0376, LP (197?): *(performers?).*

Clamos Cervi (1979) satb, org
> Priory PRCD 639, CD (1999): Christ Church Cathedral Dublin Choir, Andrew Johnstone (org), Mark Duley (cond).

Undated arrangements:

Come Back Paddy Reilly (arr.) satb, pf
> EMI CLP 3532, LP (1966): Feis Éireann Group of Singers, Eileen O'Grady (pf + cond).

David of the White Rock (arr.) v, pf
> EMI CLP 1906, LP (1965): Veronica Dunne (S), Havelock Nelson (pf).

Eileen Oge (arr.) satb, pf
> EMI CLP 3532, LP (1966): Feis Éireann Group of Singers, Eileen O'Grady (pf + cond).

Jimmy, Mo Mhile Stor (arr.) v, pf
> EMI CLP 1906, LP (1965): Veronica Dunne (S), Havelock Nelson (pf).

The Mountains of Mourne (arr.) satb, pf
> EMI CLP 3532, LP (1966): Feis Éireann Group of Singers, Eileen O'Grady (pf + cond).

The Sheep under the Snow (arr.) v, pf
> EMI CLP 1906, LP (1965): Veronica Dunne (S), Havelock Nelson (pf).

Will ye no' come back again? (arr.) v, pf
> EMI CLP 1906, LP (1965): Veronica Dunne (S), Havelock Nelson (pf).

Fanny Arthur Robinson
(* England 1831, † Dublin 1879)

Fanny Robinson was a teacher, pianist and composer of English birth. She was a pupil of William Sterndale Bennett and Sigismund Thalberg and first appeared in Ireland as a pianist in February 1849. She married Joseph Robinson four months later. Her London concerts were praised by Meyerbeer. She became a teacher at the Royal Irish Academy of Music in 1856. Her creative career was often interrupted by illness. Robinson's largest work is an orchestral cantata called *God is Love* (1872) and she wrote many piano pieces and some songs.

Recorded Work:

Constancy (18??) pf
> Hunters Moon CHMP 0589, MC (1983): Alan Etherden.
> *Re-issued on* Hunters Moon HMPCD 0183, CD (1989).

Joseph Robinson
(*Dublin 1816, † Dublin 1898)

Joseph Robinson was a baritone, conductor and composer and one of the untiring personalities of Irish musical life in the nineteenth century. He founded the Antient Concerts Society in 1834 and was conductor of Trinity College's University Choral Society from 1837 to 1847. He was instrumental in founding the Royal Irish Academy of Music and conducted an ensemble of 700 singers and musicians for the Handel centenary in 1859. He mainly wrote choral pieces, anthems and songs as well as some fine arrangements of traditional music.

Recorded Works:

Bow down thine Ear, O Lord (1853) S, T, satb. orch/org
> Priory PRCD 639, CD (1999): Sue Hemmens (S), Stuart Kinsella (T), Christ Church Cathedral Dublin Choir, Andrew Johnstone (org), Mark Duley (cond).

The Snowy-Breasted Pearl (18??) T, vn, vc, pf
> Pearl Gemm CD 9411, CD (1991, recorded in the 1920s): Tom Burke (T), anonymous piano trio:

> Nimbus NI 7854, CD (1993, recorded 1910): John McCormack (T), Victor Orchestra.

Ralph Roseingrave
(* Salisbury c. 1695, † Dublin 1747)

The second son of Daniel Roseingrave, Ralph came to live in Ireland when his father (who may have been born in Ireland, but lived in England at least since 1682) was appointed to Christ Church and St. Patrick's Cathedral in Dublin in 1698. Ralph received his first musical education from his father and succeeded him as organist of St. Patrick's in 1719 (of Christ Church additionally from 1727). He mainly composed for the church –two services and eight anthems survived in Christ Church –, but he also wrote some secular instrumental music and songs.

Recorded Works:

Fairest Charmer (c. 1720) v, hpd [basso continuo]
    Melrose Music MM CD-101, CD (1996): Frank Dunne (T), Douglas
    Gunn (fl), Carol O'Connor (vc), Brian MacKay (hpd).

Hymn on the Nativity of Our Blessed Saviour (c. 1730) v, hpd [basso continuo]
    Melrose Music MM CD-101, CD (1996): Frank Dunne (T), Carol
    O'Connor (vc), Brian MacKay (hpd).

Exaudiat te Dominus (Psalm 20) (1731?) satb, org
    Hyperion CDP 11002, CD (1994): St. Paul's Cathedral Choir, Andrew
    Lucas (org), John Scott (cond).

Bow down thine Ear (1736?) satb, org
    TCD CC 001, CD (1997): Trinity College Dublin Chapel Choir,
    Stephen Mailey (org), Kerry S. Houston (cond).

    Christ Church Cathedral Recording / Four Courts Press CCCD1, CD
    (1999): Christ Church Cathedral Dublin Choir, David Adams (org),
    Mark Duley (cond).

I will cry unto God (1736?) satb, org
    Christ Church Cathedral Recording / Four Courts Press CCCD1, CD
    (1999): Christ Church Cathedral Dublin Choir, David Adams (org),
    Mark Duley (cond).

Thomas Roseingrave
(* Winchester 1688, † Dun Laoghaire 1766)

Thomas was the elder son of Daniel Roseingrave and came to live in Ireland with the whole family in 1698. He entered Trinity College in 1707, but was sent to Italy in 1709 with financial assistance from St. Patrick's Cathedral. In Venice he became friendly with Domenico Scarlatti and was later responsible for the Scarlatti craze in England, which he furthered by his own editions of Scarlatti's music. In 1714 or 1715 he settled in England and from 1725 is mentioned as organist of St. George's, Hanover Square, London. He enjoyed an outstanding reputation as organist and teacher. A broken heart is said to be the cause for a serious personal crisis by which he neglected his duties and his pupils, composed less and from 1744 lived from half of his salary, while an assistant took over his duties. In 1753 he returned to Dublin, where he could produce his opera *Phaedra and Hippolytus* and his harpsichord concerto (c. 1740), the first keyboard concerto by a composer from the British Isles.

His music is regarded as extremely individual and although it was published and performed it did not meet with much popularity. Gerald Gifford stated in the 1980 edition of the New Grove Dictionary: "Roseingrave's fondness for chromatic intricacies, irregular phrases and flexibility of form suggests a compositional approach motivated by his brilliant powers of improvisation." He is the most important baroque composer from Ireland.

Recorded Works:

Eight Suits of Lessons for the Harpsichord or Spinnet (1728) hpd
        Excerpts (complete suites):
        No. 1: Suite in E flat
        No. 5: Suite in f
        No. 6: Suite in e
        No. 7: Suite in G
        Hyperion CDA 66564, CD (1992): Paul Nicholson.

        No. 8 in g
        Melrose Music MM CD-101, CD (1996): Douglas Gunn.

Voluntarys and Fugues made on purpose for the Organ or Harpsichord (1728) org / hpd
        Excerpts (complete works):
        (unnumbered) *Fugue in G*
        L'Oiseau Lyre OLS 114, LP (1971, recorded 1955): Thurston Dart (hpd).

Voluntary No. 4 in g
Voluntary No. 8 in g
Fugue No. 5 in d
Fugue No. 10 in G
Gemini Libra Sound LRS 126, MC (1983): Gerald Gifford (org).

Voluntary No. 2 in g
Unicorn-Kanchana DKP 9096, CD/MC (1990): Jennifer Bate (org).

Fugue No. 13 in e
Unicorn-Kanchana DKP 9104, CD/MC (1991): Jennifer Bate (org).

(unnumbered) *Voluntary in c*
Gamut Classics GAMCD 514, CD (1991): Margaret Phillips (org).

Voluntary No. 4 in g
Voluntary No. 7 in g
Voluntary No. 8 in g
Fugue No. 6 in F
Fugue No. 10 in G
Hyperion CDA 66564, CD (1992): Paul Nicholson.

(unnumbered) *Fugue and Voluntary*
TCD CC 002, CD (1998): David Adams.

Twelve Solos (1730) fl, hpd [basso continuo]
    Excerpts (complete works):
    Sonata no. 2 in D (fl, vc, hpd)
    Sonata no. 3 in G (fl, vc, hpd)
    Sonata no. 9 in D (fl, vc, hpd)
    Melrose Music MM CD-101, CD (1996): Douglas Gunn (fl), Carol
    O'Connor (vc), Brian McKay (hpd).

Introduction in g (1739) hpd
    Melrose Music MM CD-101, CD (1996): Douglas Gunn.

Concerto in D (c. 1740) org, 2trp, timp, orch
    reconstruction from hpd solo reduction:
    Hyperion CDA 66700, CD (1994): Paul Nicholson (org), Parley of
    Instruments Baroque Orchestra, Peter Holman (cond).

    reduction to hpd solo (authentic MS):
    Hyperion CDA 66564, CD (1992): Paul Nicholson.

Six Double Fugues for the Organ and Harpsichord (1750) hpd / org
    <u>Excerpts</u> (complete works):
    No. 3: Double Fugue in F (hpd)
    No. 4: Double Fugue in e (org)
    Hyperion CDA 66564, CD (1992): Paul Nicholson.

    No. 2: Double Fugue in g (hpd)
    Melrose Music MM CD-101, CD (1996): Douglas Gunn.

Allegro; Presto; Chaconne (17??; not assigned to an opus-no.) hpd
    Argo ZRG 640, LP (1970): Colin Tilney.

Charles Villiers Stanford
(* Dublin 1852, † London 1924)

Charles Villiers Stanford was the most famous composer of Irish origin before independence. Born into a musical family with many contacts to leading musicians and intellectuals, he first studied privately with Michael Quarry, Joseph Robinson and at the Royal Irish Academy of Music with Robert Prescott Stewart. In 1870 he began his academic studies at Cambridge and from 1873 at Trinity College of Music, London. The next three years he spent half a year each studying in Germany, which he did with Carl Reinecke at Leipzig and with Friedrich Kiel at Berlin and he became friendly with Brahms and Offenbach. From 1883 he was the first professor of music at the Royal College of Music, London (until his death in 1924), and occupied the same position at Cambridge, 1887-1924. He taught virtually the whole next generation of British composers including Ralph Vaughan Williams, Gustav Holst, John Ireland and some Irish composers as well.

    Stanford wrote ten operas, seven symphonies, 33 oratorios or cantatas, three piano concertos, eight string quartets and a large number of smaller works among which his large body of song compositions stands out especially. In many works he distinguishes himself by his overt use of Irish traditional elements. This, combined with the spirit of the age would have made him the ideal candidate for the fame as national Irish composer, but it was his strong unionism and protestantism as well as his residence in England which made later generations doubt his sincerity. Too Irish for the English, too English for the Irish and too German for both, he fell between all stools, where only a new appreciation in a more multicultural environment will help his position.

Recorded Works:

Magnificat and Nunc Dimittis in f (*The Queen's Service*) (1872) satb, org
   Mirabilis MMSCD 4, CD (1994): Queen's College Cambridge Choir,
   Andrew Linn (org), Ralph Woodward (cond).

   Priory PRCD 622, CD (1997): Christ Church Cathedral Dublin Choir,
   Andrew Johnstone (org), Mark Duley (cond).

Magnificat and Nunc Dimittis in E flat (1873) satb, org
   Hyperion CDA 66964, CD (1997): Winchester Cathedral Choir,
   Christopher Monks (org), David Hill (cond).

   Priory PRCD 622, CD (1997): Christ Church Cathedral Dublin Choir,
   Andrew Johnstone (org), Mark Duley (cond).

Pater Noster (1874) satb
   Hyperion CDA 66964, CD (1997): Winchester Cathedral Choir, David
   Hill (cond).

Eight Songs from 'The Spanish Gypsy' op. 1 (1872-5) v, pf
   Hyperion CDA 67123, CD (2000): Stephen Varcoe (Bar), Clifford
   Benson (pf).

Heine Songs op. 4 (1874) v, pf
   Excerpts:
   *Sterne mit den gold'nen Füsschen; Dass du mich liebst; Frühling; Der
   Schmetterling ist in die Rose verliebt*
   Hyperion CDA 67123, CD (2000): Stephen Varcoe (Bar), Clifford
   Benson (pf).

   Tragödie
   Hyperion CDA 67124, CD (2000): Stephen Varcoe (Bar), Clifford
   Benson (pf).

Symphony No. 1 in B flat (1875) orch
   Chandos CHAN 9049 (= CD), ABTD 1590 (= MC) (1992) Ulster
   Orchestra, Vernon Handley (cond).
   Re-issued on Chandos CHAN 9279-82, 4CD (1994).

Deliver Me from Mine Enemies O God (Psalm 59) (1875?) satb, org
   Hyperion CDP 11005, CD (1996): St. Paul's Cathedral Choir, Andrew
   Lucas (org), John Scott (cond).

From the Red Rose (1876) v, pf
Hyperion CDA 66937, CD (1997): Felicity Lott (S), Graham Johnson (pf).

Heine Songs op. 7 (1877) v, pf
Excerpts:
Ich lieb' eine Blume, Wie des Mondes Abbild zittert, Ich halte ihr die Augen zu, Schlummerlied
Hyperion CDA 67123, CD (2000): Stephen Varcoe (Bar), Clifford Benson (pf).

La belle dame sans merci (1877) v, pf
HMV HQS 1091, LP (1967): Janet Baker (S), Gerald Moore (pf).
Re-issued on HMV Greensleeve ESD 100642-1 (= LP), TC-ESD 100642-4 (= MC) (1983) and EMI CDM5-65009-2, CD (1994).

EMI CDC5 56830-2, CD (1999): Ian Bostridge (T), Julius Drake (pf).

Hyperion CDA 67123, CD (2000): Stephen Varcoe (Bar), Clifford Benson (pf).

The Veiled Prophet of Khorassan (1877) opera
Excerpts:
Overture, Ballet Music No. 1, There's a Bower of Roses, Ballet Music No. 2
Marco Polo 8.223580/1, 2CD (1997): Virginia Kerr (S), National Symphony Orchestra of Ireland, Colman Pearce (cond).

Service in B flat op. 10 (1879) satb, org
Priory Records PRCD 437, CD (1993): Durham Cathedral Choir, Keith Wright (org), James Lancelot (cond).

Excerpts:
Te Deum
HMV CSD 3554 (stereo), CLP 3554 (mono), LP (1966): St. Paul's Cathedral Choir (no others named in catalogue).

Abbey CDCA 929, CD (1992): Durham School Chapel Choir, Gregory Williams (org), Jonathan Newell (cond).

Conifer MCFC 214 (= MC), CDCF 214 (= CD) (1993): Trinity College Cambridge Choir, Silas Standage (org), Richard Marlow (cond).

Guild GMCD 7102, CD (1995, recorded 1978): St. Paul's Cathedral Choir, Mark Blatchly (org), Barry Rose (cond).

Chandos CHAN 9548, CD (1997): Leeds Philharmonic Chorus, Darius Battiwalla (org), BBC Philharmonic, Richard Hickox (cond).

Te Deum; Jubilate
Chandos CHAN 6603, CD (1993, recorded 1973): Ely Cathedral Choir, Gerald Gifford (org), Arthur Wills (cond).

Priory PRCD 507 (= CD), PRC 507 (= MC) (1994): Hereford Cathedral Choir, Geraint Bowen (org), Roy Massey (cond).

Te Deum; Jubilate; Magnifica; Nunc Dimittis
Hyperion CDA 66964, CD (1997): Winchester Cathedral Choir, Stephen Farr (org), David Hill (cond).

Magnificat; Nunc Dimittis
Collegium COLC 118 (= MC), COLCD 118 (= CD) (1992): Cambridge Singers, Wayne Marshall (org), John Rutter (cond).

Gamut GAMCD 527, CD (1992): Ely Cathedral Choir, Jeremy Filsell (org), Paul Trepte (cond).

Guild GMCD 7117, CD (1996) (same recording as Gamut above).

Te Deum in B flat (1879) satb, brass band, org
Pickwick IMP Classics PCD 919, CD (1989): Westminster Abbey Choir, London Brass, Martin Neary (org).

Violin Sonata No. 1 in D op. 11 (c. 1880) vn, pf
Cala United CACD 88031, CD (1996): Susanne Stanzeleit (vn), Gusztav Fenyo (pf).

Hyperion CDA 67024, CD (1999): Paul Barritt (vn), Catherine Edwards (pf).

Service in A op. 12 (1880) satb, org
Gamut GAMCD 527, CD (1992): Ely Cathedral Choir, Jeremy Filsell (org), Paul Trepte (cond).

Priory Records PRCD 514, CD (1994): Durham Cathedral Choir, Keith Wright (org), James Lancelot (cond).

Excerpts:
Te Deum; Jubilate
Guild GMCD 7117, CD (1996): Ely Cathedral Choir, Jeremy Filsell (org), Paul Trepte (cond) (from Gamut recording above).

Magnificat; Nunc Dimittis
Hyperion CDA 66030, CD (1987): Worcester Cathedral Choir, Paul Trepte (org), Donald Hunt (cond).

ASV CDQS 6019 (= CD), ZCQS 6019 (= MC) (1988): Christ Church Cathedral Oxford Choir, Francis Grier (org + cond).

Proud Sound PROU CD 121 (= CD), PROU 121 (= MC) (1990): New College Oxford Choir, David Burchell (org), Edward Higginbottom (cond).

Conifer MCFC 214 (= MC), CDCF 214 (= CD) (1993): Trinity College Cambridge Choir, Philip Rushforth (org), Richard Marlow (cond).

Priory PRCD 505 (= CD), PRC 505 (= MC) (1995): Lichfield Cathedral Choir, Andrew Lumsden (org), Mark Shepherd (cond).

Hyperion CDA 66964, CD (1997): Winchester Cathedral Choir, Stephen Farr (org), David Hill (cond).

Symphony No. 2 in d 'Elegiac' (1882) orch
Chandos CHAN 8991 (= CD), ABTD 1573 (= MC) (1992): Ulster Orchestra, Vernon Handley (cond).
Re-issued on Chandos CHAN 9279-82, 4CD (1994).

Songs of Old Ireland (1882) v, pf
Excerpts:
An Irish Lullaby
Marco Polo 8.225098, CD (1998): Bernadette Greevy (Mez), Hugh Tinney (pf).

The Confession
Hyperion A 66049, LP (1982): James Griffett (T), Clifford Benson (pf).

Jenny
Hyperion A 66049, LP (1982): James Griffett (T), Clifford Benson (pf).
Re-issued on Campion Cameo 2001, CD (1997).

The Little Red Lark
Hyperion CDA 67123, CD (2000): Stephen Varcoe (Bar), Clifford
Benson (pf).

My Love's an Arbutus
Hyperion A 66049, LP (1982): James Griffett (T), Clifford Benson (pf).
Re-issued on Campion Cameo 2001, CD (1997).

Hyperion CDA 67123, CD (2000): Stephen Varcoe (Bar), Clifford
Benson (pf).

The Poison on the Darts
Hyperion A 66058, LP (1983): James Griffett (T), Clifford Benson (pf).
Re-issued on Campion Cameo 2001, CD (1997).

The Willow Tree
Hyperion A 66049, LP (1982): James Griffett (T), Clifford Benson (pf).
Re-issued on Campion Cameo 2001, CD (1997).

If Ye Then Be Risen With Christ (1883) satb, org
CRD 3497, CD (1997): New College Oxford Choir, Paul Plummer
(org), Edward Higginbottom (cond).

Three Intermezzi op. 13 (1884) cl, pf
ASV DCA 787 (= CD), ZCDCA 787 (= MC) (1992): Emma Johnson
(cl), Malcolm Martineau (pf).

Serendipity SERCD 4000, CD (199?): Linda Merrick (cl), Benjamin
Frith (pf).

Six Songs op. 19 (1884) v, pf
Excerpts:
No. 2, *A Lullaby*; No. 3, *To the Rose*
Hyperion CDA 67124, CD (2000): Stephen Varcoe (Bar), Clifford
Benson (pf).

The Lord is my Shepherd (Psalm 23) (1886) satb, org
Hyperion CDA 66030, CD (1987): Worcester Cathedral Choir, Paul
Trepte (org), Donald Hunt (cond).

Priory PRCD 257 (= CD), PRC 257 (= MC) (1989): Guildford
Cathedral Choir, Peter Wright (org), Andrew Millington (cond).
Chandos CHAN 6519, CD (1991): Worcester Cathedral Choir, Harry
Bramma (org), Christopher Robinson (cond).

Conifer CDCF 214 (= CD), MCFC 214 (= MC) (1993): Trinity College Cambridge Choir, Richard Marlow (cond), Philip Rushforth (org).

Hyperion A 66618 (= LP), KA 666618 (= MC), CDA 66618 (= CD) (1993): St. Paul's Cathedral Choir, Andrew Lucas (org), John Scott (cond).

CRD 3497, CD (1997): New College Oxford Choir, Edward Higginbottom (cond).

EMI CDC5 55535-2, CD (1997): King's College Cambridge Choir, James Vivian (org), Stephen Cleobury (cond).

Hyperion CDA 66964, CD (1997): Winchester Cathedral Choir, Stephen Farr (org), David Hill (cond).

Symphony No. 3 in f 'Irish' op. 28 (1887) orch
HMV ASD 4221, LP (1982): Bournemouth Sinfonietta, Norman del Mar (cond).
Re-issued on EMI Greensleeve EM 291154-3 (= 2LP), EM 291154-5 (= MC) (1987) and EMI CDM5 65129-2, CD (1995).

Chandos ABRD 1253 (= LP), ABTD 1253 (= MC), CHAN 8545 (= CD) (1987): Ulster Orchestra, Vernon Handley (cond).
Re-issued on Chandos CHAN 9279-82, 4CD (1994).

Excerpt:
2nd movt.
Chandos CHAN 6525, CD (1991): [*taken from recording above*).

Oedipus Rex Prelude op. 29 (1887) orch
Chandos CHAN 8884 (= CD), ABTD 1495 (= MC) (1990): Ulster Orchestra, Vernon Handley (cond).

A Child's Garland of Songs op. 30 (pubd. 1892) v, pf
Excerpt:
No. 4, *Windy Nights*
Hyperion CDA 67124, CD (2000): Stephen Varcoe (Bar), Clifford Benson (pf).

Symphony No. 4 in F op. 31 (1888) orch
Chandos CHAN 8884 (= CD), ABTD 1495 (= MC) (1990): Ulster Orchestra, Vernon Handley (cond).
Re-issued on Chandos CHAN 9279-82, 4CD (1994).

Suite for Violin and Orchestra op. 32 (1889) vn, orch
Hyperion CDA 67208, CD (2000): Anthony Marwood (vn), BBC
Scottish Symphony Orchestra, Martyn Brabbins (cond).

Morning, Communion and Evening Services in F op. 36 (1889) satb, org
Excerpts:
Benedictus; Agnus Dei
Priory PRCD 312 (= CD), PRC 312 (= MC) (1991): Chichester
Cathedral Choir, Jeremy Suter (org), Alan Thurlow (cond).

Priory Records PRCD 437, CD (1993): Durham Cathedral Choir, Keith
Wright (org), James Lancelot (cond).

Magnificat
Priory PRCD 535, CD (1996): Hereford Cathedral Choir, Huw
Williams (org), Roy Massey (cond).

Magnificat; Nunc Dimittis
Hyperion CDA 66964, CD (1997): Winchester Cathedral Choir,
Stephen Farr (org), David Hill (cond).

Two Anthems op. 37 (1885) satb, org
Hyperion CDA 66964, CD (1997): Winchester Cathedral Choir,
Christopher Monks (org), David Hill (cond).

The Tomb (c. 1886) v, pf
Hyperion CDA 67123, CD (2000): Stephen Varcoe (Bar), Clifford
Benson (pf).

Three Motets op. 38 (pubd. 1905) satb
Argo ZRG 5423 (stereo), RG 423 (mono), LP (1965): St. Michael's
Choir (no conductor mentioned in catalogue).

Saga 5368, LP (1973, recorded 1964): Magdalen College Oxford Choir
(no conductor mentioned in catalogue).

Hyperion CDA 66030, CD (1987): Worcester Cathedral Choir, Donald
Hunt (cond).

Conifer CFC 155 (= LP), MCFC 155 (= MC), CDCF 155 (= CD)
(1987): Trinity College Cambridge Choir, Richard Marlow (cond).

EMI Eminence EMX 2161 (= CD), TC-EMX 2161 (= MC) (1990):
Vasari Singers, Jeremy Backhouse (cond).

Proudsound PROUCD 129, CD (1992): Schola Cantorum Oxford, Jeremy Summerly (cond).

Mirabilis MMSCD 4, CD (1994): Queen's College Cambridge Choir, Andrew Linn (org), Ralph Woodward (cond).

Manor MLR 0175, CD (1996): Purcell Singers, Mark Ford (cond).

EMI CDC5 55535-2, CD (1997): King's College Cambridge Choir, Stephen Cleobury (cond).

CRD 3497, CD (1997): New College Oxford Choir, Edward Higginbottom (cond).

Priory PRCD 557, CD (1997): St. Mary's Cathedral Edinburgh Choir, Timothy Byram-Wigfield (cond).

Hyperion CDA 66964, CD (1997): Winchester Cathedral Choir, David Hill (cond).

Guild GMCD 7140, CD (1998): York Minster Chapter House Choir, Jane Sturmheit (cond).

Cedille Records CDR 90000 036, CD (1998): His Majestie's Clerks, Anne Heider (cond).

Excerpts:
Nr. 1: *Justorum animae*
Hyperion CDA 66519 (= CD), KA 56519 (= MC) (1992): St. Paul's Cathedral Choir, John Scott (cond).

Collegium COLCD 113 (= CD), COLC 113 (= LP) (1992): Cambridge Singers, John Rutter (cond).

Nr. 2: *Coelos ascendit*
Abbey CACA 542, MC (1990): Southwark Cathedral Choir, John Scott (cond).

Meridian CDE 84180 (= CD), KE 77180 (= MC) (1990): Salisbury Cathedral Choir, Richard Seal (cond)

ASV CDQS 6025 (= CD), ZCQS 6025 (= MC) (1991): Winchester Cathedral Choir, Martin Neary (cond).

ASV CDQS 6036 (= CD), ZCQS 6036 (= MC) (1992): Winchester Cathedral Choir, Martin Neary (cond).

Priory PRCD 478 (= CD), PRC 478 (= MC) (1994): Lincoln Cathedral Choir, Colin Walsh (cond).

Hyperion CDA 66678 (= CD), KA 66678 (= MC) (1994): St. Paul's Cathedral Choir, John Scott (cond).

Regent REG CD 110, CD (1994): Lincoln College Choir, Alexander Chaplin (cond).

Nr. 3: *Beati quorum via*
HMV HQS 1350, LP (1966): Chichester Cathedral Choir (no conductor mentioned in catalogue).

HMV CSD 3752 (stereo), Q4CSD 3752 (quadraphonic), LP (1974): King's College Cambridge Choir (no conductor mentioned in catalogue).

ASV CDQS 6019 (= CD), ZCQS 6019 (= MC) (1988): Christ Church Cathedral Oxford Choir, Francis Grier (cond).

Collegium COLCD 107 (= CD), COLC 107 (= MC) (1988): Cambridge Singers, John Rutter (cond).
Re-issued on Collegium CSCD 500 (= CD) and CSC 500 (= MC) (1993?).

Abbey CACA 542, MC (1990): Southwark Cathedral Choir, John Scott (cond).

Hyperion CDA 66374 (= CD), KA 66374 (= MC) (1990): St. Paul's Cathedral Choir, John Scott (cond).

Regent REG CD 110, CD (1994): Lincoln College Choir, Alexander Chaplin (cond).

Priory PRCD 586, CD (1997): Marlborough Chapel Choir, Robin Nelson (cond).

For Ever Mine (1891) v, pf
Hyperion CDA 67124, CD (2000): Stephen Varcoe (Bar), Clifford Benson (pf).

Cello Sonata op. 39 (1893) vc, pf
> ASV DCA 807, CD (1993): Julian Lloyd Webber (vc), John McCabe (pf).

Prince Madoc's Farewell (1893) v. pf/orch
> Hyperion CDA 67065, CD (1999): Christopher Maltman (Bar), BBC Scottish Symphony Orchestra, Martyn Brabbins (cond).

Irish Songs and Ballads (1893) v, pf
> Excerpts:
> *Colonel Carty*
> Hyperion A 66049, LP (1982): James Griffett (T), Clifford Benson (pf). *Re-issued on* Campion Cameo 2001, CD (1997).

> *The Irish Reel*
> Hyperion A 66058, LP (1983): James Griffett (T), Clifford Benson (pf). *Re-issued on* Campion Cameo 2001, CD (1997).

> *A Lament*
> Hyperion A 66049, LP (1982): James Griffett (T), Clifford Benson (pf). *Re-issued on* Campion Cameo 2001, CD (1997).

> *Londonderry Air (The Irish Lover)*
> Hyperion A 66049, LP (1982): James Griffett (T), Clifford Benson (pf). *Re-issued on* Campion Cameo 2001, CD (1997).

> *The Ploughman's Whistle*
> Hyperion A 66049, LP (1982): James Griffett (T), Clifford Benson (pf). *Re-issued on* Campion Cameo 2001, CD (1997).

> *The Zephyrs Blest*
> Hyperion A 66049, LP (1982): James Griffett (T), Clifford Benson (pf). *Re-issued on* Campion Cameo 2001, CD (1997).

Tom Leminn (1893) v, pf
> Hyperion CDA 67124, CD (2000): Stephen Varcoe (Bar), Clifford Benson (pf).

Irish Fantasies op. 54 (1894) vn, pf
> Excerpts:
> *Boat Song; Reel*
> Continuum CCD 1051, CD (1992): Fionnuala Hunt (vn), Una Hunt (pf).

Caoine (A Lament)
Hyperion CDA 67024, CD (1999): Paul Barritt (vn), Catherine Edwards (pf).

Symphony No. 5 in D 'L'Allegro ed il penseroso' op. 56 (1894) orch
Chandos ABRD 1277 (= LP), ABTD 1277 (= MC), CHAN 8581 (= CD) (1988): Ulster Orchestra, Vernon Handley (cond).
Re-issued on Chandos CHAN 9279-82, 4CD (1994).

Fantasia and Toccata in d op. 57 (1894) org
Abbey CDCA 902 (= CD), CACA 902 (= MC) (1991): Jonathan Rees-Williams.

Priory PRCD 370, CD (1992): Keith John.

Suite of Ancient Dances op. 58 (1894) orch
Excerpts:
Morris Dance; Sarabande
Pearl GEM 123, LP (1974): anonymous orchestra, Charles V. Stanford (cond).

Piano Concerto No. 1 in G op. 59 (1895) pf, orch
Hyperion CDA 66820, CD (1995): Piers Lane (pf), BBC Scottish Symphony Orchestra, Martyn Brabbins (cond).

Moore's Irish Melodies Restored op. 60 (1895) v, pf
Excerpt:
Pearl Gemm CDS 9188, 2CD (1995, recorded 1941): John McCormack (T), Gerald Moore (pf).

Arise, Shine (1895) satb, org
Priory PRCD 733, CD (2000): St. Albans Cathedral Choir, Andrew Lucas (org + cond).

Shamus O'Brien op. 61 (1896) opera
Excerpts:
Overture
Pearl GEM 123, LP (1974): anonymous orchestra, Charles V. Stanford (cond).

Ochone! When I Used to be Young
Symposium 1093, CD (1991, recorded 1901): Joseph O'Mara (T), anonymous pianist.

Requiem op. 63 (1896) S, Mez, T, B, satb, orch
> Marco Polo 8.223580/1, 2CD (1997): Frances Lucey (S), Colette
> McGahon (Mez), Peter Kerr (T), Nigel Leeson-Williams (B), RTÉ
> Philharmonic Choir, National Symphony Orchestra of Ireland, Adrian
> Leaper (cond).

Clown's Songs from 'Twelfth Night' op. 65 (1897) v, pf
> Hyperion CDA 67124, CD (2000): Stephen Varcoe (Bar), Clifford
> Benson (pf).

> Excerpt:
> *The Rain it Raineth Every Day*
> Hyperion CDA 66480, CD (1992): Anthony Rolfe-Johnson (T),
> Graham Johnson (pf).

Violin Sonata No. 2 in A op. 70 (c. 1898) vn, pf
> Hyperion CDA 67024, CD (1999): Paul Barritt (vn), Catherine Edwards
> (pf).

Concert Variations op. 71 (1898) pf, orch
> Chandos ABRD 1376 (= LP), ABTD 1376 (= MC), CHAN 8736 (=
> CD) (1989): Margaret Fingerhut (pf), Ulster Orchestra, Vernon Handley
> (cond).
> *Re-issued on* Chandos Enchant 7099, CD (1998).

Piano Trio Nr. 2 in g op. 73 (1899) vn, vc, pf
> ASV DCA 925, CD (1995): Pirasti Trio.

Violin Concerto in D op. 74 (1899) vn, orch
> Hyperion CDA 67208, CD (2000): Anthony Marwood (vn), BBC
> Scottish Symphony Orchestra, Martyn Brabbins (cond).

Songs of Erin op. 76 (1901) v, pf
> Excerpts:
> *The Blackbird and the Wren*
> Hyperion A 66049, LP (1982): James Griffett (T), Clifford Benson (pf).
> *Re-issued on* Campion Cameo 2001, CD (1997).

> *Lullaby*
> Hyperion A 66058, LP (1983): James Griffett (T), Clifford Benson (pf).

> *More of Cloyne*
> Hyperion A 66058, LP (1983): James Griffett (T), Clifford Benson (pf).
> *Re-issued on* Campion Cameo 2001, CD (1997).

Trottin' to the Fair
Hyperion A 66049, LP (1982): James Griffett (T), Clifford Benson (pf).
Re-issued on Campion Cameo 2001, CD (1997).

Hyperion CDA 67123, CD (2000): Stephen Varcoe (Bar), Clifford Benson (pf).

An Irish Idyll in Six Miniatures op. 77 (1901) v, pf
Somm Recordings SOMMCD 214, CD (1999): Sarah Leonard (S), Malcolm Martineau (pf).

Excerpts:
No. 2, *The Fairy Lough*
Hyperion A 66058, LP (1983): James Griffett (T), Clifford Benson (pf).
Re-issued on Campion Cameo 2001, CD (1997).

Chandos CHAN 8749 (= CD), ABTD 1388 (= MC) (1989): Linda Finnie (Mez), Anthony Legge (pf).

London 430 061-2LM, CD (1991, recorded 1952): Kathleen Ferrier (Mez), Frederick Stone (pf).
Re-issued on Decca 433 473-2DM, CD (1992).

Marco Polo 8.225098, CD (1998): Bernadette Greevy (Mez), Hugh Tinney (pf).

IMP Classics 1029, CD (1998): Sarah Leonard (S), Malcolm Martineau (pf).

Hyperion CDA 67124, CD (2000): Stephen Varcoe (Bar), Clifford Benson (pf).

Orchestrated Version (1909):
Hyperion CDA 67065, CD (1999): Christopher Maltman (Bar), BBC Scottish Symphony Orchestra, Martyn Brabbins (cond).

No. 3, *Cuttin' Rushes*
Amphion PHI CD 134, CD (1996): Elsie Suddaby (S), Reginald Paul (pf).

No. 6, *Back to Ireland*
Hyperion A 66049, LP (1982): James Griffett (T), Clifford Benson (pf).
Re-issued on Campion Cameo 2001, CD (1997).

Irish Rhapsody No. 1 op. 78 (1901) orch
Pearl GEM 123, LP (1974): anonymous orchestra, Charles V. Stanford (cond).

Chandos ABRD 1316 (= LP), ABTD 1316 (= MC), CHAN 8627 (= CD) (1988): Ulster Orchestra, Verron Handley (cond).
Re-issued on Chandos CHAN 7002/3, 2CD (1994).

Clarinet Concerto op. 80 (1902) cl, orch
Hyperion CDA 66001, CD (1987): Thea King (cl), Philharmonia Orchestra, Alun Francis (cond).

ASV DCA 787 (= CD), ZCDCA 787 (= MC) (1992): Emma Johnson (cl), Royal Philharmonic Orchestra. Charles Groves (cond).

Chandos CHAN 8991 (= CD), ABTD 1573 (= MC) (1992): Janet Hilton (cl), Ulster Orchestra, Vernon Handley (cond).
Re-issued on Chandos CHAN 7002/3, 2CD (1994).

Service in G op. 81 (1903) satb, org
Priory PRC 514 (= MC), PRCD 514 (= CD) (1995): Durham Cathedral Choir, Keith Wright (org), James Lancelot (cond).

Hyperion CDA 66964, CD (1998): Winchester Cathedral Choir, Stephen Farr (org), David Hill (cond).

Excerpts:
Magnificat + Nunc Dimittis
Oryx 1806, LP (1966): Salisbury Cathedral Choir (others not named in catalogue).

Abbey LPB 716, LP (1973): New College Oxford Choir (others not named in catalogue).

Proud Sound PROU CD 121 (= CD), PROU 121 (= MC) (1987): New College Oxford Choir, David Burchell (org), Edward Higginbottom (cond).

Hyperion CDA 66439, CD (1991): St. Paul's Cathedral Choir, Andrew Lucas (org), John Scott (cond).

Collegium COLC 118 (= MC), COLCD 118 (= CD) (1992): Cambridge Singers, Wayne Marshall (org), John Rutter (cond).
Re-issued on Collegium CSCD 501 (= CD), CSC 501 (= MC) (1993?):

Conifer MCFC 214 (= MC), CDCF 214 (= CD) (1993): Trinity College Cambridge Choir, Silas Standage (org), Richard Marlow (cond).

Belart 461453-2, CD (1997, recorded c. 1956): King's College Cambridge Choir, Boris Ord (cond).

EMI CDC5 55535-2, CD (1997): King's College Cambridge Choir, James Vivian (org), Stephen Cleobury (cond).

Irish Rhapsody No. 2 in f op. 84 (1903) orch
Chandos CHAN 9049 (= CD), ABTD 1590 (= MC) (1992) Ulster Orchestra, Vernon Handley (cond).
Re-issued on Chandos CHAN 7002/3, 2CD (1994).

Six Preludes for Organ op. 88 (1903) org
Excerpts:
No. 3 "In the form of a Toccata"; No. 5 "In the form of a Pastorale"
Priory PRCD 414, CD (1994): Jane Watts.

No. 1 "In the form of a Minuet"; No. 3 "In the form of a Toccata"
Amphion PHICD 126 , CD (1995): Francis Jackson.

No. 3 "In the form of a Toccata"
Guild GMCD 7122, CD (1996): Francis Jackson.

Four Irish Dances op. 89 (1903) orch; arr. for pf by Percy Grainger
Nimbus NI 5255, CD (1990): Martin Jones.

Excerpts:
Nos. 1, 3, 4:
Nimbus NI 8809, CD (1996, recorded 1916 and 1922): Percy Grainger.

Nos. 1 and 4:
Hyperion CDA 66884, CD (1997): Marc-André Hamelin.

Songs of the Sea op. 91 (1904) Bar, ttbb, orch
Abbey LPB 689, LP (c. 1971): Benjamin Luxon (Bar) (others not named on catalogue).

HMV ASD 4401 (= LP), TCC-ASD 4401 (= MC) (1983): Benjamin Luxon (Bar), Bournemouth Symphony Chorus and Orchestra, Norman del Mar (cond).
Re-issued on EMI Greensleeve EM 291154-3 (= 2LP), EM 291154-5 (= MC) (1987) and EMI CDM5 65113-2, CD (1994).

Pearl Gemm CD 9384, CD (1990, recorded c. 1928-33): Peter Dawson (Bar), anonymous chorus, anonymous orchestra.

London 455 147-2LH (= CD), -4LH (= MC) (1997): Thomas Allen (Bar), London Philharmonic Choir and Orchestra, Roger Norrington (cond).

Reduction to v, pf:
Hyperion CDA 67124, CD (2000): Stephen Varcoe (Bar), Clifford Benson (pf).

Excerpts:
The Old Superb; Drake's Drum
Saga 5211, LP (1963): John Shirley-Quirk (Bar), Viola Tunnard (pf).

Three Rhapsodies op. 92 (1905) pf
Olympia CD 638, CD (1998): Peter Jacobs.

Five Characteristic Pieces op. 93 (1905) vn/vc, pf
Hyperion CDA 67024, CD (1999): Paul Barritt (vn), Catherine Edwards (pf).

Symphony No. 6 in E flat 'In memoriam G.F. Watts' op. 94 (1905) orch
Chandos ABRD 1316 (= LP), ABTD 1316 (= MC), CHAN 8627 (= CD) (1988): Ulster Orchestra, Vernon Handley (cond).
Re-issued on Chandos CHAN 9279-82, 4CD (1994).

Serenade in F (Nonet) op. 95 (1906) fl, ob, bn, hn, 2vn, va, vc, db
Hyperion CDA 66291 (= CD), KA 66291 (= MC) (1989): Capricorn.
Re-issued on Hyperion Helios CDH 55061, CD (2000).

Stabat Mater op. 96 (1907) S, Mez, T, Bar, org, satb, orch
Chandos CHAN 9548, CD (1997): Ingrid Attrot (S), Pamela Helen Stephen (Mez), Nigel Robson (T), Stephen Varcoe (Bar), Darius Battiwalla (org), Leeds Philharmonic Chorus, BBC Philharmonic, Richard Hickox (cond).

Six Songs of Faith op. 97 (1906, orch. 1915) v, pf/orch
Excerpts:
No. 4, *To the Soul*
EMI CDM5 55028-2, CD (1997): Thomas Hampson (Bar), Craig Rutenberg (pf).

Somm Recordings SOMM CD 214, CD (1999): Paul Leonard (Bar), Malcolm Martineau (pf).

No. 4, *To the Soul*; No. 5, *Tears*
Hyperion CDA 67065, CD (1999): Christopher Maltman (Bar), BBC Scottish Symphony Orchestra, Martyn Brabbins (cond).

No. 4, *To the Soul*; No. 6, *Joy, Shipmate, Joy!*
Hyperion CDA 67124, CD (2000): Stephen Varcoe (Bar), Clifford Benson (pf).

God and the Universe (adapted from op. 97) (1906) satb
Usk Recordings USK 1220, CD (1996): Ionian Singers, Timothy Salter (cond).

Short Preludes and Postludes (Set 1) op. 101 (1907) org
Amphion PHICD 126, CD (1995): Francis Jackson.

Excerpts:
No. 2, *Allegro non troppo e pesante*; No. 4, *Andante tranquillo*
Hyperion A 66180 (= LP), KA 66180 (= MC), CDA 66180 (= CD) (1986): Jennifer Bate.

Motette 10911 (= CD), M 10915 (= MC) (1989): Christopher Dearnley.

Prelude in E flat; Postlude in G; Postlude in F
Guild GMCD 7122, CD (1996): Francis Jackson.

Fantasia and Fugue in d op. 103 (1907) org
Amphion PHICD 126, CD (1995): Francis Jackson.

Short Preludes and Postludes (Set 2) op. 105 (1908) org
Priory PRCD 445, 2CD (1994): Desmond Hunter.

Amphion PHICD 126, CD (1995): Francis Jackson.

Excerpts:
No. 2: Prelude and Postlude on a Theme of Orlando Gibbons
Hyperion A 66180 (= LP), KA 66180 (= MC), CDA 66180 (= CD) (1986): Jennifer Bate.

No. 2: Prelude and Postlude on a Theme of Orlando Gibbons;
No. 3: Lento
Motette 10911 (= CD), M 10915 (= MC) (1989): Christopher Dearnley.

No. 6: Postlude in d
OxRecs OXCD-41 (= CD), OXCASS-41 (= MC) (1990): Magnus
Williamson.

Priory PRCD 296, CD (1991): Jonathan Bielby.

Guild GMCD 7122, CD (1996): Francis Jackson.

EMI CDC5 55535-2, CD (1997): James Vivian.

Four Part-Songs op. 106 (1908) satb
> Excerpt:
> *Autumn Leaves*
> EMI CDC 7 49765 2, CD (1988): The King's Singers.

Four Part-Songs op. 110 (1908) satb
> Excerpts:
> No. 4, *Heraclitus*
> Somm Recordings SOMM CD 204, CD (1995): Canzonetta, Jeffrey
> Wynn-Davies (cond).
>
> Usk Recordings USK 1220, CD (1996): Ionian Singers, Timothy Salter
> (cond).
>
> Arrangement for v, pf (1918):
> No. 4, *Heraclitus*
> Hyperion A 66049, LP (1982): James Griffett (T), Clifford Benson (pf).
> *Re-issued on* Campion Cameo 2001. CD (1997).
>
> Hyperion CDA 67123, CD (2000): Stephen Varcoe (Bar), Clifford
> Benson (pf).

Four Songs op. 112 (1908) v, pf
> Excerpt:
> No. 1, *The City Child*
> Hyperion A 66058, LP (1983): James Griffett (T), Clifford Benson (pf).

For All the Saints (1908) satb
> Cantoris CRCD 2367 (= CD), CRMC 2367 (= MC) (1993): Jesus
> College Choir, Daniel Phillips (cond).

O Living Will (1908) satb
> Hyperion CDA 66030, CD (1987): Worcester Cathedral Choir, Donald
> Hunt (cond).

Priory PRCD 733, CD (2000): St. Albans Cathedral Choir, Andrew Lucas (cond).

Bible Songs and Six Hymns op. 113 (1909) Bar, satb, org
Hyperion CDA 66965, CD (1998): William Kendall (Bar), Winchester Cathedral Choir, Christopher Monks (org), David Hill (cond).

Priory PRCD 733, CD (2000): Kenneth Burgess (Bar), St. Albans Cathedral Choir, Andrew Parnell (org on *Six Hymns*) Andrew Lucas (org on *Bible Songs* + cond).

Excerpts:
Bible Songs
Chandos CHAN 9548, CD (1997): Stephen Varcoe (Bar), Ian Watson (org).

Excerpts from *Bible Songs*
No. 4, *A Song of Peace*; No. 6, *A Song of Wisdom*
Regent REG CD 112, CD (1994): St. Mary's Girls Choir Warwick, Kevin Bowyer (org), Simon Lole (cond).

EMI CDC5 55535-2, CD (1997): King's College Cambridge Choir, James Vivian (org), Stephen Cleobury (cond).

Six Hymns
Priory PRCD 312 (= CD), PRC 312 (= MC) (1991): Chichester Cathedral Choir, Jeremy Suter (org), Alan Thurlow (cond).

Excerpts from *Six Hymns*
No. 4, *Pray that Jerusalem*
Meridian CDE 84140, CD (1988): Salisbury Cathedral Choir, David Halls (org), Richard Seal (cond).

Nimbus NI 5440, CD (1995): Christ Church Cathedral Oxford Choir, Stephen Farr (org), Stephen Darlington (cond).

No. 4, *Pray that Jerusalem*; No. 6, *O for a Closer Walk with God*
EMI CDC5 55535-2, CD (1997): King's College Cambridge Choir, James Vivian (org), Stephen Cleobury (cond).

No. 6, *O for a Closer Walk with God*
Collegium COLC 118 (= MC), COLCD 118 (= CD) (1992): Cambridge Singers, Wayne Marshall (org), John Rutter (cond).

Regent REG CD 111, CD (1994): Blue Coat Church of England School Choir, David Poulter (org), Christopher Howard (cond).

Abbey CDCA 589, CD (199?): St. Mary Redcliffe Choir, Colin Hunt (org), John Marsh (cond).

Service in C op. 115 (1909) satb, org

Gamut GAMCD 527, CD (1992): Ely Cathedral Choir, Jeremy Filsell (org), Paul Trepte (cond).

Priory Records PRCD 437, CD (1993): Durham Cathedral Choir, Keith Wright (org), James Lancelot (cond).

Hyperion CDA 66965, CD (1998): Winchester Cathedral Choir, Stephen Farr (org), David Hill (cond).

Hyperion CDA 66974, CD (1998): Winchester Cathedral Choir, Stephen Farr (org), David Hill (cond).

Excerpts:
Te Deum
Priory PRCD 312 (= CD), PRC 312 (= MC) (1991): Chichester Cathedral Choir, Jeremy Suter (org), Alan Thurlow (cond).

Collegium COLC 118 (= MC), COLCD 118 (= CD) (1992): Cambridge Singers, Wayne Marshall (org), John Rutter (cond).
Re-issued on Collegium CSCD 500 (= CD), CSC 500 (= MC) (1993?):

Guild GMCD 7105, CD (1996, recorded 1982): St. George's Chapel Choir, John Porter (org), Christopher Robinson (cond).

Te Deum; Benedictus; Jubilate Deo
Hyperion CDA 66974, CD (1998): Winchester Cathedral Choir, Stephen Farr (org), David Hill (cond).

Te Deum; Jubilate Deo
Priory PRCD 433 (= CD), PRC 433 (= MC) (1993): Rochester Cathedral Choir, Robert Sayer (org), Barry Ferguson (cond).

Guild GMCD 7117, CD (1996): Ely Cathedral Choir, Jeremy Filsell (org), Paul Trepte (cond) (from *Gamut* recording above).

Benedictus
Conifer MCFC 214 (= MC), CDCF 214 (= CD) (1993): Trinity College
Cambridge Choir, Silas Standage (org), Richard Marlow (cond).

Magnificat; Nunc Dimittis
Saga 5368, LP (1973, recorded 1964): Magdalen College Oxford Choir
(others not named in catalogue).

Hyperion A 66249 (= LP), KA 66249 (= MC), CDA 66249 (= CD)
(1988): St. Paul's Cathedral Choir, Christopher Dearnley (org), John
Scott (cond).

Priory PRCD 322 (= CD), PRC 322 (= MC) (1991): Truro Cathedral
Choir, Henry Doughty (org), David Briggs (cond).

Meridian CDE 84276, CD (1995, recorded in 1980s): Ely Cathedral
Choir, Stephen le Prevost (org), Arthur Wills (cond).

Priory PRCD 527, CD (1996): Portsmouth Cathedral Choir, David
Thorne (org), Adrian Lucas (cond).

EMI CDC5 55535-2, CD (1997): King's College Cambridge Choir,
James Vivian (org), Stephen Cleobury (cond).

Songs of the Fleet op. 117 (1910) Bar, ttbb, orch
Pearl GEM 123, LP (1974): Harold Williams (Bar), anonymous choir
and orchestra, Charles V. Stanford (cond).

HMV ASD 4401 (= LP), TCC-ASD 4401 (= MC) (1983): Benjamin
Luxon (Bar), Bournemouth Symphony Chorus and Orchestra, Norman
del Mar (cond).
Re-issued on EMI Greensleeve EM 291154-3 (= 2LP), EM 291154-5
(= MC) (1987) and EMI CDM5 65113-2, CD (1994).

Partsongs op. 119 (1910) satb
Excerpts:
No. 3, *The Blue Bird*
Collegium COL 104 (= LP), COLC 104 (= MC) (1986): Cambridge
Singers, John Rutter (cond).
Re-issued on Collegium CSCD 500 (= CD) and CSC 500 (= MC)
(1993?).

Somm Recordings SOMM CD 204, CD (1995): Canzonetta, Jeffrey
Wynn-Davies (cond).

Manor MLR 0175, CD (1996): Purcell Singers, Mark Ford (cond).

Naxos 8.553088 (= CD), 4.553088 (= MC) (1997), Oxford Camerata, Jeremy Summerly (cond).

Hyperion CDA 67076, CD (1999): Laudibus, Michael Brewer (cond).

No. 3, *The Blue Bird*; No. 6, *The Swallow*
Usk Recordings USK 1220, CD (1996): Ionian Singers, Timothy Salter (cond).

Idyll and Fantasia op. 121 (1910) org
Priory PRCD 414, CD (1994): Jane Watts.

Ye Choirs of New Jerusalem op. 123 (1910) satb, org
Hyperion CDA 66030, CD (1987): Worcester Cathedral Choir, Paul Trepte (org), Donald Hunt (cond).

Conifer MCFC 214 (= MC), CDCF 214 (= CD) (1993): Trinity College Cambridge Choir, Silas Standage (org), Richard Marlow (cond).

Abbey CDCA 959, CD (1994): Southwell Minster Choir, Peter Wood (org), Paul Hale (cond).

CRD 3497, CD (1997): New College Oxford Choir, Paul Plummer (org), Edward Higginbottom (cond).

Hyperion CDA 66974, CD (1998): Winchester Cathedral Choir, Stephen Farr (org), David Hill (cond).

I Heard a Voice from Heaven (1910) satb, org
Collegium COLC 118 (= MC), COLCD 118 (= CD) (1992): Cambridge Singers, Wayne Marshall (org), John Rutter (cond).

Symphony No. 7 in d op. 124 (1911) orch
Chandos CHAN 8861 (= CD), ABTD 1476 (= MC) (1990): Ulster Orchestra, Vernon Handley (cond).
Re-issued on Chandos CHAN 9279-82, 4CD (1994).

Four Songs op. 125 (1911) v, pf
Excerpt:
No. 3, *Phoebe*
Hyperion CDA 67124, CD (2000): Stephen Varcoe (Bar), Clifford Benson (pf).

Piano Concerto No. 2 op. 126 (1911) pf, orch
    Lyrita SRCS 219, LP (1985): Malcolm Binns (pf), London Symphony
    Orchestra, Nicholas Braithwaite (cond).
    Re-issued on Lyrita SRCD 219, CD (1992).

    Chandos ABRD 1376 (= LP), ABTD 1376 (= MC), CHAN 8736 (=
    CD) (1989): Margaret Fingerhut (pf), Ulster Orchestra, Vernon Handley
    (cond).
    Re-issued on Chandos Enchant 7099, CD (1998).

Festal Communion Service in B flat op. 128 (1911) satb, org
    Priory PRCD 622, CD (1997): Christ Church Cathedral Dublin Choir,
    Andrew Johnstone (org), Mark Duley (cond).

    Excerpt:
    Gloria in excelsis deo
    Polydor 2383 267, LP (1974): Westminster Abbey Choir (others not
    named in catalogue).

    Argo 411 714 1ZH (= MC), -4ZH (= LP) (1984): Canterbury Cathedral
    Choir, David Flood (org), Allan Wicks (cond).

    Conifer CDCF 214 (= CD), MCFC 214 (= MC) (1993): Trinity College
    Cambridge Choir, Silas Standage (org), Richard Marlow (cond).

    Chandos CHAN 6603, CD (1993, recorded 1974 – identical with
    Polydor above?): Westminster Abbey Choir, Timothy Farrell (org),
    Douglas Guest (cond).

    Cantoris CSACD 3050 (= CD), CSAMC 3050 (= MC) (1994):
    Westminster Abbey Choir, Martin Baker (org), Martin Neary (cond).

    Hyperion CDA 66974, CD (1998): Winchester Cathedral Choir,
    Stephen Farr (org), David Hill (cond).

    Priory PRCD 733, CD (2000): St. Albans Cathedral Choir, Simon Bell
    (org), Andrew Lucas (cond).

Clarinet Sonata op. 129 (1911) cl, pf
    RCF 009, LP (1971): John Denman (cl), Hazel Vivienne (pf).

    Hyperion A 66014, LP (1981): Thea King (cl), Clifford Benson (pf).
    Re-issued on Hyperion KA 66014 (= MC), CDA 66014 (= CD) (1989)
    and Hyperion CDD 22027, 2CD (1997).

Chandos CHAN 9079, CD (1992): Einar Jóhannesson (cl), Philip Jenkins (pf).

British Music Label BML 009, CD (1994): John Denman (cl), Paula Fan (pf).

ASV DCA 891, CD (1994): Emma Johnson (cl), Malcolm Martineau (pf).

Aurophon 34058, CD (1994): .

Continuum CCD 1074, CD (1996): Murray Khouri (cl), John McCabe (pf).

Six Characteristic Pieces op. 132 (1912) pf
Priory PRCD 449, CD (1996): Peter Jacobs.

Blessed City op. 134 (1913) satb, org/orch
Priory PRCD 733, CD (2000): St. Albans Cathedral Choir, Andrew Lucas (org + cond).

Three Motets op. 135 (1913) satb
Christ Church Cathedral Dublin Choir, Mark Duley (cond): Priory PRCD 622. CD 1997.

Excerpt:
No. 1, *Ye Holy Angels Bright*; No. 3, *Glorious and All-Powerful God*
Hyperion CDA 66030, CD (1987): Worcester Cathedral Choir, Donald Hunt (cond).

CRD 3497, CD (1997): New College Oxford Choir, Edward Higginbottom (cond).

No. 2, *Eternal Father*
Conifer CDCF 155 (= CD), MCFC 155 (= MC) (1987): Trinity College Cambridge Choir, Richard Marlow (cond).
Re-issued on Conifer CDCF 503 (= CD), MCFC 503 (= MC) (1993).

No. 2, *Eternal Father*; No. 3, *Glorious and All-Powerful God*
Hyperion CDA 66974, CD (1998): Winchester Cathedral Choir, David Hill (cond).

No. 3, *Glorious and All-Powerful God*
Abbey CDCA 9013, CD (1991): Magdalen College Oxford Choir, John Harper (cond).

Irish Rhapsody No. 3 op. 137 (1913) vc, orch
Chandos CHAN 8861 (= CD), ABTD 1476 (= MC) (1990): Raphael Wallfisch (vc), Ulster Orchestra, Vernon Handley (cond).
Re-issued on Chandos CHAN 7002/3, 2CD (1994).

A Fire of Turf op. 139 (1913) v, pf
Hyperion CDA 67124, CD (2000): Stephen Varcoe (Bar), Clifford Benson (pf).

Excerpts:
No. 1, *The Fair*
Somm Recordings SOMMCD 214, CD (1999): Paul Leonard (Bar), Malcolm Martineau (pf).

No. 2, *A Chapel on the Hill*
Hyperion A 66049, LP (1982): James Griffett (T), Clifford Benson (pf).

No. 5: *Blackberry Time*
Hyperion A 66049, LP (1982): James Griffett (T), Clifford Benson (pf).
Re-issued on Campion Cameo 2001, CD (1997).

A Sheaf of Songs from Leinster op. 140 (1913) v, pf
Marco Polo 8.225098, CD (1998): Bernadette Greevy (Mez), Hugh Tinney (pf).

Excerpts:
No. 2, *Thief of the World*
Hyperion A 66058, LP (1983): James Griffett (T), Clifford Benson (pf).
Re-issued on Campion Cameo 2001, CD (1997).

No. 3, *A Soft Day*
Hyperion A 66049, LP (1982): James Griffett (T), Clifford Benson (pf).
Re-issued on Campion Cameo 2001, CD (1997).

Hyperion A 66085, LP (1984): Graham Trew (Bar), Roger Vignoles (pf).

Max Sound MSCB 12, MC (1987): Valerie Baulard (Mez), Simon Wright (pf).

Chandos CHAN 8749 (= CD), ABTD 1388 (= MC) (1989): Linda Finnie (Mez), Anthony Legge (pf).

London 430 061-2LM, CD (1991, recorded 1952): Kathleen Ferrier (Mez), Frederick Stone (pf).
Re-issued on Decca 433 473-2DM, CD (1992).

Hyperion CDA 67123, CD (2000): Stephen Varcoe (Bar), Clifford Benson (pf).

No. 5, *The Bold Unbiddable Child*
Hyperion A 66058, LP (1983): James Griffett (T), Clifford Benson (pf).
Re-issued on Campion Cameo 2001, CD (1997).

Chandos CHAN 8749 (= CD), ABTD 1388 (= MC) (1989): Linda Finnie (Mez), Anthony Legge (pf).

Hyperion CDA 67123, CD (2000): Stephen Varcoe (Bar), Clifford Benson (pf).

No. 6, *Irish Skies*
Hyperion CDA 67123, CD (2000): Stephen Varcoe (Bar), Clifford Benson (pf).

Irish Rhapsody No. 4 in a op. 141 (1913) orch
Lyrita SRCS 123, LP (1985): London Philharmonic Orchestra, Nicholas Braithwaite (cond).

Chandos ABRD 1277 (= LP), ABTD (= MC), CHAN 8581 (= CD) (1988): Ulster Orchestra, Vernon Handley (cond).
Re-issued on Chandos CHAN 6525, CD (1991) and Chandos CHAN 7002/3, 2CD (1994).

On Time op. 142 (1913) satb
Usk Recordings USK 1220, CD (1996): Ionian Singers, Timothy Salter (cond).

St. Patrick's Breastplate (1913) satb, org
Conifer CDCF 502, CD (1993): City of Birmingham Symphony Orchestra Chorus, Peter King (org), Simon Halsey (cond).

Hyperion CDA 66974, CD (1998): Winchester Cathedral Choir, Stephen Farr (org), David Hill (cond).

The Critic op. 144 (1914) opera
> Excerpt (orchestral):
> Pearl GEM 123, LP (1974): anonymous orchestra, Charles V. Stanford (cond).

For lo I raise up op. 145 (1914) satb, org
> Abbey XPS 103, LP (1985): Guildford Cathedral Choir, Peter Wright (org), Andrew Millington (cond).
>
> Hyperion CDA 66030, CD (1987): Worcester Cathedral Choir, Paul Trepte (org), Donald Hunt (cond).
>
> Meridian CDE 84140, CD (1988): Salisbury Cathedral Choir, David Halls (org), Richard Seal (cond).
>
> ASV CDQS 6019 (= CD), ZCQS 6019 (= MC) (1988): Christ Church Cathedral Oxford Choir, Francis Grier (org + cond).
>
> Priory PRCD 351 (= CD), PRC 351 (= MC) (1992): Norwich Cathedral Choir, Neil Taylor (org), Michael Nicholas (cond).
>
> Hyperion CDA 66826, CD (1996): St. Paul's Cathedral Choir, Andrew Lucas (org), John Scott (cond).
>
> Priory PRCD 622, CD (1997): Christ Church Cathedral Dublin Choir, Andrew Johnstone (org), Mark Duley (cond).
>
> EMI CDC5 55535-2, CD (1997): King's College Cambridge Choir, James Vivian (org), Stephen Cleobury (cond).
>
> CRD 3497, CD (1997): New College Oxford Choir, Paul Plummer (org), Edward Higginbottom (cond).
>
> Hyperion CDA 66974, CD (1998): Winchester Cathedral Choir, Stephen Farr (org), David Hill (cond).

Irish Rhapsody No. 5 in g op. 147 (1917)
> Chandos ABRD 1253 (= LP), ABTD 1253 (= MC), CHAN 8545 (= CD) (1987): Ulster Orchestra, Vernon Handley (cond).
> *Re-issued on* Chandos CHAN 7002/3, 2CD (1994).

Organ Sonata No. 1 in F op. 149 (1917) org
> Priory PRCD 445, 2CD (1994): Desmond Hunter.

Organ Sonata Nr. 2 "Eroica" op. 151 (1917) org
      Priory PRCD 445, 2CD (1994): Desmond Hunter.

      Marco Polo 8.223754, CD (1994): Joseph Payne.

Organ Sonata Nr. 3 "Britannica" op. 152 (1917) org
      Priory PRCD 445, 2CD (1994): Desmond Hunter.

      Marco Polo 8.223754, CD (1994): Joseph Payne.

      Priory PRCD 680, CD (2000): David Briggs.

Organ Sonata Nr. 4 "Celtica" op. 153 (1917) org
      Priory PRCD 445, 2CD (1994): Desmond Hunter.

      Marco Polo 8.223754, CD (1994): Joseph Payne.

      Guild GMCD 7122, CD (1996): John Dexter.

Six Irish Sketches op. 154 (1917) vn, pf
      Excerpts:
      Melody; Reel
      Continuum CCD 1051, CD (1992): Fionnuala Hunt (vn), Una Hunt (pf).

Songs of a Roving Celt op. 157 (1919) v, pf
      Excerpt:
      The Pibroch
      Max Sound MSCB 13, MC (1987): Valerie Baulard (Mez), Simon
      Wright (pf).

      Hyperion CDA 67124, CD (2000): Stephen Varcoe (Bar), Clifford
      Benson (pf).

Organ Sonata No. 5 "Quasi una Fantasia" op. 159 (1918) org
      Priory PRCD 445, 2CD (1994): Desmond Hunter.

Twenty-four Preludes in all the Keys (Set 1) op. 163 (1918) pf
      Priory Records PRCD 449, CD (1996): Peter Jacobs.

Magnificat op. 164 (1918) satb, org
      Conifer CFC 155 (= LP), MCFC 155 (= MC), CDCF 155 (= CD)
      (1987): Trinity College Cambridge Choir, Richard Marlow (cond).

EMI CDC5 55535-2, CD (1997): King's College Cambridge Choir, James Vivian (org), Stephen Cleobury (cond).

Hyperion CDA 66974, CD (1998): Winchester Cathedral Choir, Stephen Farr (org), David Hill (cond).

A Japanese Lullaby (1918) v, pf
> Hyperion A 66058, LP (1983): James Griffett (T), Clifford Benson (pf).

Lighten our Darkness (1918) satb
> Hyperion CDA 66974, CD (1998): Winchester Cathedral Choir, David Hill (cond).

Six Songs from 'The Glens of Antrim' op. 174 (1920) v, pf
> Hyperion CDA 67123, CD (2000): Stephen Varcoe (Bar), Clifford Benson (pf).

Six Songs op. 175 (publd. 1921) v, pf
> Excerpts:
> No. 1, *A Song of the Bow*
> Hyperion A 66049, LP (1982): James Griffett (T), Clifford Benson (pf). *Re-issued on* Campion Cameo 2001, CD (1997).

> No. 2, *Drop me a Flower*
> Hyperion A 66049, LP (1982): James Griffett (T), Clifford Benson (pf). *Re-issued on* Campion Cameo 2001, CD (1997).

> No. 3, *The Winds of Bethlehem*
> Hyperion A 66049, LP (1982): James Griffett (T), Clifford Benson (pf). *Re-issued on* Campion Cameo 2001, CD (1997).

> No. 4, *The Monkey's Carol*
> Hyperion A 66058, LP (1983): James Griffett (T), Clifford Benson (pf). *Re-issued on* Campion Cameo 2001, CD (1997).

> No. 6, *The Unknown Sea*
> Hyperion A 66058, LP (1983): James Griffett (T), Clifford Benson (pf).

Twenty-four Preludes in all the Keys (Set 2) op. 179 (1920) pf
> Olympia CD 638, CD (1998): Peter Jacobs.

Concert Piece for Organ op. 181 (1921) org, orch
> Chandos CHAN 8861 (= CD), ABTD 1476 (= MC) (1990): Gillian Weir (org), Ulster Orchestra, Vernon Handley (cond).

Re-issued on Chandos CHAN 7002/3, 2CD (1994).

Two Fantasies (1922) cl, str-qu
Hyperion CDA 66479, CD (1992): Thea King (cl), Britten Quartet.

Six Irish Airs (arr. 1922) satb
Excerpt:
Quick, we have but a Second
Harmonia Mundi HMS 30691, LP (1965): RTÉ Singers, Waldemar
Rosen (cond).

Collegium COLCD 104 (= CD), COLC 104 (= LP) (1987): Cambridge
Singers, John Rutter (cond).

EMI CDC 7497652, CD (1988): King's Singers.

Irish Rhapsody No. 6 op. 191 (1923) vn, orch
Chandos CHAN 8884 (= CD), ABTD 1495 (= MC) (1990): Lydia
Mordkovitch (vn), Ulster Orchestra, Vernon Handley (cond).
Re-issued on Chandos CHAN 7002/3, 2CD (1994).

Prelude and Fugue op. 193 (1923) org
Excerpt:
Prelude and Fugue in c
Amphion PHICD 126, CD (1995): Francis Jackson.

Prelude and Fugue in c; Prelude and Fugue in C
CRD 3497, CD (1997): Andrew Smith.

Fairy Lures (1923) v, pf
Hyperion A 66058, LP (1983): James Griffett (T), Clifford Benson (pf).

How Beauteous are their Feet (1923) satb
CRD 3497, CD (1997): New College Oxford Choir, Paul Plummer
(org), Edward Higginbottom (cond).

Hyperion CDA 66974, CD (1998): Winchester Cathedral Choir,
Stephen Farr (org), David Hill (cond).

Priory PRCD 733, CD (2000): St. Albans Cathedral Choir, Andrew
Parnell (org), Andrew Lucas (cond).

The Earth is the Lord's (1924) satb, org
> Abbey CDCA 589, CD (199?): St. Mary Redcliffe Choir, Colin Hunt
> (org), John Marsh (cond).

Songs from 'The Elfin Pedlar' (pubd. 1925) v, pf
> Hyperion A 66058, LP (1983): James Griffett (T), Clifford Benson (pf).

The Merry Month of May (pubd. 1927) v, pf
> Hyperion A 66049, LP (1982): James Griffett (T), Clifford Benson (pf).
> *Re-issued on* Campion Cameo 2001, CD (1997).

Witches' Charms (pubd. 1928) v, pf
> Hyperion A 66058, LP (1983): James Griffett (T), Clifford Benson (pf).

John Andrew Stevenson
(Dublin 1761, † Dublin 1833)

Stevenson is the original arranger of Thomas Moore's *Irish Melodies*, published
between 1807 and 1834. Since Moore was the poet and Stevenson the composer
of the preludes and postludes ("symphonies") and accompaniment, musical
credits must mainly go to Stevenson. Stevenson, who was knighted in 1803 for
his services to music, was known for his many glee compositions, but is also the
composer of operas such as *The Patriot* (1810), other larger-scale music and also
of some liturgical music. Only very few of *Moore's Melodies* have been recorded
in the original settings by Stevenson, and only these are listed here.

Recorded Works:

Irish Melodies vol. 1 (1807) v, pf
> Excerpt:
> *Erin, the Tear and the Smile in Thine Eyes*
> Black Box Music BBM 1022, CD (1998): Kathleen Tynan (S),
> Dearbhla Collins (pf).
>
> *The Meeting of the Waters*
> Hyperion CDA 66627, CD (1993): Ann Murray (Mez), Graham
> Johnson (pf).

Irish Melodies vol. 2 (1807) v, pf
> Excerpts:

Believe Me if all those Endearing Young Charms
Hyperion CDA 66627, CD (1993): Ann Murray (Mez), Graham
Johnson (pf).

Come Send Round the Wine
Black Box Music BBM 1022, CD (1998): Kathleen Tynan (S),
Dearbhla Collins (pf).

Silent O Moyle Be the Roar of thy Water (The Song of Fionnuala)
Hyperion CDA 66774, CD (1995): Rufus Müller (T), Timothy Roberts
(pf).

Irish Melodies vol. 3 (1810) v, pf
　　Excerpts:
　　After the Battle
　　Black Box Music BBM 1022, CD (1998): Kathleen Tynan (S),
　　Dearbhla Collins (pf).

Irish Melodies vol. 5 (1813) v, pf
　　Excerpts:
　　The Last Rose of Summer
　　Hyperion CDA 66627, CD (1993): Ann Murray (Mez), Graham
　　Johnson (pf).

　　*The Valley Lay Smiling Before Me (The Song of O'Ruark, Prince of
　　Breffni)*
　　Hyperion CDA 66774, CD (1995): Christopher Purves (B), Timothy
　　Roberts (pf).

Irish Melodies vol. 6 (1815) v, pf
　　Excerpts:
　　Come O'er the Sea
　　Hyperion CDA 66774, CD (1995): Christopher Purves (B), Timothy
　　Roberts (pf).

　　Come Rest in this Bosom
　　Hyperion CDA 66774, CD (1995): Julia Gooding (S), Timothy Roberts
　　(pf).

Irish Melodies vol. 7 (1818) v, pf
　　Excerpt:
　　My Gentle Harp
　　Black Box Music BBM 1022, CD (1998): Kathleen Tynan (S),
　　Dearbhla Collins (pf).

By the Waters of Babylon (18??) satb, org
    Christ Church Cathedral Recording / Four Courts Press CCCD1, CD
    (1999): Christ Church Cathedral Dublin Choir, David Adams (org),
    Mark Duley (cond).

I looked and behold (18??) satb, org
    Christ Church Cathedral Recording / Four Courts Press CCCD1, CD
    (1999): Christ Church Cathedral Dublin Choir, David Adams (org),
    Mark Duley (cond).

Robert Prescott Stewart

(* Dublin 1824, † Dublin 1894)

Stewart was one of the few outstanding individuals in 19th-century Ireland who
kept flying the flag for classical music during difficult times. He became organist
of Christ Church Cathedral and of Trinity College, Dublin, in 1844 and conduct-
or of the University Choral Society in 1846. In 1851 he graduated MusB and
MusD and became organist of St. Patrick's Cathedral in 1852. From 1861 to
1894 he was professor of music in Trinity College and from 1871 he also taught
at the Royal Irish Academy of Music – in a word, for some decades he held all
important musical posts in the city of Dublin. Among his compositions are many
works for choir and organ, a choral fantasia for the Boston Peace Festival of
1872, and a number of other cantatas. For a very long time, his work was wholly
neglected except at the Dublin cathedrals which have now contributed to his
rediscovery.

Recorded Works:

If ye love me (pubd. 1863) S, A, T, B, satb
    Priory PRCD 639, CD (1999): Helen Roycroft (S), Sarah Lane (A),
    Michael Finlay (T), Daniel Berman (B), Christ Church Cathedral
    Dublin Choir, Mark Duley (cond).

Thou O God art Praised in Zion (pubd. 1863) satb, org
    Christ Church Cathedral Recording / Four Courts Press CCCD1. CD
    (1999): Christ Church Cathedral Dublin Choir, David Adams (org),
    Mark Duley (cond).

God Hath Spoken in His Holiness (18??) satb, org
    Hyperion CDP 11009, CD (1999): St. Paul's Cathedral Choir, Huw
    Williams (org), John Scott (cond).

O God thou hast cast us out (Psalm 60) (18??) satb, org
  Hyperion CDP 11005, CD (1996): St. Paul's Cathedral Choir, Andrew
  Lucas (org), John Scott (cond).

Eric Sweeney
(* Dublin 1948)

Sweeney studied at Trinity College, Dublin (MusB 1969), with Brian Boydell
and at Rome (1969-70). For a while he taught music at the College of Music
(Dublin) and at Trinity College. Since the mid-1980s he is Head of the music
department at the Waterford Institute of Technology – in 1994 he made his
doctorate in composition at the University of Ulster at Jordanstown. Sweeney has
composed much music for choirs and was very active for a long time as a choral
conductor: he conducted the Culwick Choral Society and the choirs of Radio
Telefís Éireann before he founded the Eric Sweeney Singers in 1981. Sweeney's
music was oriented at the continental serial and post-serial avant-garde until
about 1987 when a stylistic change during the work on his 2nd symphony made
him move in the minimalist direction. His work since then combines minimalist
procedures with elements of Irish traditional music.

Recorded Works:

Gloria (1972) satb
  New Irish Recording Co. DEB 002, LP (1974): Culwick Choral
  Society, Eric Sweeney (cond).

Figurations (1981) gui
  Black Box Music BBM 1002, CD (1998): John Feeley.

Duo (1991) sax, pf
  Contemporary Music Centre CMC CD01, Promotion-CD (1995):
  Gerard McChrystal (sax), Kathryn Page (pf).

Joan Trimble
(* Enniskillen Co. Fermanagh 1915, † Enniskillen 2000)

Joan Trimble studied music at Trinity College Dublin (BA 1936, MusB 1937) as
well as piano and violin at the R.I.A.M. From 1937 to 1940 she studied at the
London Royal College of Music with Herbert Howells and Ralph Vaughan Williams. Since her London college days she began performing in a piano duo with

her sister Valerie and within a short time they were the most sought after duo in the British Isles, making many recordings and performances with the BBC. From 1959 to 1977 she taught accompaniment and musicianship at the Royal College of Music and then returned to her native Enniskillen to take up the family newspaper business.

Trimble's compositions were mainly written between 1937 and 1943, with a remarkable piano trio following in 1949, a *Suite for Strings* (1951) as well as the first TV-opera for the BBC, *Blind Raftery* (1957). After 1969 her next composition was a wind quintet in 1990. Trimble's music is equally strongly rooted in French impressionism and Irish traditional music and this attractive mixture has, after some time, led to a justified rediscovery, with many of her works now being available.

Recorded Works:

My Grief on the Sea (1937) v, pf
> Marco Polo 8.225059, CD (1999): Patricia Bardon (Mez), Roy Holmes (pf).

Green Rain (1938) v, pf
> Marco Polo 8.225059, CD (1999): Patricia Bardon (Mez), Roy Holmes (pf).

The Humours of Carrick (1938) 2pf
> Koch International 3-7287-2H1, CD (1994): Bruce Posner & Donald Garvelmann.
>
> Marco Polo 8.225059, CD (1999): Una Hunt & Roy Holmes.

The Bard of Lisgoole (1938) 2pf
> Koch International 3-7287-2H1, CD (1994): Bruce Posner & Donald Garvelmann.
>
> Marco Polo 8.225059, CD (1999): Una Hunt & Roy Holmes.

Buttermilk Point (1938) 2pf
> Koch International 3-7287-2H1, CD (1994): Bruce Posner & Donald Garvelmann.
>
> Marco Polo 8.225059, CD (1999): Una Hunt & Roy Holmes.

Girl's Song (1938) v, pf
> Marco Polo 8.225059, CD (1999): Patricia Bardon (Mez), Roy Holmes (pf).

Phantasy Trio (1940) vn, vc, pf
    Marco Polo 8.225059, CD (1999): Dublin Piano Trio.

Sonatina (1940) 2pf
    Koch International 3-7287-2H1, CD (1994): Bruce Posner & Donald
    Garvelmann.

    Marco Polo 8.225059, CD (1999): Una Hunt & Roy Holmes.

The Green Bough (1941) 2pf
    Koch International 3-7287-2H1, CD (1994): Bruce Posner & Donald
    Garvelmann.

    Marco Polo 8.225059, CD (1999): Una Hunt & Roy Holmes.

Pastorale (1943) 2pf
    Marco Polo 8.225059, CD (1999): Una Hunt & Roy Holmes.

The Cows are a-milking (arr. 1945) 2pf
    Marco Polo 8.225059, CD (1999): Una Hunt & Roy Holmes.

The Gartan Mother's Lullaby (arr. 1949) 2pf
    Koch International 3-7287-2H1, CD (1994): Bruce Posner & Donald
    Garvelmann.

    Marco Polo 8.225059, CD (1999): Una Hunt & Roy Holmes.

The Heather Glen (arr. 1949) 2pf
    Koch International 3-7287-2H1, CD (1994): Bruce Posner & Donald
    Garvelmann.

    Marco Polo 8.225059, CD (1999): Una Hunt & Roy Holmes.

The County Mayo (1949) Bar, 2pf
    Marco Polo 8.225059, CD (1999): Joe Corbett (Bar), Una Hunt (pf),
    Roy Holmes (pf).

Suite for Strings (1951) str-orch
    Black Box Music BBM 1003, CD (1997): Irish Chamber Orchestra,
    Fionnuala Hunt (cond).

Puck Fair (1953) 2pf
    Marco Polo 8.225059, CD (1999): Una Hunt & Roy Holmes.

Gerard Victory
(* Dublin 1921, † Dublin 1995)

Gerard Victory was one of the most versatile and prolific composers in 20th-century Ireland. He studied French, German and Celtic Studies at Trinity College Dublin (1939-42), but was active musically for a long time, studying privately with Walter Beckett (1951-3), also performing as an actor and singer in various musical theatre groups. From 1948 he filled several positions at Radio (Telefís) Éireann, being the music director from 1967 to 1982. His work-list includes more than 230 compositions, among them ten operas, four symphonies and 70 more orchestral pieces.

Victory was a strong eclecticist; there is an equal share of easy listening tonal music and of more modern music sometimes bordering on the avant-garde, especially during the 1960s. His largest work is the 90-minute requiem *Ultima Rerum* (1981), which combines his many styles in one work.

Recorded Works:

The Dreaming of the Bones (1948) fl, perc
    Argo ZRG 5469 (stereo) RG 469 (mono), LP (1965): André Prieur (fl),
    Janos Keszei (perc).

At the Hawk's Well (1949) fl, b-cl, perc
    Argo ZRG 5469 (stereo) RG 469 (mono), LP (1965): André Prieur (fl),
    David Lloyd (b-cl), Janos Keszei (perc).

An Old Woman of the Roads (1954) v, pf
    Marco Polo 8.225098, CD (1998): Bernadette Greevy (Mez), Hugh
    Tinney (pf).

The Fairy Builder (1956) orch
    Ember ERL 3319, LP (c. 1963): anonymous orchestra and conductor.

Gaelic March (1956) orch
    Ember ERL 3319, LP (c. 1963): anonymous orchestra and conductor.

The Sea King (1956) orch
    Ember ERL 3319, LP (c. 1963): anonymous orchestra and conductor.

Patrician Theme (1956) orch
    Ember ERL 3319, LP (c. 1963): anonymous orchestra and conductor.

Gaelic Galop (1956) orch
  EMI Ireland STAL (I) 1003, LP (1971): Irish Concert Orchestra,
  Éimear Ó Broin (cond).

Balladeer (1961) orch
  Ember ERL 3319, LP (c. 1963): anonymous orchestra and conductor.

Postman's Knock (1961) orch
  Ember ERL 3319, LP (c. 1963): anonymous orchestra and conductor.

Prelude and Toccata (1962) pf
  New Irish Recording Co. NIR 001, LP (1971): Charles Lynch.

String Quartet (1963) str-qu
  New Irish Recording Co. NIR 002, LP (1972): RTÉ String Quartet.

Valse Aigrette (1963) orch
  Ember ERL 3319, LP (c. 1963): anonymous orchestra and conductor.

Dilin O Deamhas (1964) satb
  Harmonia Mundi HMS 30691, LP (1965): RTÉ Singers, Waldemar
  Rosen (cond).

Resurrection (1965) 2perc
  Argo ZRG 5469 (stereo) RG 469 (mono), LP (1965): Janos Keszei &
  Friedemann Lembens.

The Cat and the Moon (1965) cl, perc, pf
  Argo ZRG 5469 (stereo) RG 469 (mono), LP (1965): Sidney Egan (cl),
  Janos Keszei (perc), Deirdre McNulty (pf).

Miroirs (1969) orch
  New Irish Recording Co. NIR 004, LP (1972): New Irish Chamber
  Orchestra, André Prieur (cond).

Jonathan Swift: A Symphonic Portrait (1970) orch
  New Irish Recording Co. NIR 011, LP (1975): RTÉ Symphony
  Orchestra, Albert Rosen (cond).

Three Irish Pictures (1980) orch
  Marco Polo 8.223804, CD (1996): RTÉ Sinfonietta, Proinnsías
  Ó Duinn (cond).

Ultima Rerum (1981) S, Mez, T, Bar, satb, children's ch, orch
> Marco Polo 8.223532-3, 2CD (1994): Virginia Kerr (S), Bernadette
> Greevy (Mez), Adrian Thompson (T), Alan Opie (Bar), RTÉ
> Philharmonic Choir, National Chamber Choir, RTÉ Cór na nÓg,
> National Symphony Orchestra of Ireland, Colman Pearce (cond).

Songs from Lyonnesse (1984) satb, pf
> Black Box Music BBM 1030, CD (2000): National Chamber Choir of
> Ireland, Colin Mawby (pf + cond).

Mayo Rhapsody (199?) brass band
> Torc Music TOLCD2, CD (1997): Band of An Garda Síochána.

Kevin Volans
(* Pietermaritzburg 1949)

Outside Ireland, Kevin Volans is known as a South African composer and he is possibly one of the better known composers in this volume. He is living in Ireland since 1986 and became an Irish citizen in 1994. He first studied at Johannesburg, then changed to Aberdeen (Scotland) and finally to Cologne, Germany, where he became the teaching assistant of Karlheinz Stockhausen (1975-6). He lived in Cologne until 1981, then returned to Durban (until 1984) and came to Ireland via Paris (1984-5). He taught at Queen's University, Belfast (1986-9), and lives near Dublin since 1992.

Volans' individual mixture of minimalism and indigenous African soundscapes has made him a popular composer in classical music terms, the CD *Pieces of Africa* by the Kronos Quartet featuring Volans' *White Man Sleeps* (1986) running high in the sales charts. His 2nd string quartet *Hunting: Gathering* (1987) was the first ever classical CD-single. His largest works are the opera *The Man with Footsoles of Wind* (1993) and the orchestral work *One Hundred Frames* (1991).

Recorded Works:

Mbira (1980) 2hpd, perc
> Landor/Barcelona DTL CD 111, CD (1991): Kevin Volans (hpd),
> Deborah James (hpd), Robyn Schulkowsky (perc).
> *Re-issued on* Cala-United CACD 88034, CD (1994).

Kneeling Dance (1982/85) 6pf
> Argo 440 294-2ZH, CD (1993): Piano Circus.

White Man Sleeps (1982) 2hpd, va da gamba, perc
Landor/Barcelona DTL CD 111, CD (1991): Kevin Volans (hpd),
Robert Hill (hpd), Margriet Tindemans (va da gamba), Robyn
Schulkowsky (perc).
Re-issued on Cala-United CACD 88034, CD (1994).

Walking Song (1984) fl, hpd, perc
Chandos CHAN 9563, CD (1997): Marieke Schneemann (fl), Menno
van Delft (hpd), Peter Prommel (perc), Rene Oussoren (perc).

Leaping Dance (1984 rev. 1996) wind orch
Chandos CHAN 9563, CD (1997): Netherlands Wind Ensemble, Wim
Steinmann (cond).

White Man Sleeps (String Quartet No. 1) (1985) str-qu
Elektra Nonesuch 79 163-2 (= CD), -1 (= LP), -4 (MC) (1987): Kronos
Quartet.
Re-issued on Elektra Nonesuch 79 171-2 (= CD), -4 (MC) (1990), and
Elektra Nonesuch 79 275-2 (= CD), -4 (MC) (1992), Elektra Nonesuch
79 504-2, 10CD (1999).

Landor/Barcelona DTL CD 111, CD (1991): Smith Quartet.
Re-issued on Cala-United CACD 88034, CD (1994).

Excerpt:
Movt. IV, arranged for 3gui:
Signum 071, CD (1996): Tilman Hoppstock, Goldau, Markert.

She who Sleeps With a Small Blanket (1986) perc
Landor/Barcelona DTL CD 111, CD (1991): Robyn Schulkowsky
(perc).
Re-issued on Cala-United CACD 88034, CD (1994).

Sony 1985B 3634, CD (1990):

Artifact ART-004, CD (1991): Arraymusic.

Hunting: Gathering (String Quartet No. 2) (1987) str-qu
Elektra Nonesuch 79253-2, CD (1991): Kronos Quartet.

Argo 440 687-2ZH, CD (1994): Balanescu Quartet.

Movement for String Quartet (1987) str-qu
Collins 14172, CD (1995): Duke Quartet.

The Songlines (String Quartet No. 3) (1988) strqu
Argo 440 687-2ZH, CD (1994): Balanescu Quartet.

The Ramanujan Notebooks (String Quartet No. 4) (1990-94) str-qu
Collins 14172, CD (1995): Duke Quartet.

This is how it is (1993 rev. 1996) wind orch
Chandos CHAN 9563, CD (1997): Netherlands Wind Ensemble, Wim
Steinmann (cond).

Dancers on a Plane (String Quartet No. 5) (1994) str-qu, tape
Collins 14172, CD (1995): Duke Quartet.

Cicada (1994) 2pf
Black Box Music BBM 1029, CD (2000): Mathilda Hornsveld & Jill
Richards.

Duets (1995) 2pf, tape
Black Box Music BBM 1029, CD (2000): Kevin Volans & Matteo
Fargion.

Concerto for Piano and Wind Instruments (1995) pf, wind orch
Chandos CHAN 9563, CD (1997): Peter Donohoe (pf), Netherlands
Wind Ensemble, Daniel Harding (cond).

Untitled (1996) pf, wind orch
Chandos CHAN 9563, CD (1997): Kevin Volans (pf), Netherlands
Wind Ensemble, Wim Steinmann (cond).

(William) Vincent Wallace
(* Waterford 1812, † Chateau de Haget 1865)

The Irishmen Michael William Balfe and Vincent Wallace were the most
successful composers of English-language operas in the 19th century. Wallace's
adventurous life did not leave him much room for composition – he only wrote
seven operas, the most popular being *Maritana* (1845) and *Lurline* (1847). He
emigrated to Tasmania in 1835 and further to Sydney, Australia, in 1836, where
he led an active musical life. He left Australia in bankruptcy and after 1838
travelled to Chile, Argentina, Peru, Jamaica, Cuba, reaching Mexico City in
1841, then further to New Orleans, Philadelphia (1842), Boston (1843) and New
York, before he went on to London in 1845. He continued his travels in later

years, marrying in New York for a second time. His travels did affect his music and Wallace was to first to introduce South American flair into European opera. Otherwise his music sounds vaguely like Donizetti or early Verdi, albeit with worse libretti and less drama.

Recorded Works:

Maritana (1845) opera
> Marco Polo 8.223406-7, 2CD (1996): Majella Cullagh (S), Lynda Lee (Mez), Paul Charles Clarke (T), Ian Caddy (Bar), Damien Smith (Bar), Quentin Hayes (B), RTÉ Philharmonic Choir, RTÉ Concert Orchestra, Proinnsías Ó Duinn (cond).
> *Re-issued on* Naxos 8.554080-1, 2CD (1996).

> Excerpts:
> *Overture*
> Decca SXL 6235 (stereo), LXT 6235 (mono), LP (1966): London Symphony Orchestra, Richard Bonynge (cond).

> *Overture; In Happy Moments; Yes, let me like a Soldier fall; Scenes that are the Brightest*
> EMI CSD 3651, LP (1968): Veronica Dunne (S), Uel Deane (T), Eric Hinds (Bar), unnamed orchestra, Havelock Nelson (cond).

> *Scenes that are the Brightest; 'Tis the Harp in the Air*
> Melba 301082, CD (2000): Deborah Riedel (S), Australian Opera and Ballet Orchestra, Richard Bonynge (cond).

> *There is a Flower that Bloometh*
> Symposium 1163, CD (1996, recorded 1908): John McCormack (T), anonymous orchestra.

> *Yes, let me like a Soldier fall*
> Pearl Gemm CD 9319, CD (1989, recorded 1931): Heddle Nash (T), anonymous orchestra.

> Claremont CDGSE 78-50-46, CD (1992, recorded 1930)): Walter Widdop (T), anonymous orchestra, Lawrance Collingwood (cond).

Lurline (1847) opera
> Excerpts:
> *The Naiad's Spell; The Night Winds*
> Melba 301082, CD (2000): Deborah Riedel (S), Australian Opera and Ballet Orchestra, Richard Bonynge (cond).

The Amber Witch (1861) opera
> Excerpt:
> *My long Hair is Braided*
> Melba 301082, CD (2000): Deborah Riedel (S), Australian Opera and
> Ballet Orchestra, Richard Bonynge (cond).

Love's Triumph (1862) opera
> Excerpt:
> *These Withered Flowers*
> Melba 301082, CD (2000): Deborah Riedel (S), Australian Opera and
> Ballet Orchestra, Richard Bonynge (cond).

Ian Wilson
(* Belfast 1964)

Of the younger generation of Irish composers Ian Wilson is certainly the most
successful so far. His music is published by Universal Edition and several of his
chamber pieces have been recorded on CD. Wilson studied at the University of
Ulster at Jordanstown and received a doctorate for his orchestral score *Running,
Thinking, Finding* (1989), which was the key work to his early fame. In 1992 he
received the Macauley Fellowship and in 1998 was elected to Aosdána, Ireland's
academy of the arts. His music has been played at many Irish and international
music festivals. Wilson's largest works have been the organ concerto *Rich
Harbour* (1995) and two violin concertos (both 1999).

> Wilson's music is characterised by strong contrasts. He does not dismiss
diatonic, even pastoral writing, but may also sound harsh and dissonant. Much
of his inspiration stems from his deeply felt Christianity.

Recorded Works:

Timelessly This (1992) fl/cl, vn, vc, pf
> Contemporary Music Centre CMC CD02, promotion-CD (1997):
> Concorde.

Winter's Edge (1992) str-qu
> Chandos CHAN 9295, CD (1994): Vanbrugh Quartet.
>
> Black Box Music BBM 1031, CD (2000): Vanbrugh Quartet.

The Capsizing Man and Other Stories (1994) str-qu
> Black Box Music BBM 1031, CD (2000): Vanbrugh Quartet.

The Seven Last Words (Piano Trio No. 2) (1995) vn, vc, pf
Timbre Records DMHCD 4, CD (1997): Kammerspiel.

Towards the Far Country (1996) str-qu
Black Box Music BBM 1031, CD (2000): Vanbrugh Quartet.

Six Days at Jericho (1996) vc, pf
Timbre Records DMHCD 4, CD (1997): Robin T. Clarke (vc), Paul Bateman (pf).

I Sleep at Waking (1995) alto sax
Silva Classics SILKD 6010, CD (1996): Gerard McChrystal.

Catalan Tales (Piano Trio No. 3) (1996) vn, vc, pf
Timbre Records DMHCD 4, CD (1997): Kammerspiel.

James Wilson
(* London 1922)

James Wilson was born in London, studied for two years with Alec Rowley at Trinity College of Music, London, and came to live in Ireland in 1948. His first step to fame was the children's opera *The Hunting of the Snark* (1963), the culmination of an early work phase in tonal styles. He later embraced more adventurous playing techniques and a more contemporary musical language. For a long time he was one of the most productive composers in Ireland. He taught composition at the Royal Irish Academy of Music (1969-80) and in 1983 co-founded the Ennis Summer School for composition. He was one of the directors of the Irish Music Rights Organisation (1982-92). His deep interest in music theatre resulted in seven large-scale operas. Other large scores include two symphonies, concertos for violin, viola (*Menorah*, 1989), piano, clarinet and a triple concerto for violin, viola and cello, the *Concerto for Sarajevo* (1996).

Recorded Works:

Thermagistris op. 29 (1968) pf
New Irish Recording Co. NIR 001, LP (1971): Charles Lynch.

Capricci op. 33 (1969) pf
Goasco GXX 003-4, MC (1985): Nicholas O'Halloran.

Upon Silence (1972) S
    Altarus AIR-CD-9010, CD (1996): Penelope Price Jones.

Arlecchino op. 75a (1979) fl
    Association of Irish Composers AIC 001, Promotion-CD (1999): Anne
    O Briain.

Pearl and Unicorn op. 120 (1989) vn, orch
    Marco Polo 8.225027, CD (2000): Alan Smale (vn), National
    Symphony Orchestra of Ireland, Colman Pearce (cond).

Menorah op. 122 (1989) va, orch
    Marco Polo 8.225027, CD (2000): Constantin Zanidache (va), National
    Symphony Orchestra of Ireland, Colman Pearce (cond).

Concertino op. 137 (1992) orch
    Marco Polo 8.225027, CD (2000): National Symphony Orchestra of
    Ireland, Colman Pearce (cond).

For Cliodhna (1992) vc
    Contemporary Music Centre CMC CD02, Promotion-CD (1997): David
    James.

Charles Wood
(* Armagh 1866, † Cambridge 1926)

Charles Wood stood for most of his life in the shadow of Charles V. Stanford, with whom he studied at the Royal College of Music and whose teaching duties at Cambridge were taken over by Wood. Only after Stanford's death did Wood become professor at Cambridge for the remaining two years of his life. Though living in England, Wood preserved a lively interest in Ireland and in 1904 co-founded the Irish Folk-Song-Society of London. Several of his chamber works and songs use Irish material. Wood, however, is mainly remembered as a fine composer for the church and together with Stanford is the most often played composer in the Church of England. This is reflected in his discography, which mainly concentrates on his liturgical music and does not quite represent his real work-list, in which his eight string quartets stand out.

Recorded Works:

O Lord, Rebuke Me Not (c. 1885) satb
  Priory PRCD 754, CD (2001): Gonville and Caius College Cambridge
  Choir, Geoffrey Webber (cond).

If Love be Dead (1886) satb
  Priory PRCD 622, CD (1998): National Youth Choir of Great Britain,
  Michael Brewer (cond).

Full Fathom Five (1891) satb
  Somm Recordings SOMM CD 204, CD (1995): Canzonetta, Jeffrey
  Wynn-Davies (cond).

  Priory PRCD 622, CD (1998): National Youth Choir of Great Britain,
  Robert Isaacs (cond).

I will arise (1894) satb, org
  Priory Records PRCD 484, CD (1995): Blackburn Cathedral Choir,
  David Goodenough (org), David Cooper (cond).

This Joyful Eastertide (1895) satb
  Word UK WST 9636 (= LP), WC 9636 (= MC) (1984): Cambridge
  Singers, John Rutter (cond).

  Alpha ACA 556, LP (1986): The Abbey Singers, Andrew Seivewright
  (cond).

  Collegium COLCD 107 (= CD), COLC 107 (= MC) (1988): Cambridge
  Singers, John Rutter (cond).
  Re-issued on Collegium CSCD 500 (= CD) and CSC 500 (= MC)
  (1993?).

  Hyperion CDA 66916, CD (1997): St. Paul's Cathedral Choir, John
  Scott (cond).

The Widow Bird (1896) satb
  Priory PRCD 622, CD (1998): National Youth Choir of Great Britain,
  Robert Isaacs (cond).

Magnificat and Nunc Dimittis in D (1897-8) satb, org
  Priory PRCD 554 (= CD), PRC 554 (= MC) (1996): St. Edmondsbury
  Cathedral Choir, Scott Farrell (org), Mervyn Cousins (cond).

Nights of Music (1899) satb
> Priory PRCD 622, CD (1998): National Youth Choir of Great Britain,
> Michael Brewer (cond).

Nunc dimittis in c (1900) satb, org
> Priory Records PRCD 484, CD (1995): Blackburn Cathedral Choir,
> David Goodenough (org), David Cooper (cond).

As the Moon's Soft Splendour (1905) satb
> Priory PRCD 622, CD (1998): National Youth Choir of Great Britain,
> Michael Brewer (cond).

I Will Call upon God (1905) satb
> Priory PRCD 754, CD (2001): Gonville and Caius College Cambridge
> Choir, Geoffrey Webber (cond).

The Whispering Waves (1905) satb
> Priory PRCD 622, CD (1998): National Youth Choir of Great Britain,
> Michael Brewer (cond).

How Sweet the Tuneful Bells (1906) satb
> Priory PRCD 622, CD (1998): National Youth Choir of Great Britain,
> Michael Brewer (cond).

There Comes a New Moon (c. 1907) male v choir
> EMI EL 749 765-1 (= LP), -4 (= MC) CDC7 49765-2 (= CD) (1988):
> The King's Singers.

Magnificat and Nunc Dimittis in F (1907-8) satb, org
> Hyperion A 66249 (= LP), KA 66249 (= MC), CDA 66249 (= CD)
> (1988): St. Paul's Cathedral Choir, Christopher Dearnley (org), John
> Scott (cond).

Come, Sleep (1908) satb
> Priory PRCD 622, CD (1998): National Youth Choir of Great Britain,
> Robert Isaacs (cond).

Music When Soft Voices Die (1908) satb
> Priory PRCD 622, CD (1998): National Youth Choir of Great Britain,
> Michael Brewer (cond).

The Nymph's Fawn (1908) ssaa
> Priory PRCD 622, CD (1998): National Youth Choir of Great Britain,
> Michael Brewer (cond).

King Jesus Hath a Garden (before 1910) satb
    Alpha ACA 556, LP (1986): The Abbey Singers, Andrew Seivewright (cond).

Glorious and Powerful God (1910) satb, org
    Argo 421 218-1ZH (LP), -4ZH (= MC), -2ZH (= CD) (1988): Massed Choirs of the RSCM, Martin How (org), Michael Laird (cond).

String Quartet in a (1911) str-qu
    ASV DCA 879, CD (1993): The Lindsays.

Sixteen Preludes Founded on Melodies from the English and Scottish Psalters (1911-2) org
        Excerpts:
    Martyrs
            Priory PRCD 754, CD (2001): Timothy Uglow.

    Nunc Dimittis
            ASV DCA 702, CD (1990): Jane Parker-Smith.

    Old 104th Psalm
            Priory PRCD 754, CD (2001): Timothy Uglow.

    Old 132th Psalm
            Priory PRCD 754, CD (2001): Timothy Uglow.

    Old 136th Psalm
            Alpha ACA 556, LP (1985): Andrew Shaw.

            Priory PRCD 754, CD (2001): Timothy Uglow.

    Psalm 23
            Priory PRCD 754, CD (2001): Timothy Uglow.

    St. Mary's
            HMV CSD 3678, LP (1970): Philip Marshall.

            Hyperion A 66180 (= LP), KA 66180 (= MC), CDA 66180 (= CD) (1986): Jennifer Bate.

            Motette 10911 (= CD), M 10915 (= MC) (1989): Christopher Dearnley.

            Priory Records PRCD 484, CD (1995): David Goodenough.

Guild GMCD 7122, CD (1996): Francis Jackson.

York

Alpha ACA 556, LP (1986): Andrew Shaw.

Priory Records PRCD 484, CD (1995): David Goodenough.

Guild GMCD 7122, CD (1996): Francis Jackson.

Priory PRCD 754, CD (2001): Timothy Uglow.

Hail, Gladdening Light (c. 1912) satb
Saga 5368, LP (1973, recorded 1964): Magdalen College Oxford Choir
(no conductor mentioned in catalogue).

HMV CSD 3752 (stereo), Q4CSD 3752 (quadraphonic), LP (1974):
King's College Cambridge Choir (no conductor mentioned in
catalogue).

Alpha ACA 556, LP (1986): The Abbey Singers, Andrew Shaw (org),
Andrew Seivewright (cond).

ASV CDQS 6019 (= CD), ZCQS 6019 (= MC) (1988): Christ Church
Cathedral Oxford Choir, Francis Grier (org + cond).

Hyperion CDA 66374 (= CD) KA 66374 (= MC) (1990): St. Paul's
Cathedral Choir, John Scott (cond).

EMI Eminence EMX 2161 (= CD), TC-EMC 2161 (= MC) (1990):
Vasari Singers, Jeremy Backhouse (cond).

Classics for Pleasure CFP CD-CFP 4570 (= CD), TC-CFP 4570 (= MC)
(1990): King's College Cambridge Choir, David Willcocks (cond).

Abbey CDCA 913, CD (1991): Magdalen College Oxford Choir, John
Harper (cond).

Collegium COLCD 113 (= CD), COLC 113 (= LP) (1992): Cambridge
Singers, John Rutter (cond).

EMI CDC7 54418-2, CD (1993): King's College Cambridge Choir,
Stephen Cleobury (cond).

Conifer CDCF 219 (= CD), MCFC 219 (= MC) (1993): Trinity College Cambridge Choir, Richard Marlow (cond).

Priory PRCD 435 (= CD), PRC 435 (= MC) (1993): Southwark Cathedral Choir, Peter Wright (cond).

Mirabilis MMSCD 4, CD (1994): Queen's College Cambridge Choir, Ralph Woodward (cond).

Meridian CDE 84276, CD (1995, recorded in 1980s): Ely Cathedral Choir, Stephen le Prevost (org), Arthur Wills (cond).

Collegium COLCD 125, CD (1999): Clare College Cambridge Choir, Timothy Brown (cond).

Glory and Honour and Laud (c. 1912) satb
Saga 5368, LP (1973, recorded 1964): Magdalen College Oxford Choir (no conductor mentioned in catalogue).

Alpha ACA 556, LP (1986): The Abbey Singers, Andrew Seivewright (cond).

Hyperion CDA 66758, CD (1995): St. Paul's Cathedral Choir, John Scott (cond).

O King Most High (c. 1912) satb
Priory PRCD 754, CD (2001): Gonville and Caius College Cambridge Choir, Geoffrey Webber (cond).

Father all-holy (1912) satb
Priory Records PRCD 484, CD (1995): Blackburn Cathedral Choir, David Cooper (cond).

'Tis the Day of Resurrection (1912) satb
Saga 5368, LP (1973, recorded 1964): Magdalen College Oxford Choir (no conductor mentioned in catalogue).

Priory Records PRCD 484, CD (1995): Blackburn Cathedral Choir, David Cooper (cond).

Hyperion CDA 66826, CD (1996): St. Paul's Cathedral Choir, John Scott (cond).

Priory PRCD 639, CD (1999): Christ Church Cathedral Dublin Choir, Mark Duley (cond).

Priory PRCD 754, CD (2001): Gonville and Caius College Cambridge Choir, Geoffrey Webber (cond).

Great Lord of Lords (1912) male ch
Priory PRCD 351 (= CD), PRC 351 (= MC) (1992): Norwich Cathedral Choir, Michael Nicholas (cond).

Priory PRCD 484, CD (1995): Blackburn Cathedral Choir, David Cooper (cond).

When Winds that Move Not (1913) attb
EMI EL 749 765-1 (= LP), -4 (= MC) CDC7 49765-2 (= CD) (1988): The King's Singers.

Priory PRCD 622, CD (1998): National Youth Choir of Great Britain, Robert Isaacs (cond).

True Love's the Gift (1914) satb
Priory PRCD 754, CD (2001): Gonville and Caius College Cambridge Choir, Geoffrey Webber (cond).

O Thou the Central Orb (1915) satb, org
Alpha ACA 556, LP (1986): The Abbey Singers, Andrew Shaw (org), Andrew Seivewright (cond).

Priory PRCD 257 (= CD), PRC 257 (= MC) (1989): Guildford Cathedral Choir, Peter Wright (org), Andrew Millington (cond).

Abbey CDCA 913, CD (1991): Magdalen College Oxford Choir, Michael Stoddart (org), John Harper (cond).

Abbey CDCA 922, CD (1992): Giggleswick School Choir, Timothy Harvey (org), Peter Read (cond).

Hyperion CDA 66678 (= CD), KA 66678 (= MC) (1994): St. Paul's Cathedral Choir, Andrew Lucas (org), John Scott (cond).

Mirabilis MMSCD 4, CD (1994): Queen's College Cambridge Choir, Andrew Linn (org), Ralph Woodward (cond).

Nimbus NI 5440, CD (1995): Christ Church Cathedral Oxford Choir, Stephen Farr (org), Stephen Darlington (cond).

Carlton Classics 30366 00532, CD (1996): Christ's Hospital Choir, Mark Wardell (org), Peter Allwood (cond).

Priory PRCD 586, CD (1997): Marlborough Chapel Choir, Christopher Rathbone (org), Robin Nelson (cond).

Evening Service in F (Collegium Regale) (1915) satb, org
Saga 5368, LP (1973, recorded 1964): Magdalen College Oxford Choir (no conductor mentioned in catalogue).

Hyperion A 66249 (= LP), KA 66249 (= MC), CDA 66249 (= CD) (1988): St. Paul's Cathedral Choir, Christopher Dearnley (org), John Scott (cond).

Priory PRCD 484 (= CD), PRC 484 (= MC) (1995): Blackburn Cathedral Choir, David Goodenough (org), David Cooper (cond).

Priory PRCD 632, CD (1999): Peterborough Cathedral Choir, Mark Duthie (org), Christopher Gower (cond).

Suite in the Ancient Style (c. 1915) org
Excerpts:
Bourrée I and II
Priory PRCD 569, CD (1999): Ian le Grice.

Summer ended (1917) satb, org
Priory Records PRCD 484, CD (1995): Blackburn Cathedral Choir, David Goodenough (org), David Cooper (cond).

Magnificat and Nunc Dimittis in E flat no. 2 (1918) satb, org
Alpha ACA 556, LP (1986): The Abbey Singers, Andrew Shaw (org), Andrew Seivewright (cond).

Priory PRCD 553, CD (1997): Truro Cathedral Choir, Simon Morley (org), Andrew Nethsingha (cond).

Expectans expectavi (1919) satb, org
Alpha ACA 556, LP (1986): The Abbey Singers, Andrew Shaw (org), Andrew Seivewright (cond).

EMI Eminence EMX 2161 (= CD), TC-EMC 2161 (= MC) (1990): Vasari Singers, Ian Curror (org), Jeremy Backhouse (cond).

Abbey CDCA 913, CD (1991): Magdalen College Oxford Choir, Michael Stoddart (org), John Harper (cond).

Hyperion A 66618 (= LP), KA 666618 (= MC), CDA 66618 (= CD) (1993): St. Paul's Cathedral Choir, Andrew Lucas (org), John Scott (cond).

Mirabilis MMSCD 4, CD (1994): Queen's College Cambridge Choir, Andrew Linn (org), Ralph Woodward (cond).

Priory PRCD 429 (= CD), PRC 429 (= MC) (1994): Truro Cathedral Choir, Simon Morley (org), David Briggs (cond).

Priory PRCD 484, CD (1995): Blackburn Cathedral Choir, David Goodenough (org), David Cooper (cond).

Priory PRCD 754, CD (2001): Gonville and Caius College Cambridge Choir, Gavin Roberts (org), Geoffrey Webber (cond).

Haec Dies (1919) satb
   Priory PRCD 484, CD (1995): Blackburn Cathedral Choir, David Cooper (cond).

   Priory PRCD 754, CD (2001): Gonville and Caius College Cambridge Choir, Geoffrey Webber (cond).

O Lord that Seest from Yon Starry Height (1919) satb, org
   Priory PRCD 754, CD (2001): Gonville and Caius College Cambridge Choir, Gavin Roberts (org), Geoffrey Webber (cond).

Sunlight All Golden (1919) ssaa, pf/org
   Priory PRCD 754, CD (2001): Gonville and Caius College Cambridge Choir, Gavin Roberts (org), Geoffrey Webber (cond).

The Passion of our Lord according to St. Mark (1920) vv, satb, org
   ASV DCA 854, CD (1993): William Kendall (T), Peter Harvey (B), Paul Robinson (v), Kwamé Ryan (v), Richard Hill (org), Gonville and Caius College Cambridge Choir, Geoffrey Webber (cond).

   Excerpts:
   Part 1

Alpha ACA 556, LP (1986): Anthony Peacock (T), James Johnson (B), The Abbey Singers, Andrew Shaw (org), Elizabeth Lamb (cond).

Short Communion Service in the Phrygian Mode (1923) satb
Excerpts:
Sanctus; Benedictus
HMV HQS 1350, LP (1966): Chichester Cathedral Choir (no conductor mentioned in catalogue).

Kyrie; Gloria; Sanctus; Benedictus; Agnus Dei
Priory PRCD 341 (= CD), PRC 341 (= MC) (1991): Wakefield Cathedral Choir, Jonathan Bielby (cond).

Four Antiphons (1926?) satb, org
Priory PRCD 754, CD (2001): Gonville and Caius College Cambridge Choir, Timothy Uglow (org), Geoffrey Webber (cond).

How Dear to Me (1926) ttbb
Priory PRCD 622, CD (1998): National Youth Choir of Great Britain, Robert Isaacs (cond).

Magnificat and Nunc Dimittis in G (pubd. 1926) satb, org
Priory PRCD 555, CD (1996): Ripon Cathedral Choir, Robert Marsh (org), Kerry Beaumont (cond).

Priory PRCD 592, CD (1998): Ely Cathedral Choir, David Price (org), Paul Trepte (cond).

A Clear Midnight (pubd. 1926) ttbb
Priory PRCD 622, CD (1998): National Youth Choir of Great Britain, Robert Isaacs (cond).

Ascension Hymn (pubd. 1927) satb, org
Priory PRCD 754, CD (2001): Gonville and Caius College Cambridge Choir, Timothy Uglow (org), Geoffrey Webber (cond).

Jesu, the Very Thought is Sweet (pubd. 1927) satb
Alpha ACA 556, LP (1986): The Abbey Singers, Andrew Seivewright (cond).

Magnificat and Nunc Dimittis in C (pubd. 1927) satb, org
Priory PRCD 664, CD (1999): Keble College Oxford Chapel Choir, Stephen Bullamore (org), Philip Stopford (cond).

Magnificat in E flat no. 2 (pubd. 1927) satb, org
>Priory PRCD 484 (= CD), PRC 484 (= MC) (1995): Blackburn
>Cathedral Choir, David Goodenough (org), David Cooper (cond).

God Omnipotent Reigneth (pubd. 1927) satb, org
>Priory PRCD 484 (= CD), PRC 484 (= MC) (1995): Blackburn
>Cathedral Choir, David Goodenough (org), David Cooper (cond).

>Priory PRCD 754, CD (2001): Gonville and Caius College Cambridge
>Choir, Gavin Roberts (org), Geoffrey Webber (cond).

Jesu, the Very Thought is Sweet (pubd. 1927) satb
>Priory PRCD 754, CD (2001): Gonville and Caius College Cambridge
>Choir, Geoffrey Webber (cond).

Two Introits: O Most Merciful + Oculi Omnium (pubd. 1927) satb, org
>Priory PRCD 484 (= CD), PRC 484 (= MC) (1995): Blackburn
>Cathedral Choir, David Goodenough (org), David Cooper (cond).

>Excerpt:
>*O Most Merciful*
>Priory PRCD 754, CD (2001): Gonville and Caius College Cambridge
>Choir, Gavin Roberts (org), Geoffrey Webber (cond).

Song for a Dance (pubd. 1927) satb
>Priory PRCD 622, CD (1998): National Youth Choir of Great Britain,
>Michael Brewer (cond).

When thou art Nigh (pubd. 1927) ttbb
>Priory PRCD 622, CD (1998): National Youth Choir of Great Britain,
>Robert Isaacs (cond).

Hence Away, Begone! (pubd. 1929) satb
>Priory PRCD 622, CD (1998): National Youth Choir of Great Britain,
>Robert Isaacs (cond).

O thou Sweetest Source (pubd. 1931) satb, org
>Priory PRCD 754, CD (2001): Gonville and Caius College Cambridge
>Choir, Gavin Roberts (org), Geoffrey Webber (cond).

Prelude and Fugue (pubd. 1933) org
>Priory PRCD 484 (= CD), PRC 484 (= MC) (1995): David
>Goodenough.

An Easter Carol (not dated) satb
>> Priory PRCD 484 (= CD), PRC 484 (= MC) (1995): Blackburn
>> Cathedral Choir, David Cooper (cond).

Richard Woodward
(* Dublin c. 1744, † Dublin 1777)

The early death of Richard Woodward undoubtedly deprived Irish music of one
her most talented musicians. He was a choir boy at Christ Church, Dublin, from
1751 and was appointed organist in 1765. In 1771 he published a collection of
church music, on the basis of which he was awarded a doctorate from Trinity
College. His very recent discography consists of anthems and psalm settings.

Recorded Works:

Veni Creator Spiritus (1767) satb, org
>> Priory PRCD 639, CD (1999): Christ Church Cathedral Dublin Choir,
>> Andrew Johnstone (org), Mark Duley (cond).

Sing O ye Heavens (1771) satb, org
>> Christ Church Cathedral Recording / Four Courts Press CCCD1, CD
>> (1999): Christ Church Cathedral Dublin Choir, David Adams (org),
>> Mark Duley (cond).

O Lord God, to whom Vengeance belongeth (Psalm 94) (17??) satb, org
>> Hyperion CDP 11008, CD (1998): St. Paul's Cathedral Choir, Andrew
>> Lucas (org), John Scott (cond).

I will give thanks unto the Lord (Psalm 111) (17??) satb, org
>> Hyperion CDP 11009, CD (1999): St. Paul's Cathedral Choir, Huw
>> Williams (org), John Scott (cond).

I was Glad (Psalm 122) (17??) satb, org
>> EMI CDM5 66784-2, CD (1999): King's College Cambridge Choir,
>> David Willcocks (org + cond).

PART II

Recorded "Irish" Music by Non-Irish Composers

Note: Part II is meant to demonstrate the breadth of Irish influence internationally; it does not aim at completeness. Instead it concentrates on CDs, many of which are still available.

Leroy Anderson
(* Cambridge, Massachusetts 1908, † Woodbury, Connecticut 1975)

Leroy Anderson studied with George Enescu and Walter Piston at Harvard University (1926-30) and worked in Boston and New York as an arranger (1935-42). He then developed a talent for light, entertaining orchestral music and his *Irish Suite* is one such example – a potpourri of Irish favorites for an American audience.

Recorded "Irish" Work:

Irish Suite (1947) orch
> Naxos International 8.990018, CD (1990): Richard Hayman and His Symphony Orchestra.

> Mercury 434 376 MM, CD (1995, recorded 1956): Eastman-Rochester Pops Orchestra, Frederick Fennell (cond).

> Excerpts:
> *The Irish Washerwoman + The Rakes of Mallow*
> K-Tel Celtic Collections CCD 135, CD (1999): RTÉ Concert Orchestra, (no conductor named).

Malcolm Arnold
(* Northampton 1921)

Arnold studied with Gordon Jacob at the Royal College of Music, London. In 1941 he joined the London Philharmonic Orchestra as a trumpeter leaving in 1948 to devote his time fully to composition. A brilliant orchestrator, Arnold's music is mainly light-weight, but with a profound sense for drama and effect.

Recorded "Irish" Work:

Four Irish Dances op. 126 (1986) orch
   Chandos CHAN 8867 (=CD), ABTD 1482 (= MC) (1990):
   Philharmonia Orchestra, Bryden Thomson (cond).

   Lyrita SRCD 201, CD (1990): London Philharmonic Orchestra,
   Malcolm Arnold (cond).

   Naxos 8.553526, CD (1996): Queensland Symphony Orchestra,
   Andrew Penny (cond)

Arnold Bax
(* Streatham 1883, † Cork 1953)

Arnold Bax regretted more than once not to have Irish blood in his veins, and indeed he would have served Irish music well. He studied at the Royal Academy of Music, London (1900-5), when he came under influence of the poetical works of W. B. Yeats. He owned a house in Rathgar, Dublin, from 1905 to 1914 and strongly identified with Celtic Irish culture – he even published some widely respected Irish short stories using the pseudonym Dermot O'Byrne. His early tone poems for orchestra were all shaped by his Celtic type of impressionism and several of his later works take up elements of Irish folklore, musical or otherwise. His largest works are the seven symphonies (1922-39) and he has written in many genres, excluding opera. It was on one of his adjudication journeys to musical competitions in Ireland that he died in the house of the Irish composer Aloys Fleischmann.

Recorded "Irish" Works:

A Celtic Song Cycle (1904) v, pf
   Centaur CRC 2075, CD (1990): Ellen Frohnmayer (S), Philip
   Frohnmayer (Bar), Logan Skelton (pf).

Cathaleen-ni-Hoolihan (1905) orch
>   Chandos CHAN 9879, CD (2001): BBC Philharmonic, Martyn
>   Brabbins (cond).

Into the Twilight (1908) orch
>   Chandos ABRD 1133 (=LP), ABTD (= MC), CHAN 8367 (= CD)
>   (1985): Ulster Orchestra, Bryden Thomson (cond).

In the Faery Hills (1909) orch
>   Chandos ABRD 1133 (=LP), ABTD (= MC), CHAN 8367 (= CD)
>   (1985): Ulster Orchestra, Bryden Thomson (cond).
>   *Re-issued on* Chandos CHAN 6525, CD (1991).

Rosc-Catha (1910) orch
>   Chandos ABRD 1133 (=LP), ABTD (= MC), CHAN 8367 (= CD)
>   (1985): Ulster Orchestra, Bryden Thomson (cond).
>   *Re-issued on* Chandos CHAN 6525, CD (1991).

To Éire (1910) v, pf
>   Continuum CCD 1046, CD (1993): Patricia Wright (S), Rosemary
>   Barnes (pf).

The Pleasant Plain: an Irish Tone Poem (1917) 2pf
>   Cabaletta CON 5002, LP (1984, recorded early 1970s): Frank Merrick
>   & Michael Round.

Five Irish Songs (1921) v, pf
>   Excerpts:
>   *I Heard a Piper Piping* (1921) v, pf
>   Continuum CCD 1046, CD (1993): Patricia Wright (S), Rosemary
>   Barnes (pf).
>
>   Forlane 16784, CD (1998): Ann Murray (Mez), Graham Johnson (pf).

Three Irish Songs (1922) v, pf
>   Excerpts:
>   *Cradle Song*
>   Simax PSC 1824, CD (1996, recorded 1954): Kirsten Flagstad (S),
>   Waldemar Alme (pf).
>
>   *Rann of Exile*
>   Continuum CCD 1046, CD (1993): Christopher Keyte (B), Rosemary
>   Barnes (pf).

Irish Landscape (from *Three Pieces*) (1928) orch
    Lyrita SCRS 99, LP (1978): Royal Philharmonic Orchestra, Vernon
    Handley (cond).

    EMI CDC7 47945-2 (= CD), EL 270592-1 (= LP), EL 270592-4 (=
    MC) (1987): English Chamber Orchestra, Jeffrey Tate (cond).

Amy Marcy Beach

(* Henniker, New Hampshire 1867, † New York 1944)

Amy Beach was a pianist and composer, the first American woman composer to
succeed with large-scale art music. As a pianist she toured Europe in 1911-14.
She spent many summers in the MacDowell Colony and came under the influence of MacDowell and Debussy. When she used folk music elements as a
melodic or harmonic basis she preferred Irish material since she considered this
the most important ingredient of American folk music.

Recorded "Irish" Works:

Symphony in e 'Gaelic' op. 32 (1896) orch
    Chandos CHAN 8958, CD (1991): Detroit Symphony Orchestra,
    Neeme Järvi (cond).

    Bridge 9086, CD (1999, recorded 1968): Royal Philharmonic
    Orchestra, Karl Krueger (cond).

Suite for two Pianos founded upon old Irish Melodies op. 104 (1924) 2pf
    Koch International 3-7254-2H1, CD (1995): Virginia Eskin & Kathleen
    Supove.

Ludwig van Beethoven

(* Bonn 1770, † Vienna 1827)

Beethoven is certainly one of the best-known classical composers of all time and
possibly the popular prototype of musical genius. After his education and early
musical experiences at Bonn, Germany, he settled in Vienna in 1792. He is best
known for his nine symphonies, five piano concertos, 17 string quartets and

piano music. It is lesser known, however, that his most often employed genre was folk music arrangements and that, among these, Irish songs formed the majority. He arranged the Irish melodies for the Scottish publisher George Thomson and the words were commissioned by Thomson from various English and Scottish poets of his day. There is a complete recording of all of Beethoven's folk-song settings on a 7CD-Box with Deutsche Grammophon and a number of others scattered among different recordings.

Recorded "Irish" Works:

Irish Songs I (1814) (later listed as *Twenty-five Irish Songs*, WoO 152, and *Twenty Irish Songs*, WoO 153, 1-4) v, vn, vc, pf
> Deutsche Grammophon 453 786-2, 7CD (1997): Felicity Lott (S), Ann Murray (Mez), John Mark Ainsley (T), Christopher Maltman (Bar), Thomas Allen (Bar), Marieke Blankestijn (vn), Elizabeth Layton (vn), Ursula Smith (vc), Malcolm Martineau (pf).

> Excerpts:
> WoO 152, No. 1: *The Return to Ulster*
>> Channel Classics CCS 1491, CD (1990): Marjanne Kweksilber (S), Vera Beths (vn), Anner Bijlsma (vc), Stanley Hoogland (pf).

>> Philips 442 784-2PH, CD (1998): Wolfgang Holzmair (Bar), Fontenay Trio.

> WoO 152, No. 2: *Sweet Power of Song*
>> EMI CDC7 49930-2 (= CD), EL 749930-4 (= MC) (1990): Felicity Lott (S), Ann Murray (Mez), Galina Solodchin (vn), Jonathan Williams (vc), Graham Johnson (pf).
>> *Re-issued on* HMV Classics 5 73043 2, CD (1998).

>> Berlin Classics 0091322BC, 3CD (1996, recorded 1976-7): Renate Krahmer (S), Ingeborg Springer (Mez), Brahms Trio.

> WoO 152, No. 5: *On the Massacre of Glencoe*
>> Channel Classics CCS 1491, CD (1990): Marjanne Kweksilber (S), Vera Beths (vn), Anner Bijlsma (vc), Stanley Hoogland (pf).

>> Berlin Classics 0091322BC, 3CD (1996, recorded 1976-7): Siegfried Lorenz (Bar), Brahms Trio.

>> Philips 442 784-2PH, CD (1998): Wolfgang Holzmair (Bar), Fontenay Trio.

WoO 152, No. 6: *What Shall I Do to Shew How Much I Love Her?*
Berlin Classics 0091322BC, 3CD (1996, recorded 1976-7):
Eberhard Büchner (T), Siegfried Lorenz (Bar), Brahms Trio.

WoO 152, No. 7: His Boat Comes on the Sunny Tide
Sony Classical SK 64301, CD (1995): Carolyn Watkinson
(Mez), Christian Altenburger (vn), Julius Berger (vc), Helmut
Deutsch (pf).

WoO 152, No. 8: *Come Draw We Round a Cheerful Ring*
Channel Classics CCS 1491, CD (1990): Marjanne Kweksilber
(S), Vera Beths (vn), Anner Bijlsma (vc), Stanley Hoogland
(pf).

Alienor AL 1065, CD (1991): Mario Hacquard (Bar), Franck
della Valle (vn), Frederic Deville (vc), Claude Collet (pf).

Sony Classical SK 64301, CD (1995): Josef Protschka (T),
Christian Altenburger (vn), Julius Berger (vc), Helmut Deutsch
(pf).

Berlin Classics 0091322BC, 3CD (1996, recorded 1976-7):
Siegfried Lorenz (Bar), Brahms Trio.

WoO 152, No. 10: *The Deserter*
Berlin Classics 0091322BC, 3CD (1996, recorded 1976-7):
Eberhard Büchner (T), Berliner Solisten, Brahms Trio.

Philips 442 784-2PH, CD (1998): Wolfgang Holzmair (Bar),
Fontenay Trio.

WoO 152, No. 11: *Thou Emblem of Faith*
Channel Classics CCS 1491, CD (1990): Marjanne Kweksilber
(S), Vera Beths (vn), Anner Bijlsma (vc), Stanley Hoogland
(pf).

Berlin Classics 0091322BC, 3CD (1996, recorded 1976-7):
Siegfried Lorenz (Bar), Brahms Trio.

WoO 152, No. 12: *English Bulls, or The Irishman in London*
EMI CDC7 49930-2 (= CD), EL 749930-4 (= MC) (1990):
Felicity Lott (S), Ann Murray (Mez), Galina Solodchin (vn),
Jonathan Williams (vc), Graham Johnson (pf).
Re-issued on HMV Classics 5 73043 2, CD (1998).

WoO 152, No. 13: *Musing on the Roaring Ocean*
Berlin Classics 0091322BC, 3CD (1996, recorded 1976-7):
Renate Krahmer (S), Brahms Trio.

WoO 152, No. 15: *Let Brainspinning Swains*
Berlin Classics 0091322BC, 3CD (1996, recorded 1976-7):
Siegfried Lorenz (Bar), Brahms Trio.

WoO 152, No. 17: *In Vain to this Desert*
Berlin Classics 0091322BC, 3CD (1996, recorded 1976-7):
Renate Krahmer (S), Armin Ude (T), Brahms Trio.

WoO 152, No. 18: *They Bid Me Slight My Dermot Dear*
EMI CMS5 65061-2(2), 4CD (1994, recorded 1960): Victoria
de los Angeles (S), Dietrich Fischer-Dieskau (T), Gerald
Moore (pf).

WoO 152, No. 19: *Wife, Children and Friends*
Berlin Classics 0091322BC, 3CD (1996, recorded 1976-7):
Renate Krahmer (S), Eberhard Büchner (T), Brahms Trio.

WoO 152, No. 20: *Farewell Bliss and Farewell Nancy*
Sony Classical SK 64301, CD (1995): Josef Protschka (T),
Richard Salter (Bar), Christian Altenburger (vn), Julius Berger
(vc), Helmut Deutsch (pf).

Berlin Classics 0091322BC, 3CD (1996, recorded 1976-7):
Renate Krahmer (S), Siegfried Lorenz (Bar), Brahms Trio.

WoO 152, No. 21: *Morning a Cruel Turmoiler is*
Berlin Classics 0091322BC, 3CD (1996, recorded 1976-7):
Siegfried Lorenz (Bar), Brahms Trio.

Philips 442 784-2PH, CD (1998): Wolfgang Holzmair (Bar),
Fontenay Trio.

WoO 152, No. 23: *A Wand'ring Gipsey, Sirs, am I*
Orfeo C 378 951 A, CD (1995): Julie Kaufmann (S), Neues
Münchner Klaviertrio.

Berlin Classics 0091322BC, 3CD (1996, recorded 1976-7):
Renate Krahmer (S), Brahms Trio.

WoO 153, No. 24: *The Traugh Welcome*
Berlin Classics 0091322BC, 3CD (1996, recorded 1976-7):
Siegfried Lorenz (Bar), Brahms Trio.

WoO 153, No. 1: *When Eve's Last Rays in Twilight Die*
Berlin Classics 0091322BC, 3CD (1996, recorded 1976-7):
Armin Ude (T), Siegfried Lorenz (Bar), Brahms Trio.

WoO 153, No. 2: *No Riches from his Scanty Store*
Orfeo C 378 951 A, CD (1995): Julie Kaufmann (S), Neues
Münchner Klaviertrio.

WoO 153, No. 3: *The British Light Dragoons*
Deutsche Harmonia Mundi 069-99 940, LP (1982): James
Griffett (T), Franzjosef Maier (vn), Rudolf Mandalka (vc),
Bradford Tracey (pf).
Re-issued on Ars Musici AM 1142-2, CD (1982).

WoO 153, No. 4: *Since Greybeards Inform Us that Youth Will Decay*
Alienor AL 1065, CD (1991): Mario Hacquard (Bar), Franck
della Valle (vn), Frederic Deville (vc), Claude Collet (pf).

Berlin Classics 0091322BC, 3CD (1996, recorded 1976-7):
Eberhard Büchner (T), Brahms Trio.

Irish Songs II (1816) (later listed as *Twenty Irish Songs*, WoO 153, 5-20, *Twelve Irish Songs*, WoO 154, 1, 3-6, 8-12, *Twelve Songs of Various Nationalities*, WoO 157, 2, 6, 8, 11) v, vn, vc, pf
Deutsche Grammophon 453 786-2, 7CD (1997): Felicity Lott (S),
Janice Watson (S), Ann Murray (Mez), Ruby Philogene (Mez), Sarah
Walker (Mez), John Mark Ainsley (T), Toby Spence (T), Thomas Allen
(Bar), Christopher Maltman (Bar), Marieke Blankestijn (vn), Elizabeth
Layton (vn), Krysia Osostowicz (vn), Ursula Smith (vc), Malcolm
Martineau (pf).

Excerpts:
WoO 153, No. 5: *I Dream'd I Lay Where Flow'rs were Springing*
Berlin Classics 0091322BC, 3CD (1996, recorded 1976-7):
Renate Krahmer (S), Ingeborg Springer (Mez), Brahms Trio.

WoO 153, No. 6: *Sad and Luckless was the Season*
Sony Classical SK 64301, CD (1995): Carolyn Watkinson
(Mez), Christian Altenburger (vn), Julius Berger (vc), Helmut
Deutsch (pf).

WoO 153, No. 7: *O Soothe Me, My Lyre*
Berlin Classics 0091322BC, 3CD (1996, recorded 1976-7):
Renate Krahmer (S), Brahms Trio.

WoO 153, No. 8: *Norah of Balamagairy*
Berlin Classics 0091322BC, 3CD (1996, recorded 1976-7):
Siegfried Lorenz (Bar), Berliner Solisten, Brahms Trio.

WoO 153, No. 9: *The Kiss, Dear Maid, Thy Lip has Left*
Philips 442 784-2PH, CD (1998): Wolfgang Holzmair (Bar),
Fontenay Trio.

WoO 153, No. 10: *The Hapless Soldier*
Berlin Classics 0091322BC, 3CD (1996, recorded 1976-7):
Renate Krahmer (S), Ingeborg Springer (Mez), Brahms Trio.

WoO 153, No. 11: *When Far from the Home*
Philips 442 784-2PH, CD (1998): Wolfgang Holzmair (Bar),
Fontenay Trio.

WoO 153, No. 12: *I'll Praise the Saints with Early Song*
Sony Classical SK 64301, CD (1995): Elaine Woods (S),
Christian Altenburger (vn), Julius Berger (vc), Helmut Deutsch
(pf).

WoO 153, No. 13: *'Tis Sunshine at Last*
Sony Classical SK 64301, CD (1995): Josef Protschka (T),
Christian Altenburger (vn), Julius Berger (vc), Helmut Deutsch
(pf).

WoO 153, No. 15: *'Tis But in Vain, for Nothing Thrives*
Berlin Classics 0091322BC, 3CD (1996, recorded 1976-7):
Renate Krahmer (S), Brahms Trio.

WoO 153, No. 16: *O Might I but My Patrick Love*
Orfeo C 378 951 A, CD (1995): Julie Kaufmann (S), Neues
Münchner Klaviertrio.

Arabesque Z 6672, CD (1996): New York Vocal Arts
Ensemble.

WoO 153, No. 17: *Come Darby Dear*
Deutsche Harmonia Mundi 069-99 940, LP (1982): James
Griffett (T), Franzjosef Maier (vn), Rudolf Mandalka (vc),
Bradford Tracey (pf).

Re-issued on Ars Musici AM 1142-2, CD (1982).

Berlin Classics 0091322BC, 3CD (1996, recorded 1976-7):
Armin Ude (T), Brahms Trio.

WoO 153, No. 20: *Thy Ship Must Sail, My Henry Dear*
Orfeo C 378 951 A, CD (1995): Julie Kaufmann (S), Neues
Münchner Klaviertrio.

Berlin Classics 0091322BC, 3CD (1996, recorded 1976-7):
Renate Krahmer (S), Brahms Trio.

WoO 154, No. 1: *The Elfin Fairies*
Deutsche Grammophon 2530 262, LP (1972): Dietrich
Fischer-Dieskau (Bar), Andreas Rohn (vn), Georg Donderer
(vc), Karl Engel (pf).

EMI CDC7 49930-2 (= CD), EL 749930-4 (= MC) (1990):
Felicity Lott (S), Ann Murray (Mez), Galina Solodchin (vn),
Jonathan Williams (vc), Graham Johnson (pf).
Re-issued on HMV Classics 5 73043 2, CD (1998).

Philips 442 784-2PH, CD (1998): Wolfgang Holzmair (Bar),
Fontenay Trio.

WoO 154, No. 3: *The Farewell Song*
Deutsche Harmonia Mundi 069-99 940, LP (1982): James
Griffett (T), Franzjosef Maier (vn), Rudolf Mandalka (vc),
Bradford Tracey (pf).
Re-issued on Ars Musici AM 1142-2, CD (1982).

WoO 154, No. 4: *The Pulse of an Irishman*
Deutsche Grammophon 2530 262, LP (1972): Dietrich
Fischer-Dieskau (Bar), Andreas Rohn (vn), Georg Donderer
(vc), Karl Engel (pf).

Alienor AL 1065, CD (1991): Mario Hacquard (Bar), Franck
della Valle (vn), Frederic Deville (vc), Claude Collet (pf).

Sony Classical SK 64301, CD (1995): Richard Salter (Bar),
Christian Altenburger (vn), Julius Berger (vc), Helmut Deutsch
(pf).

Arabesque Z 6672, CD (1996): New York Vocal Arts
Ensemble.

Philips 442 784-2PH, CD (1998): Wolfgang Holzmair (Bar), Fontenay Trio.

WoO 154, No. 5: *O Who, My Dear Dermot*
Philips 442 784-2PH, CD (1998): Wolfgang Holzmair (Bar), Fontenay Trio.

WoO 154, No. 6: *Put Round the Bright Wine*
Deutsche Grammophon 2530 262, LP (1972): Dietrich Fischer-Dieskau (Bar), Andreas Rohn (vn), Georg Donderer (vc), Karl Engel (pf).

WoO 154, No. 8: *Save Me from the Grave and Wise*
Sony Classical SK 64301, CD (1995): Elaine Woods (S), Josef Protschka (T), Richard Salter (Bar), Christian Altenburger (vn), Julius Berger (vc), Helmut Deutsch (pf).

WoO 154, No. 9: *O Would I Were but that Sweet Linnet*
EMI CDC7 49930-2 (= CD), EL 749930-4 (= MC) (1990): Felicity Lott (S), Ann Murray (Mez), Galina Solodchin (vn), Jonathan Williams (vc), Graham Johnson (pf).
Re-issued on HMV Classics 5 73043 2, CD (1998).

Alienor AL 1065, CD (1991): Mario Hacquard (Bar), Franck della Valle (vn), Frederic Deville (vc), Claude Collet (pf).

EMI CMS5 65061-2(2), 4CD (1994, recorded 1960): Victoria de los Angeles (S), Dietrich Fischer-Dieskau (T), Gerald Moore (pf).

Forlane 16784, CD (1998): Ann Murray (Mez), Graham Johnson (pf).

WoO 154, No. 11: *The Soldier in a Foreign Land*
Arabesque Z 6672, CD (1996): New York Vocal Arts Ensemble.

WoO 154, No. 12: *He Promis'd Me at Parting*
Deutsche Grammophon 2530 262, LP (1972): Dietrich Fischer-Dieskau (Bar), Andreas Rohn (vn), Georg Donderer (vc), Karl Engel (pf).

EMI CMS5 65061-2(2), 4CD (1994, recorded 1960): Victoria de los Angeles (S), Dietrich Fischer-Dieskau (T), Gerald Moore (pf).

> Sony Classical SK 64301, CD (1995): Elaine Woods (S), Josef
> Protschka (T), Christian Altenburger (vn), Julius Berger (vc),
> Helmut Deutsch (pf).
>
> Forlane 16784, CD (1998): Ann Murray (Mez), Graham
> Johnson (pf).

Seven British Songs WoO 158b (18??, unpubl.) v, vn, vc, pf
> (Irish) Excerpts:
> *Lament for Owen Roe O'Neill*
>> Deutsche Grammophon 453 786-2, 7CD (1997): Krysia
>> Osostowicz (vn), Ursula Smith (vc), Malcolm Martineau (pf).

> *Erin! O Erin!*
>> Deutsche Grammophon 453 786-2, 7CD (1997): Timothy
>> Robinson (T), Krysia Osostowicz (vn), Ursula Smith (vc),
>> Malcolm Martineau (pf).

> *Castle O'Neill*
>> Deutsche Grammophon 453 786-2, 7CD (1997): Krysia
>> Osostowicz (vn), Ursula Smith (vc), Malcolm Martineau (pf).

Julius Benedict
(* Stuttgart 1804, † London 1885)

Benedict studied with Johann Nepomuk Hummel and Carl Maria von Weber
(1821-4), was active as a conductor at Naples before he settled in London in
1835. His main post as conductor there was at the Drury Lane Theatre (1838-
48), but he also conducted at Her Majesty's Theatre and at successive Norwich
Festivals (1845-78), where he also presented his own works. The year 1862 saw
the production of his most successful opera, *The Lily of Killarney*, based on an
Irish theme and making use of Irish musical material. Together with Balfe's *The
Bohemian Girl* (1843) and Wallace's *Maritana* (1845) this work constituted the
so-called "English Ring" in allusion to Wagner's *Ring of the Nibelung* cycle of
operas. Of course, this *Ring* is much more Irish than English, if anything of the
two at all.

Recorded "Irish" Work:

The Lily of Killarney (1862) opera
> Excerpts:

The moon hath raised her lamp; 'Tis a charming girl I love; I'm alone; Eily Mavourneen
EMI CSD 3651, LP (1968): Veronica Dunne (S), Uel Deane (T), Eric Hinds (Bar), anonymous orchestra, Havelock Nelson (cond).

The moon hath raised her lamp
Meridian DUOCD 89009 (= CD), KD 89009 (= MC) (1991): Hilliard Ensemble, Lena-Luis Kiesel (org).

Eily Mavourneen
ASV CD AJA 5227, CD (1999, recorded 1931): Heddle Nash (T), Gerald Moore (pf).

Hector Berlioz
(* La Côte-St.-André 1803, † Paris 1869)

Berlioz was self-taught on a number of instruments and studied composition at the Paris Conservatoire in the mid-1820s. In 1831-2 he worked in Rome as a winner of the Prix de Rome. Just the year previously he completed one of his most famous works, the *Symphonie fantastique*. He was later celebrated for his three operas and his brilliant orchestral technique as well as for much of his vocal music. One of his major non-musical influences was the Irish actress Harriet Smithson whom he married in 1830. Through her he got to know the poetry of Thomas Moore and his *Irish Melodies* and this influence is reflected in his early song cycle *Irlande* op. 2.

Recorded "Irish" Work:

Irlande op. 2 (1829, rev. 1850) v, pf
    Excerpts:
    No. 1: *Le coucher du soleil*; No. 4: *La Belle Voyageuse*; No. 7: *L'Origine de la Harpe*
    Saga 5388, LP (1974): Jill Gomez (S), John Constable (pf).

    No. 1: *Le coucher du soleil*; No. 4: *La Belle Voyageuse*; No. 9: *Elégie*
    Dorian DOR 90128, CD (1990): Janice Taylor (Mez), Dalton Baldwin (pf).

    No. 4: *La Belle Voyageuse*
    Deutsche Grammophon 445 823-2GH, CD (1992): Anne Sofie von Otter (Mez), Cord Garben (pf).

No. 2: *Hélène*; No. 3: *Chant Guerrier*; No. 4: *La Belle Voyageuse*;
No. 5: *Chanson a Boire*; No. 7: *L'Origine de la Harpe*; No. 9: *Elégie*
Deutsche Grammophon 435 860-2GH2, 2CD (1994): (singers share
items in various combinations) Françoise Pollet (S), Anne Sofie von
Otter (Mez), John Aler (T), Thomas Allen (Bar), Cord Garben (pf).

No. 1: *Le coucher du soleil*; No. 4: *La Belle Voyageuse*; No. 7:
L'Origine de la Harpe; No. 8: *Adieu, Bessy!*; No. 9: *Elégie*
EMI 7243 5 55047 2, CD (1994): Thomas Hampson (Bar), Geoffrey
Parsons (pf).

No. 7: *L'Origine de la Harpe*
Black Box Music BBM 1022, CD (1998): Kathleen Tynan (S),
Dearbhla Collins (pf).

No. 4: *La Belle Voyageuse*; No. 7: *L'Origine de la Harpe*
Forlane 16784, CD (1998): Ann Murray (Mez), Graham Johnson (pf).

Version partly arranged for soloists with satb:
L'Oiseau Lyre SOL 305, LP (1968): (items shared in various
combinations) April Cantelo (S), Helen Watts (Mez), Robert Tear (T),
Viola Tunnard (pf), Monteverdi Choir, John Eliot Gardiner (cond).
Re-issued on Decca 448 113-2DF2, 2CD (1996).

> Excerpts:
> No. 3: *Chant Guerrier*; No. 6: *Chant Sacre*
> Argo ZRG 635, LP (1969): Heinrich Schütz Choir.
>
> No. 2: *Hélène*; No. 5: *Chanson a Boire*; No. 6: *Chant Sacre*
> Harmonia Mundi HMP 390 1293, CD (1989): Bruce Brewer
> (T), Lyon National Choir, Noël Lee (pf), Bernard Tetu (cond).

Version with orchestra:
> Excerpts:
> No. 4: *La Belle Voyageuse*
> Phonogram 6500009, LP (1970): Sheila Armstrong (S),
> London Symphony Orchestra, Carl Davis (cond).
>
> Erato 4509-99768-2, CD (1990): Diana Montague (Mez), Lyon
> Opera Orchestra, John Eliot Gardiner (cond).

Lorenzo Bocchi
(* Italy late 17th century, † England? early 18th century)

Of Bocchi's life and work not much is known except for the fact that he was a composer and a player of the bass-viol who around 1720 worked for a short while in Edinburgh before settling in Ireland. In 1724 he published an arrangement of a tune by Turlough Carolan with the Dublin publishers John and William Neal. Within a year his partially recorded piece for bass-viol, a predecessor of the violoncello, was published. By 1729 he was back in Edinburgh after which he disappeared from view.

Recorded "Irish" Work:

A Musicall Entertainment for a Chamber (c. 1724-5) 2 bass-viols, archlute
Hyperion CDA 67088, CD (1999): The Parley of Instruments: Mark Caudle (solo bass-viol), Susanne Heinrich (continuo bass-viol), Elizabeth Kenny (archlute).

William Brade
(* England 1560, † Hamburg 1630)

English-born William Brade spent most of his life at German courts, notably at Berlin, Bückeburg and Hamburg, also at the Danish court at Copenhagen. He was acclaimed as one the finest violinists of his time. He published many dance compositions, and by introducing them to Germany, contributed to the development of the baroque suite.

Recorded "Irish" Work:

Irish Dance (after 1600) hpd
Hyperion CDA 66894, CD (1997): Timothy Roberts.

Frank Bridge
(* Brighton 1879, † Eastbourne 1941)

Bridge studied with Irish composer Charles V. Stanford at the Royal College of Music in London (1899-1903) and made a reputation as a chamber musician and conductor. His early music showed the influence of Bax and Delius but after

World War I his works became more chromatic and adventurous. Although a competent and innovative composer in his own right, his fame largely rests on having been Benjamin Britten's teacher. The Irish air he used in a string quartet of 1908 was very popular at the time having previously been used by Stanford and Grainger among others.

Recorded "Irish" Work:

An Irish Melody: Londonderry Air (1908) str-qu
> Chandos ABRD 1073 (= LP), ABTD 1073 (= MC) (1983): Delmé Quartet.
> *Re-issued on* Chandos CHAN 8426, CD (1987).

> Naxos 8.553718, CD (1995): Maggini Quartet.

> Version for str-orch (1908):
> Nimbus NI 5366, CD (1993): English String Orchestra, William Boughton (cond).

Benjamin Britten
(* Lowestoft 1913, † Aldeburgh 1976)

Britten was one of the most important English composers of the mid-20th century. He studied with Frank Bridge and at the Royal College of Music, London. In the 1930s Britten worked on a number of film scores, including some with the poet W.H. Auden. He wrote twelve operas of which *Peter Grimes* (1945) and *Billy Budd* (1951) became the most influential. He also wrote a large number of orchestral and choral works as well as songs. Among the latter are several settings of folk song arrangements and among these are a number of Irish ones, including new settings to some of the *Irish Melodies* by Thomas Moore.

Recorded "Irish" Works:

Around the Village Green – Irish Reel (c. 1930s) orch
> Beulah 1PD14, CD (1996, recorded 1938): Charles Brill Orchestra, Charles Bril (cond).

Folksong Arrangements vol. 1: The British Isles (1943) v, pf
> Excerpt:
> *Down By the Sally Gardens*
> Musica Rara MUS 25, LP (1967): Raimund Gilvan (T), Frederic Capon (pf).

Re-issued on Oryx 1925, LP (197?).

Decca SXL 6413, LP (1970): Bernadette Greevy (Mez), Paul Hamburger (pf).

Saga 5345, LP (1973): Sheila Armstrong (S), Martin Isepp (pf).

HMV HQS 1341, LP (1975): Robert Tear (T), Philip Ledger (pf).

Max Sound MSCB 13, MC (1987): Valerie Baulard (Mez), Simon Wright (pf).

Etcetera KTC 1046 (= CD), XTC 1046 (= MC) (1988): Carolyn Watkinson (Mez), Tan Crone (pf).

Globe GLO 5017, CD (1989): Glenda Maurice (Mez), David Garvey (pf).

Hyperion CDA 66209, CD (1990): Anthony Rolfe Johnson (T), Graham Johnson (pf).

Delos DE 3029, CD (1989): Arleen Auger (S), Dalton Baldwin (pf).

Chandos CHAN 8946, CD (1992): Benjamin Luxon (Bar), David Willison (pf).

Hyperion CDA 66941/2, 2CD (1994): Jamie MacDougall (Bar), Malcolm Martineau (pf).
Re-issued on Hyperion Dyad CDD 22042, 2CD (2000).

Pearl Gemm CD 9177, CD (1995, recorded 1944): Peter Pears (T), Benjamin Britten (pf).

Collins 7039-2, 3CD (1995): Thomas Allen (Bar), Graham Johnson (pf).

Version with string orchestra:
Collins 7039-2, 3CD (1995): Thomas Allen (Bar), Northern Sinfonia, Steuart Bedford (cond).

Folksong Arrangements vol. 4: Moore's Irish Melodies (1957-8) v, pf
Hyperion CDA 66941/2, 2CD (1994): Regina Nathan (S), Malcolm Martineau (pf).
Re-issued on Hyperion Dyad CDD 22042, 2CD (2000).

Collins 7039-2, 3CD (1995): Felicity Lott (S), Graham Johnson (pf).

Excerpts:
No. 3: *How Sweet the Answer*; No. 7: *Dear Harp of My Country*; No. 8: *Oft in the Stilly Night*; No. 9: *The Last Rose of Summer*
Classics for Pleasure CD-CFP 4636, CD (1987): Sarah Brightman (S), Geoffrey Parsons (pf).

No. 3: *How Sweet the Answer*; No. 4: *The Minstrel Boy*
Etcetera KTC 1046 (= CD), XTC 1046 (= MC) (1988): Yvonne Kenny (S), Tan Crone (pf).

No. 1: *Avenging and Bright*; No. 3: *How Sweet the Answer*; No. 4: *The Minstrel Boy*; No. 8: *Oft in the Stilly Night*; No. 9: *The Last Rose of Summer*
London 430 063-2LM, CD (1991, recorded 1961): Peter Pears (T), Benjamin Britten (pf).
No. 9: *The Last Rose of Summer* re-issued on Belart 450 020-2, CD (1992?).

No. 3: *How Sweet the Answer*; No. 8: *Oft in the Stilly Night*; No. 9: *The Last Rose of Summer*; No. 10: *O the Sight Entrancing*
Hyperion CDA 66627, CD (1993): Ann Murray (Mez), Graham Johnson (pf).

John Bull
(* Old Radnor c. 1562-3, † Antwerp 1628)

John Bull was one of the leading English renaissance composers and keyboard virtuosos. He was active at Hereford Cathedral and the Chapel Royal, London (from 1574) and made doctorates at Cambridge (1589) and Oxford (1592). He taught at Gresham College, London, between 1597 and 1607. In 1613 he fled to the Netherlands on charges of adultery and was active at Antwerp Cathedral until his death. Bull is chiefly remembered for his keyboard music, but there also survived some anthems and many canons. Much of his music was lost, when he left England.

Recorded "Irish" music:

Irish Toy (date unknown) hpd
    Astree Auvidis E 8543, CD (1995): Pierre Hantai.

William Byrd
(* Lincoln 1543, † Stondon Massey 1623)

Byrd was brought up in London and was a pupil of Thomas Tallis. In 1563 he became organist and master of the choristers at Lincoln Cathedral and, though he remained there, was also Gentleman at the Chapel Royal, London, and its organist from 1575. In 1593 he moved to Essex where he remained for the rest of his life. He was described as the "Father of British Music"; Thomas Morley and Thomas Tomkins were his most famous pupils. Byrd was a prolific composer, a traditionalist and an innovator at the same time. Much of his vocal and instrumental music was published during his lifetime.

Recorded "Irish" music:

Callino Casturame (date unknown) hpd
> Pan PAN 6202 (= mono), SPAN 6202 (= stereo), LP (1966): Michael Thomas.

> Hyperion A 66067 (= LP), KA 66067 (= MC) (1983): Christopher Kite. *Re-issued on* Hyperion CDA 66067, CD (198?).

> Meridian DUOCD 89027 (= CD), KD 89027 (= MC) (1993): Michael Bailey.

The Irish March (date unknown) wind consort, hpd
> Astree Auvidis E 8611, CD (1997): Capriccio Stravagante, Skip Sempe (hpd + cond).

John Cage
(* Los Angeles 1912, † New York 1992)

John Cage traveled Europe in 1930-1 before he studied with Henry Cowell in New York (1933-4) and Arnold Schönberg in Los Angeles (1934). In 1937 he moved to Seattle where he founded a percussion orchestra and began to use electronic devices as early as 1939. He later lived in San Francisco, Chicago and New York (from 1942) and became interested in Eastern philosophies, especially Zen, resulting in many works featuring indeterminacy instead of creative purpose. Cage became known as one the greatest experimentalists in twentieth-century music including the invention of the "prepared piano". He also wrote music for twelve radios and the famous silent piece *4'33"* (1952). His *Roaratorio*

(1979) on excerpts from James Joyce's *Finnegan's Wake* is a collaboration with Irish traditional musicians.

Recorded "Irish" Work:

Roaratorio – An Irish Circus on "Finnegan's Wake" (1979) spkr, v, vn, 2Bdn, fl, U.P.
>   Wergo WER 6303-2, CD (1994): John Cage (spkr), Joe Heaney (v), Paddy Glackin (vn), Peadar Mercier (Bdn), Mel Mercier (Bdn), Matt Molloy (fl), Seamus Ennis (U.P.).
>   *Also issued on* Mode 28/9, 2CD (1994).

Rebecca Clarke
(* Harrow 1886, † New York 1979)

Clarke studied with Irish composer C.V. Stanford at the Royal College of Music, London (1907-10), She began a distinguished career as a viola player in chamber groups and as a composer, particularly of vocal and chamber music. In 1912 she was among the first six women to get an orchestra position in Henry Wood's Queen's Hall Orchestra. In 1939 she settled in the USA and lived in New York from 1944. She was the President of the Chautaqua Society of New York from 1949 and read many papers at the Chautaqua Institution between 1945 and 1956.

Recorded "Irish" Works:

Three Irish Country Songs (19??) S, vn, pf
>   Gamut GAMCD 534, CD (1993): Patricia Wright (S), Jonathan Rees (vn), Kathreen Sturrock (pf).

Eric Coates
(* Hucknall 1886, † Chichester 1957)

Eric Coates studied at the Royal Academy of Music at London and worked as an orchestral viola player. He was an outstanding composer of so-called light music, a specific English phenomenon ignoring international harmonic develop-ments of the early twentieth century in favor of a light and often humorous tonal romanticism. Coates wrote a lot of orchestral music and many songs.

Recorded "Irish" Work:

The Fairy Tales of Ireland (1918) v, pf
        Marco Polo 8.223806, CD (1996): Richard Edgar-Wilson (T), Eugene
        Asti (pf).

John Corigliano
(* New York 1938)

Corigliano studied at Columbia University and worked mainly in radio and television. His music is in an accessible, romantic style, with tonal harmony and outstanding orchestration. He became known for his "electric rock opera" *The Naked Carmen* (1970, after Bizet), the opera *A Figaro for Antonio* (1985), presented by the Metropolitan Opera, a clarinet concerto (1977) and for his film music.

Recorded "Irish" Work:

Three Irish Folk-Song Settings (19??) T, 2fl, ob, cl, str-qu, hpd
        RCA Victor Red Seal GD 60395, CD (1991): Robert White (T),
        Ransom Wilson (fl), Thomas Nyfenger (fl), Humbert Lucarelli (ob),
        Joseph Rabbai (cl), American Quartet, Maurice Peress (hpd).

Jean Coulthard
(* Vancouver 1908, † Vancouver 2000)

Jean Coulthard was the first Canadian woman composer to achieve international recognition. She studied in London with Ralph Vaughan Williams (1929-31) and taught music theory and composition at the University of British Columbia (1947-73). She wrote symphonies, concertos, choral music and an opera. Her music is mostly in a tonal, lyrical mood.

Recorded "Irish" work:

Four Irish Poems (19??) S, orch
        CBC Records , CD (1995): Linda Maguire (S), CBC Vancouver
        Orchestra, Mario Bernadi (cond).

Henry Cowell
(* Menlo Park, California 1897, † Shady, New York 1965)

Before he had any formal training in music, Cowell wrote a number of piano pieces using clusters, direct playing on the strings of a grand piano and other new effects. A large number of these early experimental works use Irish traditional melodies or are based on Irish legends that he heard in his home (his parents came from Ireland). He later studied in California and New York (1916-1918) but continued an individual path, which was later regarded as groundbreaking, although his works between 1936 and 1950 were less adventurous. Later in life he taught at the Peabody Conservatory (1951-6) and Columbia University (1949-65). Cowell wrote more than 140 orchestral works (including 21 symphonies), about 170 chamber and more than 200 piano works apart from operas, choral and film music.

Recorded "Irish" Works:

The Tides of Manaunaun (c. 1912) pf
        Folkways 3349, LP (1963): Henry Cowell.
        Re-issued on Smithsonian Folkways SF 40801, CD (1993).

        Acta 7, CD (1993): Chris Burn.

        Hat-Hut ART CD 6144, CD (1995): Steffen Schleiermacher.

        Town Hall THCD 48, CD (1997): Sorrel Hays.

        New Albion NA 103, CD (1999): Sorrel Hays.

Exultation (1919) pf
        Folkways 3349, LP (1963): Henry Cowell.
        Re-issued on Smithsonian Folkways SF 40801, CD (1993).

        Argo 436 925-2ZH, CD (1993): Alan Feinberg.

Voice of Lir (1919) pf
        Folkways 3349, LP (1963): Henry Cowell.
        Re-issued on Smithsonian Folkways SF 40801, CD (1993).

        Acta 7, CD (1993): Chris Burn.

        Hat-Hut ART CD 6144, CD (1995): Steffen Schleiermacher.

        Town Hall THCD 48, CD (1997): Sorrel Hays.

The Hero Sun (1922) pf
> Town Hall THCD 48, CD (1997): Sorrel Hays.

Harp of Life (1924) pf
> Folkways 3349, LP (1963): Henry Cowell.
> *Re-issued on* Smithsonian Folkways SF 40801, CD (1993).

The Trumpet of Angus Og (1924) pf
> Folkways 3349, LP (1963): Henry Cowell.
> *Re-issued on* Smithsonian Folkways SF 40801, CD (1993).

> Acta 7, CD (1993): Chris Burn.

> Town Hall THCD 48, CD (1997): Sorrel Hays.

(Slow) Jig (1925) pf
> Folkways 3349, LP (1963): Henry Cowell.
> *Re-issued on* Smithsonian Folkways SF 40801, CD (1993).

> New Albion NA 103, CD (1999): Sarah Cahill.

Lilt of the Reel (1925) pf
> Folkways 3349, LP (1963): Henry Cowell.
> *Re-issued on* Smithsonian Folkways SF 40801, CD (1993).

> Acta 7, CD (1993): Chris Burn.

> Town Hall THCD 48, CD (1997): Sorrel Hays.

> Composers Recordings Inc. CRI 750, CD (1997, recorded 1956): Henry Cowell.

> New Albion NA 103, CD (1999): Sorrel Hays.

The Banshee (c. 1925) pf
> Folkways 3349, LP (1963): Henry Cowell.
> *Re-issued on* Smithsonian Folkways SF 40801, CD (1993).

> Acta 7, CD (1993): Chris Burn.

> Hat-Hut ART CD 6144, CD (1995): Steffen Schleiermacher.

> Town Hall THCD 48, CD (1997): Sorrel Hays.

Composers Recordings Inc. CRI 750, CD (1997, recorded 1956): Henry Cowell.

New Albion NA 103, CD (1999): Chris Brown.

The Fairy Bells (1928) pf
Acta 7, CD (1993): Chris Burn.

Fairy Answer (1929) pf
Folkways 3349, LP (1963): Henry Cowell.
Re-issued on Smithsonian Folkways SF 40801, CD (1993).

Acta 7, CD (1993): Chris Burn.

New Albion NA 103, CD (1999): Sarah Cahill.

Fiddler's Jig (1952) vn, orch
CPO 999 222-2, CD (1994): Marjorie Kransberg Talvi (vn), Seattle Northwest Chamber Orchestra, Alun Francis (cond).

Koch 37282-2, CD (1995): unnamed soloist, Manhattan Chamber Orchestra, Richard Auldon Clark (cond).

Frederick Nicholls Crouch
(* London 1808, † Portland ME 1896)

Crouch was an English cellist, singer and composer who settled as a singing teacher in the USA from 1849. He wrote two operas and hundreds of songs, of which the Irish-style *Kathleen Mavourneen* became the most popular.

Recorded "Irish" Work:

Kathleen Mavourneen (c. 1838) v, pf
Pearl Gemm CD 9312, CD (1990, recorded 1906): Adelina Patti (S), Alfredo Barili (pf).

Memoir Classics CDMOIR 418, CD (1992, recorded 1927): John McCormack (T), Edwin Schneider (pf).

Centaur CRC 2243, CD (1995): Gary Lakes (T), Kevin Murphy (pf).

Pearl GEM 0086, CD (2000, recorded 1930): Clara Butt (Mez), anonymous pianist.

Naxos Nostalgia 8.120504, CD (2000) (same recording as *Memoir* above).

Arrangement with orchestra:
Pearl Gemm CD 9411, CD (1991, recorded in the 1920s): Tom Burke (T), anonymous orchestra.

Nimbus NI 7854, CD (1993, recorded 1911): John McCormack (T), Victor Orchestra.

Romophone 82006-2, 2CD (1996) (same recording as *Nimbus* above).

Heinrich Wilhelm Ernst
(* Brno 1814, † Nice 1865)

Ernst was a Moravian violinist and composer educated at the Vienna Conservatory. He was one of the outstanding virtuoso violinists of his time, often compared to Paganini and sometimes surpassing him. His positively romantic music included many works for violin among them the *Concerto Pathétique* op 23 and the famous *Élégie* op. 10.

Recorded "Irish" Work:

Variations on 'The Last Rose of Summer' (18??) vn
        Biddulph LAW 001, CD (1990): Maxim Vengerov.

Sony Classical SK 467 42, CD (1991?): Midori.

Koch Discover International DICD 920 241, CD (1995): Juliette Kang.

Claves CD 50-9613, CD (1996): Ingolf Turban.

Friedrich von Flotow
(* Teutendorf 1812, † Darmstadt 1883)

Von Flotow studied at the Paris Conservatoire and became influenced by Auber, Rossini, Meyerbeer and Donizetti, later by Gounod and Offenbach. None of 17 operas surpassed the popularity of *Martha* (1847), a delightful romantic work

with much period charm. It contains an aria with the tune and German trans-
lation of Thomas Moore's *The Last Rose of Summer*, one of his famous *Irish
Melodies*. The following list is very selective, only listing the complete recordings – the Moore aria, however, is contained in basically all highlights selections
from *Martha*.

Recorded "Irish" Works:

Martha (1847) opera
        EMI SLS 944, 2LP (1969): Anneliese Rothenberger (S) Brigitte
        Fassbaender (Mez), Nicolai Gedda (T), Hermann Prey (Bar), Dieter
        Weller (B), Bavarian State Opera Choir, Bavarian State Orchestra,
        Robert Heger (cond).
        Re-issued on EMI CMS7 69339-2, 2CD (1989).

        Deutsche Grammophon 25422XGR, LP (1982, recorded 1977): Lucia
        Popp (S), Doris Soffel (Mez), Siegfried Jerusalem (T), Karl Ridder-
        busch (B), Bavarian Radio Choir, Munich Radio Orchestra, Heinz
        Wallberg (cond).
        Re-issued on Eurodisc 352 878, 2CD (1988) *and on* RCA Victor 74321
        32231-2, 2CD (1989).

        Berlin Classics 0021 632BC, 2CD (1994, recorded 1944): Erna Berger
        (S), Else Tegetthoff (Mez), Peter Anders (T), Josef Greindl (Bar),
        Eugen Fuchs (B), Berlin State Opera Choir, Berlin Staatskapelle,
        Johannes Schüler (cond).

John Gardner
(* Manchester 1917)

John Gardner studied at Oxford and has mostly been active as a music teacher.
He was also on the music staff of the Royal Opera House, London (1946-52). He
excels as a composer of vocal music, especially operatic and choral. He is mostly writing light music in a diatonic style. His *Irish Suite* (1996) is dedicated to
Irish composer/conductor Michael Bowles (1909-1998) and his wife Kathleen.

Recorded "Irish" Works:

Irish Suite op. 231 (1996) orch
        ASV WHL 2125, CD (2000): Royal Ballet Sinfonia, Gavin Sutherland
        (cond).

George Gershwin
(* Brooklyn 1898, † Hollywood 1937)

Gershwin was largely self-taught as a composer and began his career as a song-writer, also producing a series of musicals between 1919 and 1933. When his *Rhapsody in Blue* (1924) became a success, he turned more to "serious" music, the most ambitious pieces being the Piano Concerto in F (1925) and the orchestral tone poem *An American in Paris* (1928). He continued to write music for the stage; one of the most successful pieces was *Porgy and Bess* (1935).

Recorded "Irish" Work:

Irish Waltz (c. 1925-30) pf
    ASV WHL 2077, CD (1993): Jack Gibbons (pf).

Mauro Giuliani
(* Bisceglie 1781, † Naples 1829)

Giuliani was one of the most famous and most important early nineteenth-century composers for the guitar. He lived in Vienna from 1806 to 1819. As a cellist, he played in the orchestra in the premiere of Beethoven's seventh symphony (1813). Among his works are three guitar concertos, many sonatas, studies and variations for guitar solo as well as some chamber music involving a guitar.

Recorded "Irish" Works:

Variations on Three Irish Airs op. 125 (18??) gui
    Max Sound MSCB/C 29, MC (1988): Timothy Walker.

Percy Grainger
(* Melbourne 1882, † White Plains, New York 1961)

Grainger left his native Australia early to study at Frankfurt, Germany (1895-9), where he became linked to the English composers Henry Balfour Gardiner, Roger Quilter and Cyril Scott. He settled in London in 1901, appeared widely as a concert pianist and took part in the folksong movement. In 1914 he moved to the USA where he taught at Chicago and New York, visiting Australia several times and helping to establish the Grainger Museum at Melbourne. He often made several versions of one piece, most of which undated, and his *Irish Tune from County Derry* was his most often used item for experiments in instrument-ation and technique. It exists in innumerable versions (and recordings) and the ones listed here are probably far from complete.

Recorded "Irish" Works:

Irish Tune from County Derry
> Version for satb (1902)
>> Collegium COLCD 104 (= CD), COLC 104 (= LP) (1987): Cambridge Singers, John Rutter (cond).
>>
>> Conifer 75605 51752-2, 2CD (1988): City of Birmingham Symphony Orchestra Chorus, Simon Halsey (cond).
>>
>> Hyperion CDA 66793, CD (1994): Polyphony, Stephen Layton (cond).
>
> Version for pf (1911)
>> Nimbus NI 5244, CD (1990): Martin Jones.
>>
>> Priory PRCD 335, CD (1991): Peter King (org).
>>
>> Hyperion CDA 66884, CD (1997): Marc-André Hamelin.
>>
>> Chandos CHAN 9895, CD (2001): Penelope Thwaites.
>
> Version for str-orch (1913)
>> Telarc CD 80059, CD (1983): St. Louis Symphony Orchestra, Leo Slatkin (cond).
>>
>> London 425 159-2LM, CD (1989, recorded 1972): English Chamber Orchestra, Steuart Bedford (cond).
>>
>> Koch 37003-2, CD (1990): Melbourne Symphony Orchestra, Geoffrey Simon (cond).
>>
>> Mercury 434 330-2MM, CD (1993, recorded 1959): Eastman-Rochester Orchestra, Frederick Fennell (cond).
>>
>> Chandos CHAN 9346, CD (1994): Academy of St. Martin-in-the-Fields Chamber Ensemble.

RCA Victor 09026 68511-2, CD (1995) (same recording as
Telarc above).

Dutton Laboratories CDSJB 1006, CD (1997, recorded 1957):
Hallé Orchestra, John Barbirolli (cond).

Chandos CHAN 9584, CD (1998): BBC Philharmonic,
Richard Hickox (cond).
Re-issued on Chandos CHAN 9839, CD (2000).

Version for large wind ensemble (1917)
Phoenix (USA) PHCD 119, CD (198?, recorded 1980): UCLA
Wind Ensemble, James Westbrook (cond).

EMI CDM5 65122-2, CD (1985): Royal Air Force Central
Band, Eric Banks (cond).

ASV CD WHL 2067, CD (1992): London Wind Orchestra,
Denis Wick (cond).

Chandos CHAN 9549, CD (1997): Royal Northern College of
Music Wind Orchestra, Timothy Reynish (cond).
Re-issued on Chandos CHAN 9630, CD (1998).

Version for satb, orch (1920)
Philips 446 657-2PH (= CD), -4PH (= MC) (1996):
Monteverdi Choir, English Country Gardiner Orchestra, John
Eliot Gardiner (cond).

Chandos CHAN 9499, CD (1996): Joyful Company of
Singers, City of London Sinfonia, Richard Hickox (cond).
Re-issued on Chandos CHAN 9653, CD (1998):

Other versions (without date)
ASV CD WHL 2103, CD (1997): Bernard Gregor-Smith (vc),
Yolande Wrigley (pf).

Victor Herbert
(* Dublin 1859, † New York 1924)

Herbert was born in Ireland but his family emigrated to Germany, where he studied at the Stuttgart Conservatory and began a career as a cellist, teacher and composer. In 1886 he moved to New York where he taught at the National Conservatory. He also conducted the Pittsburgh Symphony Orchestra (1898-1904) and was an active propagandist for copyrights in music. Although he wrote some orchestral and chamber music he is mainly remembered as the first really significant Broadway composer – he wrote more than 40 operettas including *Babes in Toyland* (1903) and *Naughty Marietta* (1910). After the Easter Rising in Ireland he composed an Irish operetta, *Eileen* (1917).

Recorded "Irish" Works:

Irish Rhapsody (1892) orch
  Naxos International 8.990018, CD (1990): Richard Hayman and His Symphony Orchestra.

  Newport Classic NPD 85572, CD (1994): Manhattan Chamber Orchestra, Richard Auldon Clark (cond).

  Marco Polo 8.225109, CD (2000): Slovak Radio Symphony Orchestra, Keith Brion (cond).

Eileen (1917) opera
  Newport Classic NPD 85615/2, 2CD (1998): Suzanne Woods (S), John Pickle (T), Catherine Robison (Mez), Alan Payne (Bar) and other singers, Ohio Light Opera Chorus and Orchestra, Michael Butterman (cond), James Stuart (Art.-Dir.).

  Excerpts:
  The Irish Have a Great Night Tonight
  Naxos International 8.990018, CD (1990): Richard Hayman and His Symphony Orchestra.

  Sony Classical SK 52491, CD (1992): Pittsburgh Symphony Orchestra, Lorin Maazel (cond)

  The Irish Have a Great Night Tonight; Ireland My Sireland; Free Trade and a Misty Moon
  Pearl Gemm CDS 9059/61, 3CD (1994, recorded 1917): Greek Evans (v), Vernon Stiles (v), Scott Welsh (v), Original Broadway Cast, Victor Herbert (cond).

Thine Alone
Newport Classic NPD 85572, CD (1994): Andrea Matthews (S),
Manhattan Chamber Orchestra, Richard Auldon Clark (cond).

Paul Hindemith

(* Hanau 1895, † Frankfurt 1963)

Paul Hindemith was one of the most important German composers in the first
half of the twentieth century. He studied at Hoch's Conservatory in Frankfurt
(1908-17) and made an early reputation through his chamber music and express-
ionist operas. He was a noted viola player and was involved in promoting contemporary chamber music, e.g. during the early years of the Donaueschingen
festival. From 1927 Hindemith taught at the Musikhochschule Berlin. Under the
Nazis his music was disapproved of and he emigrated to Switzerland in 1938
and to the USA, where he taught at Yale (1940-53). His music after about 1930
was less adventurous than before and than most of his orchestral output. Apart
from his *Nine English Songs,* which include an Irish one, he also wrote an Irish
piece that still awaits recording, the *Old Irish Air* (1940) for choir, harp and
string orchestra or piano.

Recorded "Irish" Work:

Nine English Songs (1944) v, pf
    Excerpt:
    On Hearing "The Last Rose of Summer"
    Orfeo C 156 861 A, CD (1987): Dietrich Fischer-Dieskau (Bar), Aribert
    Reimann (pf).

Augusta Holmès

(* Paris 1847, † Paris 1903)

Augusta Holmès was born in Paris of Irish parents and is reputed to have been
an ardent Irish nationalist. She frequently mixed with high society and was
admired by Camille Saint-Saëns, César Franck (with whom she studied) and
Stephane Mallarmé. She wrote several operas, dramatic symphonies and
symphonic poems as well as successful choral works (*Ode triomphale*, 1889)
and many songs. After her symphonic poem *Irlande* was performed at the first

Dublin Feis Ceoil in 1897 she donated the rights to the Gaelic League. One year before her death she became a Catholic.

Recorded "Irish" Work:

Irlande (1882) orch
        Marco Polo 8.223449, CD (1994): Rheinland-Pfalz Philharmonic,
        Samuel Friedmann (cond).

Charles Herbert Kitson
(* Yorkshire 1874, † London 1944)

Kitson is primarily remembered as a theorist – he wrote many books on harmony, counterpoint and similar subjects. Born in England, he lived in Dublin from 1913 to 1935 as professor of music at University College and Trinity College successively.

Recorded "Irish" Works:

Communion on an Irish Air (19??) org
        Guild GMCD 7122, CD (1996): John Dexter.

Friedrich Kuhlau
(* Uelzen 1786, † Copenhagen 1832)

Kuhlau is regarded as a Danish composer of German birth. He studied at Hamburg, but made a name for himself in Copenhagen as a pianist and composer. He also traveled to Stockholm and Vienna where he met Beethoven. He is mainly remembered for his piano and his flute music but also wrote an opera *Lulu* (1824) and some incidental music to plays. His recorded "Irish" piece shows the influence of Moore.

Recorded "Irish" Works:

Variations on an Irish folksong op. 105 (1829) fl, pf
        Kontrapunkt 32237, CD (1996): Toke Lund Christiansen (fl), Elisabeth
        Westenholz (pf).

Charles Martin Loeffler
(* Schöneberg or Mulhouse 1861, † Medfield, Massachusetts 1935)

Loeffler studied at Berlin and Paris and emigrated to the USA in 1881. He became assistant leader of the Boston Symphony Orchestra (1882-1903) and a noted proponent of contemporary music. In 1910 he retired to the country. He wrote music in all genres, at first in a romantic impressionist style, later influenced by jazz. His *Five Irish Fantasies* on words by W. B. Yeats are only partly folkloristic and were first performed in the USA by the Irish tenor John McCormack.

Recorded "Irish" Work:

Five Irish Fantasies (1920) T, orch
New World NW 332-2, LP/MC/CD (1985): Neil Rosenshein (T), Indianapolis Symphony Orchestra, John Nelson (cond).

Frank Martin
(* Geneva 1890, † Naarden 1974)

Frank Martin is one of the most important Swiss composers of the twentieth century. His early work is in an extended tonal style; from c. 1934 he adopted Schönbergian serialism while from the early 1940s he developed an individual style marked by dissonant chords and smooth part-writing. In 1946 he moved to the Netherlands and also taught at Cologne, Germany (1950-7). He wrote several operas, oratorios and many orchestral works.

Recorded "Irish" Work:

Trio sur des mélodies populaires irlandaises (1925) vn, vc, pf
Jecklin-Disco JD 646-2, CD (1990): Brenton Langbein (vn), Raffaele Altwegg (vc), Hanni Schmid-Wyss (pf).

Chandos CHAN 9016, CD (1992): Borodin Trio.

Ottavo OTRC 28922, CD (1993): Guarneri Trio.

Gallo CD-633, CD (1993): Musiviva Trio.

Channel Classics 13098, CD (1998): Osiris Trio.

Centaur CRC 2318, CD (1999): Primavera Trio.

William Thomas McKinley
(* New Kensington, Pennsylvania 1938)

McKinley is an American composer of Irish extraction. He studied at Carnegie-Mellon University and completed a doctorate in 1969 at Yale University. He pursues a career in classical composition and jazz, and teaches both subjects at the New England Conservatory of Music.

Recorded "Irish" Work:

Symphony No. 5 'Irish' (1989) orch
> Vienna Modern Masters VMM 3005, CD (1991): Warsaw National Philharmonic Orchestra, Robert Black (cond).

Felix Mendelssohn-Bartholdy
(* Hamburg 1809, † Leipzig 1847)

Mendelssohn-Bartholdy is one of the most important German composers of the nineteenth century. In his short life he wrote five symphonies, many other orchestral works, some famous oratorios, six string quartets and a large body of songs, piano and chamber music. A period of travel allowed him to visit England, Scotland (1829) and Italy (1830-1); he was in Paris and London several times and conducted at Düsseldorf, Germany (1833-5). As a conductor and music organizer his most significant achievement was in Leipzig (1835-45), where he also founded and directed the Conservatory (1843). As a festival organizer he was associated with the Lower Rhine and Birmingham festivals.

Recorded "Irish" Work:

Fantasia on 'The Last Rose of Summer' op. 15 (1827) pf
> Nimbus NI 5072, CD (1988): Martin Jones.

> Meridian DUOCD 89024 (= CD), KD89024 (= MC) (1993): Trudelies Leonhardt.

> Albany TROY 183, CD (1995): Anthony Goldstone.

> Koch Discover International DICD 920415, CD (1997): Dana Protopopescu.

Bertrand Walton O'Donnell
(* England 1887, † England 1939)

Not much is known today of the work of O'Donnell. He was one of three brothers who all devoted their lives to military music. His last appointment was in 1927 with the BBC Wireless Military Band. He contributed much to set new standards of serious band music. On this recording he is joined by music of Ralph Vaughan Williams and Gustav Holst.

Recorded "Irish" Works:

Two Irish Tone Sketches op. 20 (19??) brass band
> Bandleader BNC 3002, LP (1985): Regimental Band of the Coldstream Guards, Richard A. Ridings (cond).

Two Songs of the Gael (A Gaelic Fantasy) op. 31 (19??) brass band
> Bandleader BNC 3002, LP (1985): Regimental Band of the Coldstream Guards, Richard A. Ridings (cond).

Chauncey Olcott
(* Buffalo, New York 1860, † Monte Carlo 1932)

Olcott was an extremely popular song writer and musical composer who wrote Irish-style music with great ease without ever having been to Ireland – his mother, however, came from Ireland as a young child. The leading Irish-American performer of his day, he staged many pseudo-Irish works and toured successfully through the whole country. Olcott perfected the image of the stage Irishman. When John McCormack began singing his music, Olcott's name began to spread beyond American shores.

Recorded "Irish" Works:

The Irish Artist (1894) musical
> Excerpt:
> *My Beautiful Irish Maid*
> Pearl Gemm CDS 9050/2, 3CD (1994, recorded 1913): Chauncey Olcott (T), Original Broadway Cast.

Sweet Inniscarra (1897) musical
> Excerpt:
> *Sweet Inniscarra*
> Pearl Gemm CDS 9050/2, 3CD (1994, recorded 1913): Chauncey Olcott (T), Original Broadway Cast.

A Romance of Athlone (1899) musical
> Excerpt:
> *My Wild Irish Rose*
> RCA Victor GD 60720 (= CD), GK 60720 (= MC) (1992): Mario
> Lanza (T), anonymous orchestra.
>
> Pearl Gemm CDS 9050/2, 3CD (1994, recorded 1913): Chauncey
> Olcott (T), Original Broadway Cast.
>
> Preiser 91081, CD (2000): Robert Brooks (Bar), Ingrid Hedlund (pf).

Barry of Ballymore (1910) musical (in collaboration with Ernest R. Ball)
> Excerpts:
> *I Love the Name of Mary; Mother Machree*
> Pearl Gemm CDS 9053/5, 3CD (1994, recorded 1913): Chauncey
> Olcott (T), Original Broadway Cast.
>
> *Mother Machree*
> Memoir Classics CDMOIR 418, CD (1992, recorded 1927): John
> McCormack (T), Edwin Schneider (pf).
>
> Hyperion CDA 66627, CD (1993): Ann Murray (Mez), Graham
> Johnson (pf).
>
> Centaur CRC 2243, CD (1995): Gary Lakes (T), Kevin Murphy (pf).
>
> Symposium 1166, CD (1998): (same recording as *Memoir* above)
>
> Preiser 91081, CD (2000): Robert Brooks (Bar), Ingrid Hedlund (pf).
>
> > Arrangement with orchestra:
> > Romophone 82006-2, 2CD (1996): John McCormack (T),
> > Victor Orchestra.
> >
> > HMV Classics 5 73043 2, CD (1998, recorded 1952): Josef
> > Locke (T), anonymous orchestra, Woolf Phillips (cond).

Macushla (1912) musical (in collaboration with Ernest R. Ball)
> Excerpts:
> *That's How the Shannon Flows; I'll Miss You Old Ireland; God Bless*
> *You, Goodbye; 'Tis an Irish Girl I Love*
> Pearl Gemm CDS 9053/5, 3CD (1994, recorded 1913): Chauncey
> Olcott (T), Original Broadway Cast.

The Isle o' Dreams (1913) musical (in collaboration with Ernest R. Ball)
  Excerpts:
  When Irish Eyes are Smiling
  Preiser 91081, CD (2000): Robert Brooks (Bar), Ingrid Hedlund (pf).

    Arrangement with orchestra:
    ASV CD AJA 5119, CD (1993, recorded 1916): John
    McCormack (T), anonymous orchestra, Rosario Bourdon
    (cond).

    Naxos Nostalgia 8.120504, CD (2000) (same recording as *ASV*
    above).

Too-Ra-Loo-Ra-Loo-Ral (1914), v, pf
  Centaur CRC 2243, CD (1995): Gary Lakes (T), Kevin Murphy (pf).

George Frederick Pinto
(* Lambeth 1785, † Chelsea 1806)

Pinto's early death of an unknown cause at the age of twenty undoubtedly robbed England of one its greatest musical talents. He studied violin in London with Salomon and also the piano but seems to have been a natural talent as a composer. Some of his works show astonishing stylisitic anticipations of Beethoven and Schubert. He mainly wrote for the piano, and his "Irish" piece is a rondo on a very popular Irish melody.

Recorded "Irish" Work:

Rondo on an Irish Air, 'Cory Owen' (1801) pf
  Chandos CHAN 9798, CD (2000): Micheál O'Rourke.

Henry Purcell
(* England 1659, † Westminster 1695)

Henry Purcell was the most outstanding 17th-century English composer. He began his career as a chorister in the Chapel Royal, London, and became an organ maker. In 1679 he succeeded his teacher John Blow as organist of Westminster Abbey and he became organist of the Chapel Royal in 1682. From about 1680 he began to write music for the theater, notably Dido and Aeneas (1689).

Recorded "Irish" Work:

A New Irish Tune "Lilliburlero" (c. 1690) hpd
        CRD 1047, LP (1978): Trevor Pinnock.
        Re-issued on CRD 3347 (= CD), CRDC 4047 (= MC) (1989).

        Vanguard Classics 08.2003.72, 2CD (1993, recorded 1959): George Malcolm.

        Erato 0630-10695-2, CD (1996): Olivier Baumont.

        Version for bass viol:
        Albany Troy 127-2, CD (1995): Brent Wissick.

Ernest Schelling
(* Belvidere, New Jersey 1876, † USA 1939)

Reliable biographical information about American composer Ernest Schelling is hard to get: He was a child prodigy who gave his first piano recital at age four at the Philadelphia Academy of Music. As a pianist he was a pupil of Paderewsky and Leschetizky in Vienna (?). As a conductor he became Music Director of the Baltimore Symphony Orchestra and, from the mid-1920s, the founder of the Young People's Concerts of the New York Philharmonic.

Recorded "Irish" Work:

Irlandaise (date unknown) pf, arr. by Fritz Kreisler for vn, pf
        Caprice CAP 21496, CD (1995): Tobias Ringborg (vn), Anders Kilström (pf).

Cyril Scott
(* Oxton 1879, † Eastbourne 1970)

Scott studied at Hoch's Conservatory in Frankfurt, Germany (1892-3, 1895-8), with Engelbert Humperdinck and Iwan Knorr. His early works show some affinity with Scriabin and Debussy, an example being his *Piano Concerto* from

1915. His output includes operas and ballets, three symphonies, a second piano concerto, some chamber music and numerous piano pieces. He was also a noted writer on occultism, a poet and an internationally known pianist.

Recorded "Irish" Work:

Two Passacaglias on Irish Themes (1912) orch
>   Marco Polo 8.223485, CD (1994) South African Broadcasting Corp.
>   Symphony Orchestra, Peter Marchbank (cond).

Arthur Sullivan
(* London 1842, † London 1900)

Sullivan had Irish ancestors in his grandfather's generation (hence his Irish name). He studied with William Sterndale Bennett at the Royal Academy of Music (1856) and at the Leipzig Conservatory (1858-61). From 1866 he began to develop an interest in comic opera and in his ensuing partnership with William S. Gilbert he became an extremely popular composer of light operas, mainly produced from 1881 at the Savoy Theatre in London. He wrote 24 operas (*The Pirates of Penzance, The Mikado, The Gondoliers, Ivanhoe* etc.) seven pieces for spoken stage works, two ballets, two oratorios, many orchestral pieces, some liturgical and choral music but only nine chamber pieces.

Recorded "Irish" Works:

Irish Symphony in E (1866) orch
>   HMV ASD 2435, LP (1968): Royal Liverpool Philharmonic Orchestra,
>   Charles Groves (cond).
>   *Re-issued on* EMI CDM7 64726-2, CD (1993); EMI CMS7 64406-2,
>   2CD (1993).
>
>   CPO 999 171-2, CD (1994): BBC Concert Orchestra, Owain Arwel
>   Hughes (cond).
>
>   Chandos CHAN 9859, CD (2000): BBC Philharmonic, Richard Hickox
>   (cond).

The Emerald Isle (1901; *completed after Sullivan's death by Edward German*) opera
>   Pearl SHE 574/5, 2LP (1982): The Prince Consort, Gilbert & Sullivan
>   Society of Edinburgh Chorus, The Consort Orchestra, David Lyle
>   (cond).
>   *Re-issued on* Sounds on CD VGS 207, CD (1999).

Raymond Warren
(* England 1928)

Warren studied music at Cambridge with Robin Orr and composition privately with Lennox Berkeley and Michael Tippett. He was Professor of Music at Queen's University Belfast (1970-2) and at the University of Bristol (1972-94). His work-list contains many operas, oratorios, three symphonies and liturgical music. His *Wexford Bells* was commissioned for the BBC Northern Ireland Light Orchestra.

Recorded "Irish" Work:

Wexford Bells – Suite on Old Irish Tunes (1970) orch
        ASV CD WHL 2126, CD (2000): Royal Ballet Sinfonia, Gavin
        Sutherland (cond).

Index

About the Author

AXEL KLEIN has co-edited two volumes of essays on Irish music and is an advisor
to the German encyclopedia *Die Musik in Geschichte und Gegenwart*. His other writing includes the monograph *Die Musik Irlands im 20. Jahrhundert*, on the subject of
twentieth-century Irish music.